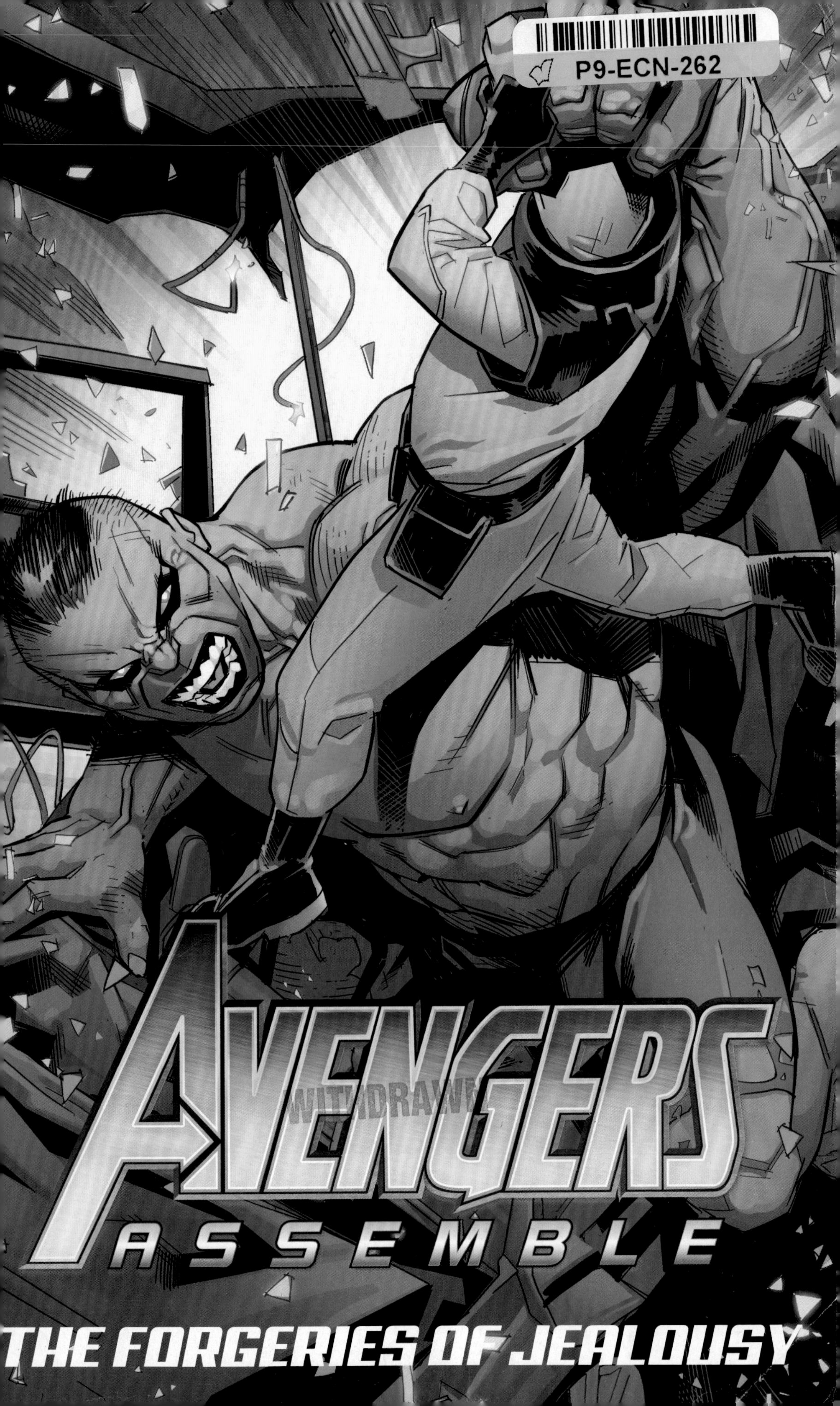
AVENGERS
ASSEMBLE
THE FORGERIES OF JEALOUSY

Collection Editor: Jennifer Grünwald • Assistant Editor: Sarah Brunstad
Associate Managing Editor: Alex Starbuck • Editor, Special Projects: Mark D. Beazley
Senior Editor, Special Projects: Jeff Youngquist • SVP Print, Sales & Marketing: David Gabriel

Editor in Chief: Axel Alonso • Chief Creative Officer: Joe Quesada
Publisher: Dan Buckley • Executive Producer: Alan Fine

AVENGERS ASSEMBLE: THE FORGERIES OF JEALOUSY. Contains material originally published in magazine form as AVENGERS ASSEMBLE #21, #22.INH-23.INH and #24-25. First printing 2014. ISBN# 978-0-7851-6798-3. Published by MARVEL WORLDWIDE, INC., a subsidiary of MARVEL ENTERTAINMENT, LLC. OFFICE OF PUBLICATION: 135 West 50th Street, New York, NY 10020. Copyright © 2013 and 2014 Marvel Characters, Inc. All rights reserved. All characters featured in this issue and the distinctive names and likenesses thereof, and all related indicia are trademarks of Marvel Characters, Inc. No similarity between any of the names, characters, persons, and/or institutions in this magazine with those of any living or dead person or institution is intended, and any such similarity which may exist is purely coincidental. **Printed in Canada.** ALAN FINE, EVP - Office of the President, Marvel Worldwide, Inc. and EVP & CMO Marvel Characters B.V.; DAN BUCKLEY, Publisher & President - Print, Animation & Digital Divisions; JOE QUESADA, Chief Creative Officer; TOM BREVOORT, SVP of Publishing; DAVID BOGART, SVP of Operations & Procurement, Publishing; C.B. CEBULSKI, SVP of Creator & Content Development; DAVID GABRIEL, SVP Print, Sales & Marketing; JIM O'KEEFE, VP of Operations & Logistics; DAN CARR, Executive Director of Publishing Technology; SUSAN CRESPI, Editorial Operations Manager; ALEX MORALES, Publishing Operations Manager; STAN LEE, Chairman Emeritus. For information regarding advertising in Marvel Comics or on Marvel.com, please contact Niza Disla, Director of Marvel Partnerships, at ndisla@marvel.com. For Marvel subscription inquiries, please call 800-217-9158

AVENGERS ASSEMBLE

THE FORGERIES OF JEALOUSY

WRITERS
KELLY SUE DeCONNICK & **WARREN ELLIS**

ARTISTS, #21-24
MATTEO BUFFAGNI WITH **PACO DIAZ** (#22)

ARTISTS, #25
MATTEO BUFFAGNI & **DAVE MEIKIS** (PP. 1-13),
NEIL EDWARDS (PP. 14-18) AND **RAFFAELE IENCO** (PP. 19-20)

COLOR ARTISTS
NOLAN WOODARD (#21-23) & **RUTH REDMOND** (#24-25)

LETTERER
VC'S CLAYTON COWLES

COVER ART
JORGE MOLINA

ASSISTANT EDITOR
JON MOISAN

EDITOR
LAUREN SANKOVITCH

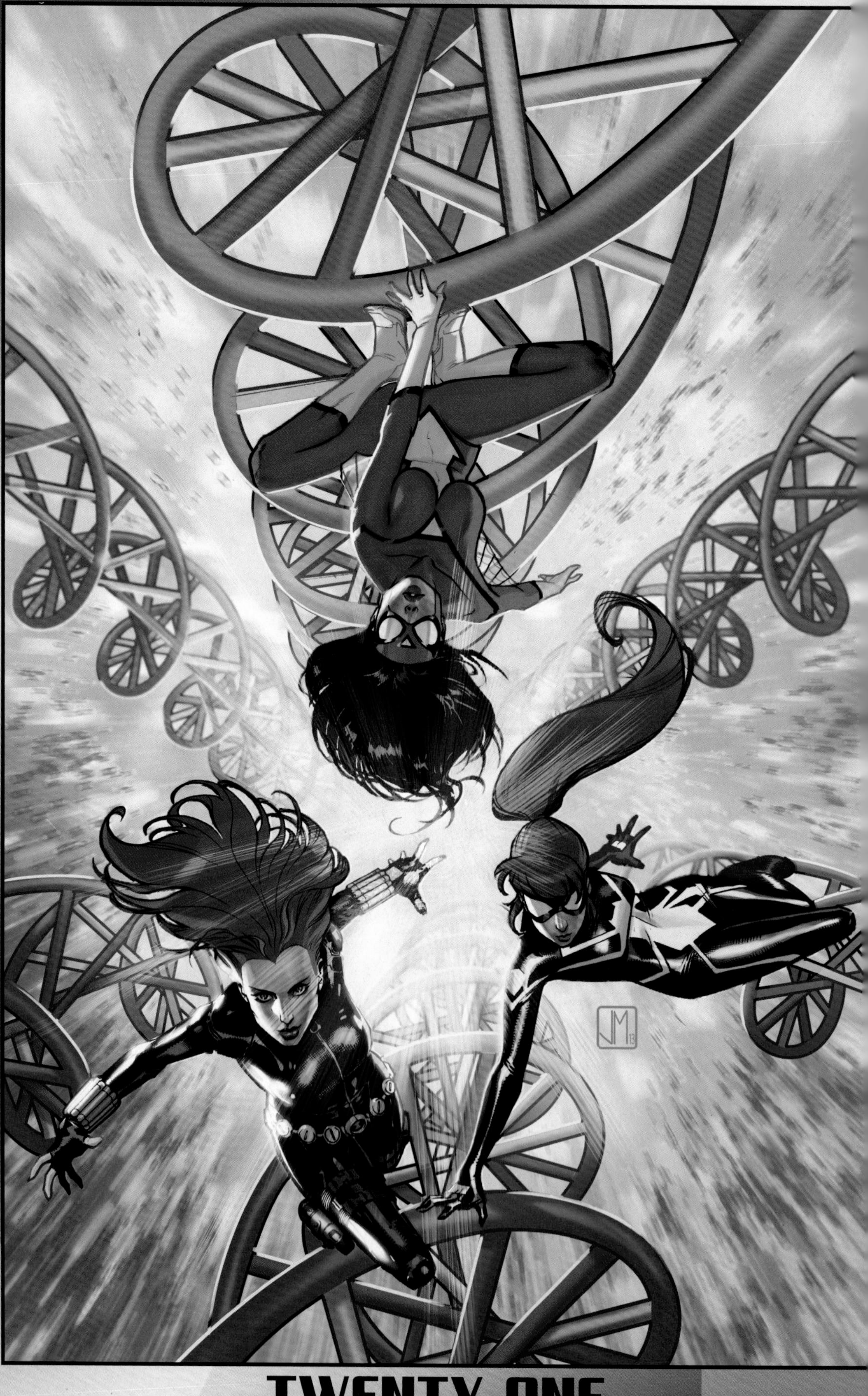

TWENTY-ONE

AND THERE CAME A DAY, A DAY UNLIKE ANY OTHER, WHEN EARTH'S MIGHTIEST HEROES FOUND THEMSELVES UNITED AGAINST A COMMON THREAT! ON THAT DAY, THE AVENGERS WERE BORN, TO FIGHT THE FOES NO SINGLE SUPER HERO COULD WITHSTAND!

AVENGERS ASSEMBLE

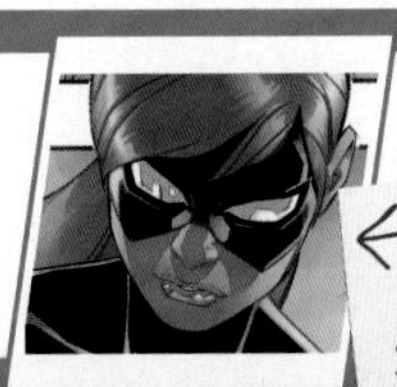

← Is not, NOT an Avenger
–The Superior Spider-Man

SPIDER-GIRL
ANYA CORAZON
SPIDER-POWERED SUPER STUDENT

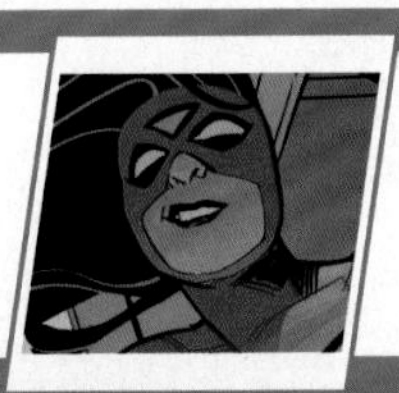

SPIDER-WOMAN
JESSICA DREW
SPIDER-POWERED SECRET AGENT

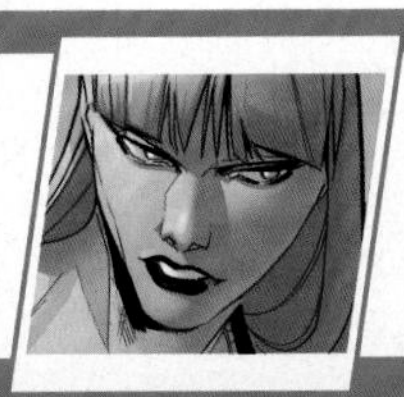

BLACK WIDOW
NATASHA ROMANOFF
PLAIN OL' COVERT SPECIALIST

FILE: INFINITY_04

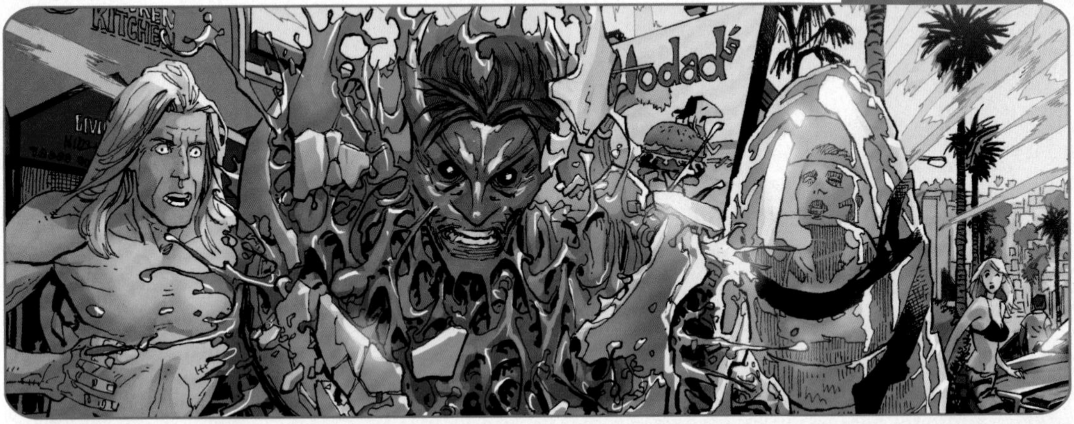
Hodad's

While most of the Avengers were off Earth fighting an alien threat, the Mad Titan Thanos led an invasion force to attack their home planet. Scouring the Earth to locate his own Inhuman son, Thane, Thanos sought to destroy Thane and raze the planet. Black Bolt, King of the Inhumans, in an effort to protect his people, detonated a Terrigen bomb, causing latent Inhumans hidden and scattered around Earth to undergo the Terrigen mists' mutating effects. Some were affected immediately; others were trapped in cocoons, the extent of their newly activated abilities yet to be seen...

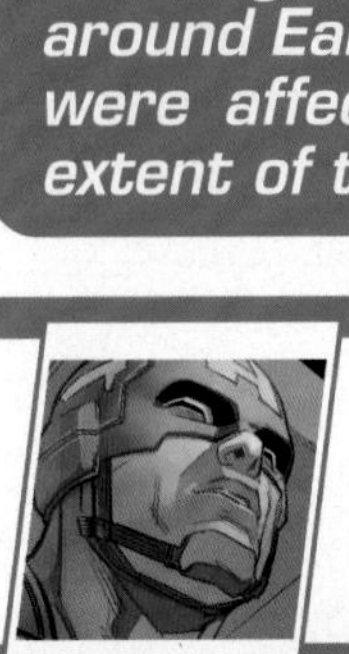

CAPTAIN AMERICA
STEVE ROGERS

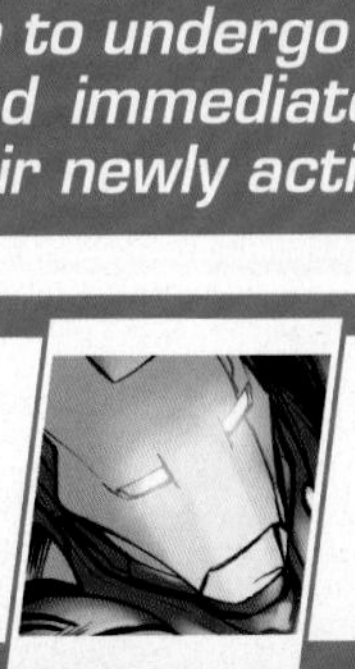

IRON MAN
TONY STARK

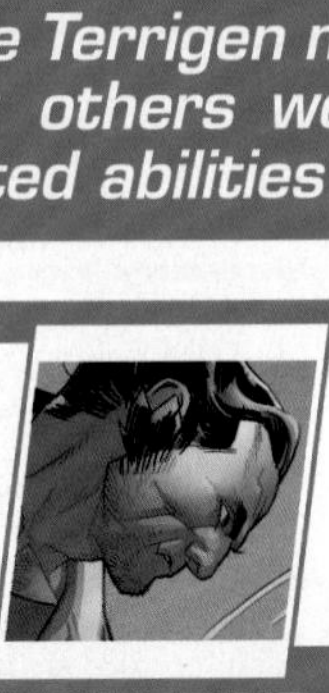

WOLVERINE
JAMES "LOGAN" HOWLETT

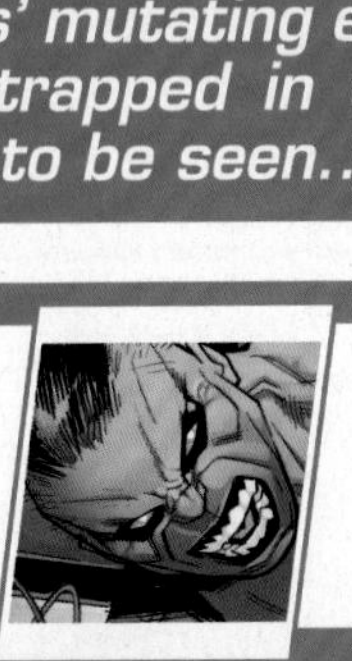

HULK
DR. BRUCE BANNER

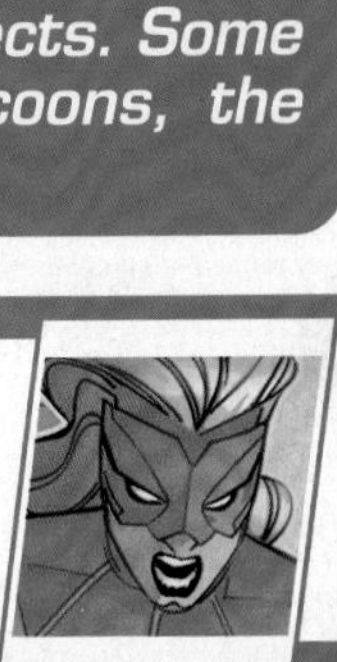

CAPTAIN MARVEL
CAROL DANVERS

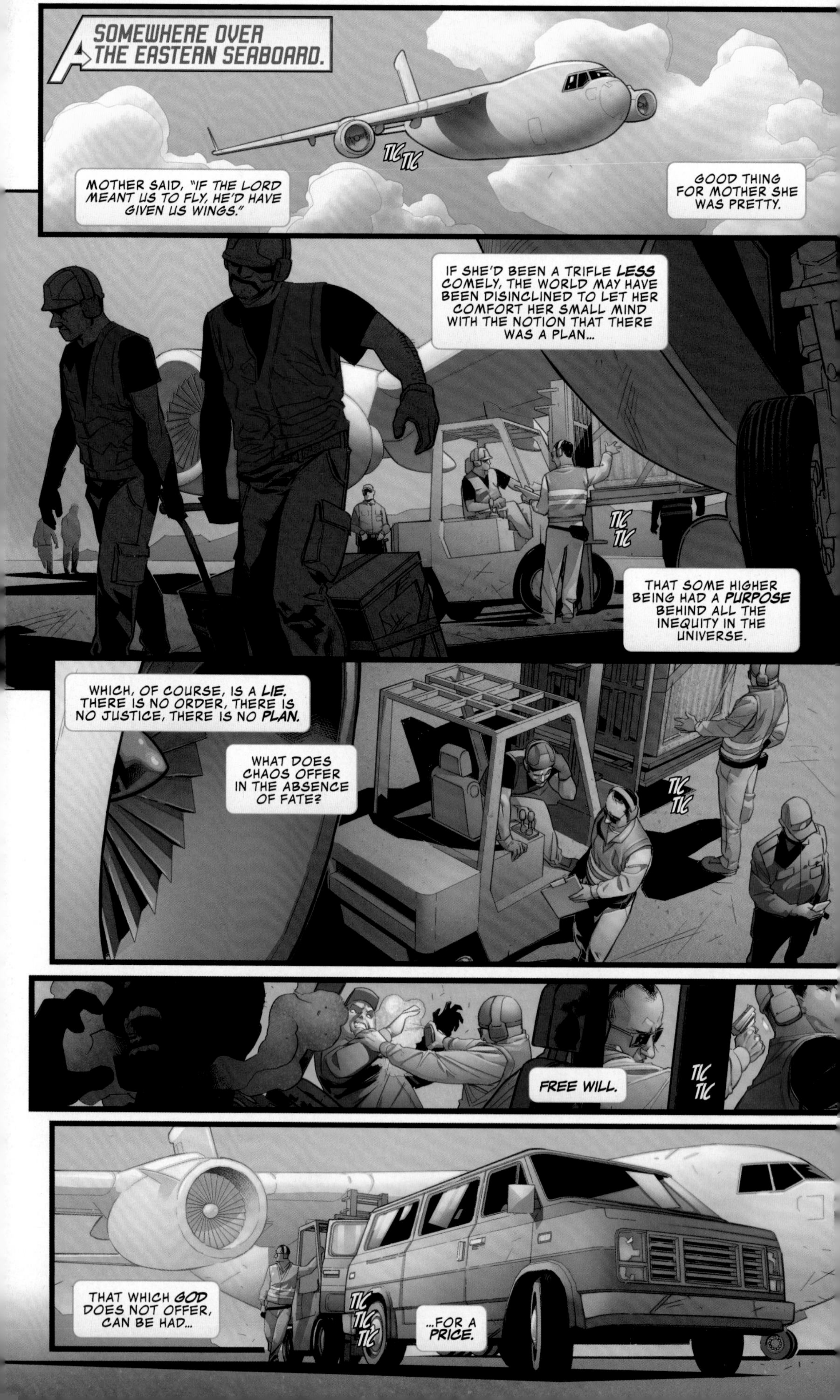
SOMEWHERE OVER THE EASTERN SEABOARD.
TIC TIC
MOTHER SAID, "IF THE LORD MEANT US TO FLY, HE'D HAVE GIVEN US WINGS."
GOOD THING FOR MOTHER SHE WAS PRETTY.
IF SHE'D BEEN A TRIFLE LESS COMELY, THE WORLD MAY HAVE BEEN DISINCLINED TO LET HER COMFORT HER SMALL MIND WITH THE NOTION THAT THERE WAS A PLAN...
TIC TIC
THAT SOME HIGHER BEING HAD A PURPOSE BEHIND ALL THE INEQUITY IN THE UNIVERSE.
WHICH, OF COURSE, IS A LIE. THERE IS NO ORDER, THERE IS NO JUSTICE, THERE IS NO PLAN.
WHAT DOES CHAOS OFFER IN THE ABSENCE OF FATE?
TIC TIC
FREE WILL.
TIC TIC
THAT WHICH GOD DOES NOT OFFER, CAN BE HAD...
TIC TIC TIC
...FOR A PRICE.

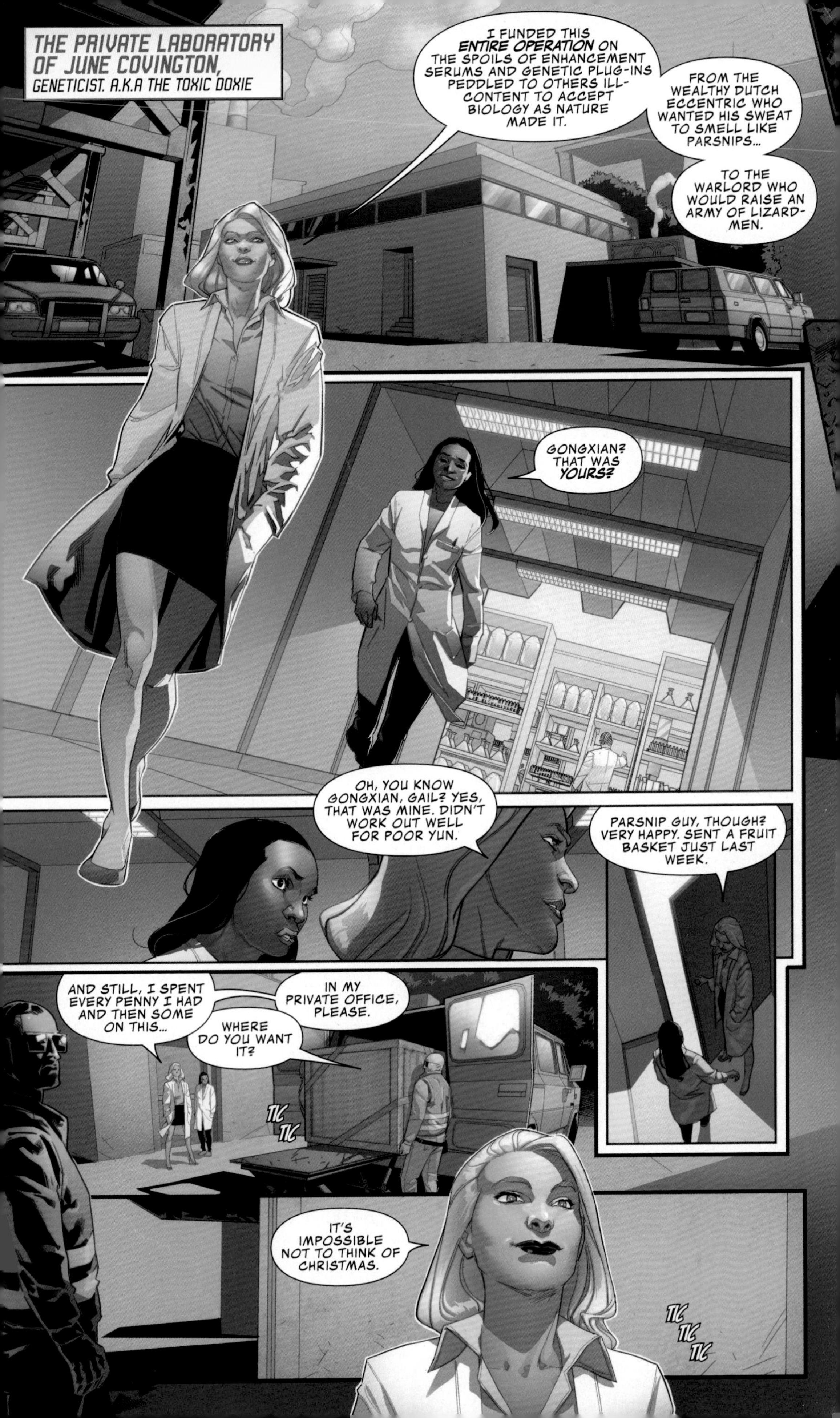
THE PRIVATE LABORATORY OF JUNE COVINGTON, GENETICIST. A.K.A THE TOXIC DOXIE
I FUNDED THIS ENTIRE OPERATION ON THE SPOILS OF ENHANCEMENT SERUMS AND GENETIC PLUG-INS PEDDLED TO OTHERS ILL-CONTENT TO ACCEPT BIOLOGY AS NATURE MADE IT.
FROM THE WEALTHY DUTCH ECCENTRIC WHO WANTED HIS SWEAT TO SMELL LIKE PARSNIPS...
TO THE WARLORD WHO WOULD RAISE AN ARMY OF LIZARD-MEN.
GONGXIAN? THAT WAS YOURS?
OH, YOU KNOW GONGXIAN, GAIL? YES, THAT WAS MINE. DIDN'T WORK OUT WELL FOR POOR YUN.
PARSNIP GUY, THOUGH? VERY HAPPY. SENT A FRUIT BASKET JUST LAST WEEK.
AND STILL, I SPENT EVERY PENNY I HAD AND THEN SOME ON THIS...
WHERE DO YOU WANT IT?
IN MY PRIVATE OFFICE, PLEASE.
TIC TIC
IT'S IMPOSSIBLE NOT TO THINK OF CHRISTMAS.
TIC TIC TIC

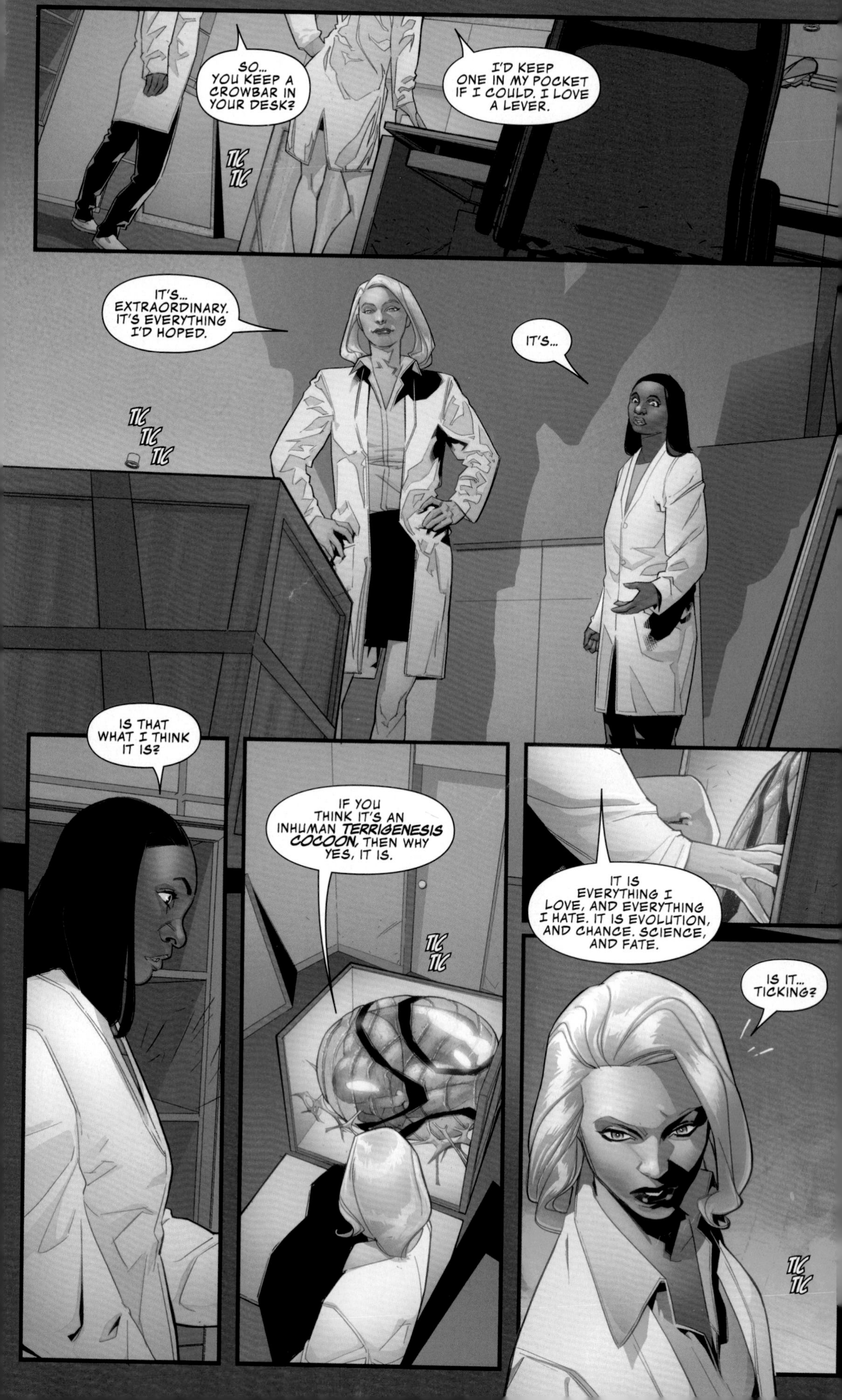
SO... YOU KEEP A CROWBAR IN YOUR DESK?
I'D KEEP ONE IN MY POCKET IF I COULD. I LOVE A LEVER.
TIC TIC
IT'S... EXTRAORDINARY. IT'S EVERYTHING I'D HOPED.
IT'S...
TIC TIC TIC
IS THAT WHAT I THINK IT IS?
IF YOU THINK IT'S AN INHUMAN TERRIGENESIS COCOON, THEN WHY YES, IT IS.
TIC TIC
IT IS EVERYTHING I LOVE, AND EVERYTHING I HATE. IT IS EVOLUTION, AND CHANCE. SCIENCE, AND FATE.
IS IT... TICKING?
TIC TIC

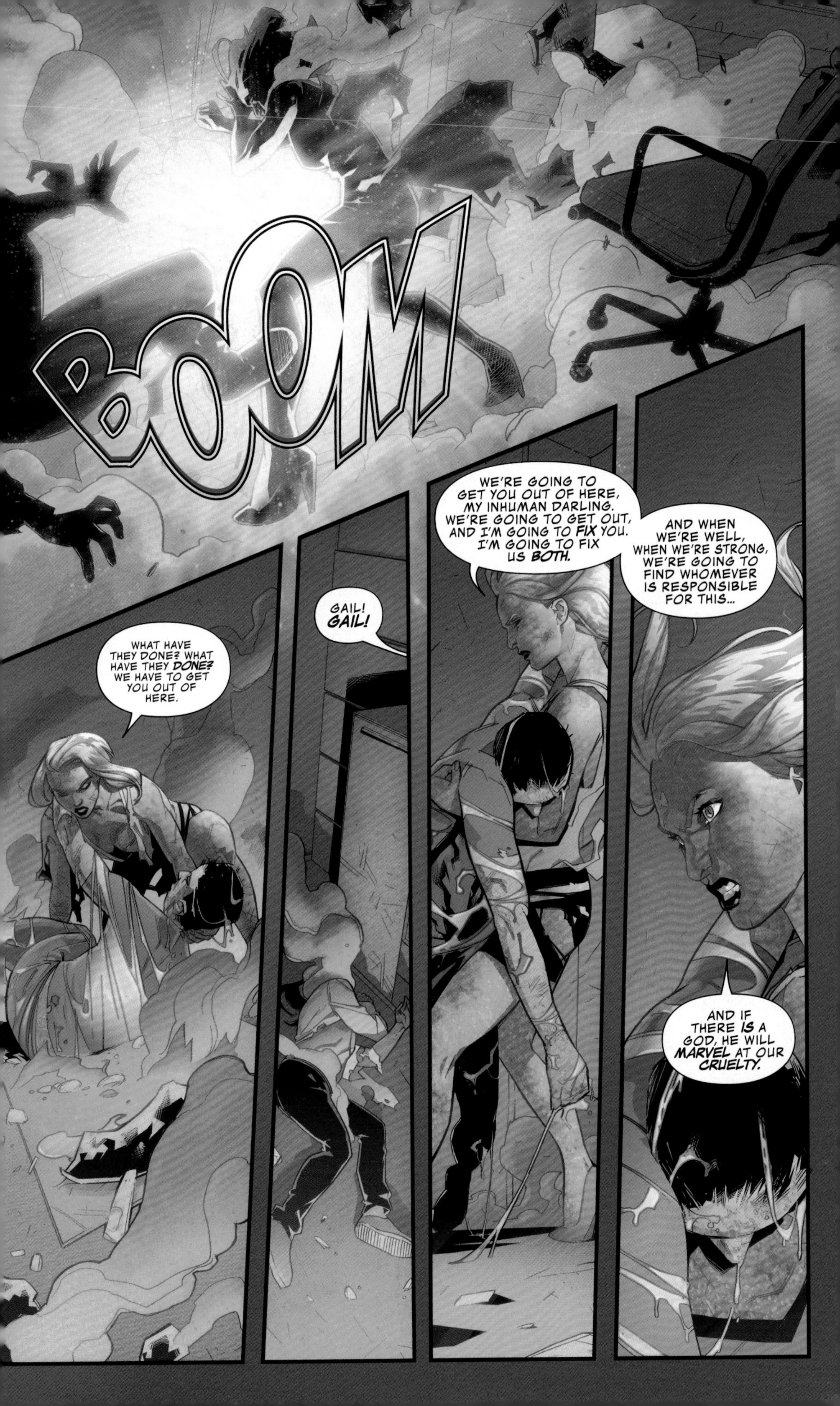
BOOM
WHAT HAVE THEY DONE? WHAT HAVE THEY DONE? WE HAVE TO GET YOU OUT OF HERE.
GAIL! GAIL!
WE'RE GOING TO GET YOU OUT OF HERE, MY INHUMAN DARLING. WE'RE GOING TO GET OUT, AND I'M GOING TO FIX YOU. I'M GOING TO FIX US BOTH.
AND WHEN WE'RE WELL, WHEN WE'RE STRONG, WE'RE GOING TO FIND WHOMEVER IS RESPONSIBLE FOR THIS...
AND IF THERE IS A GOD, HE WILL MARVEL AT OUR CRUELTY.

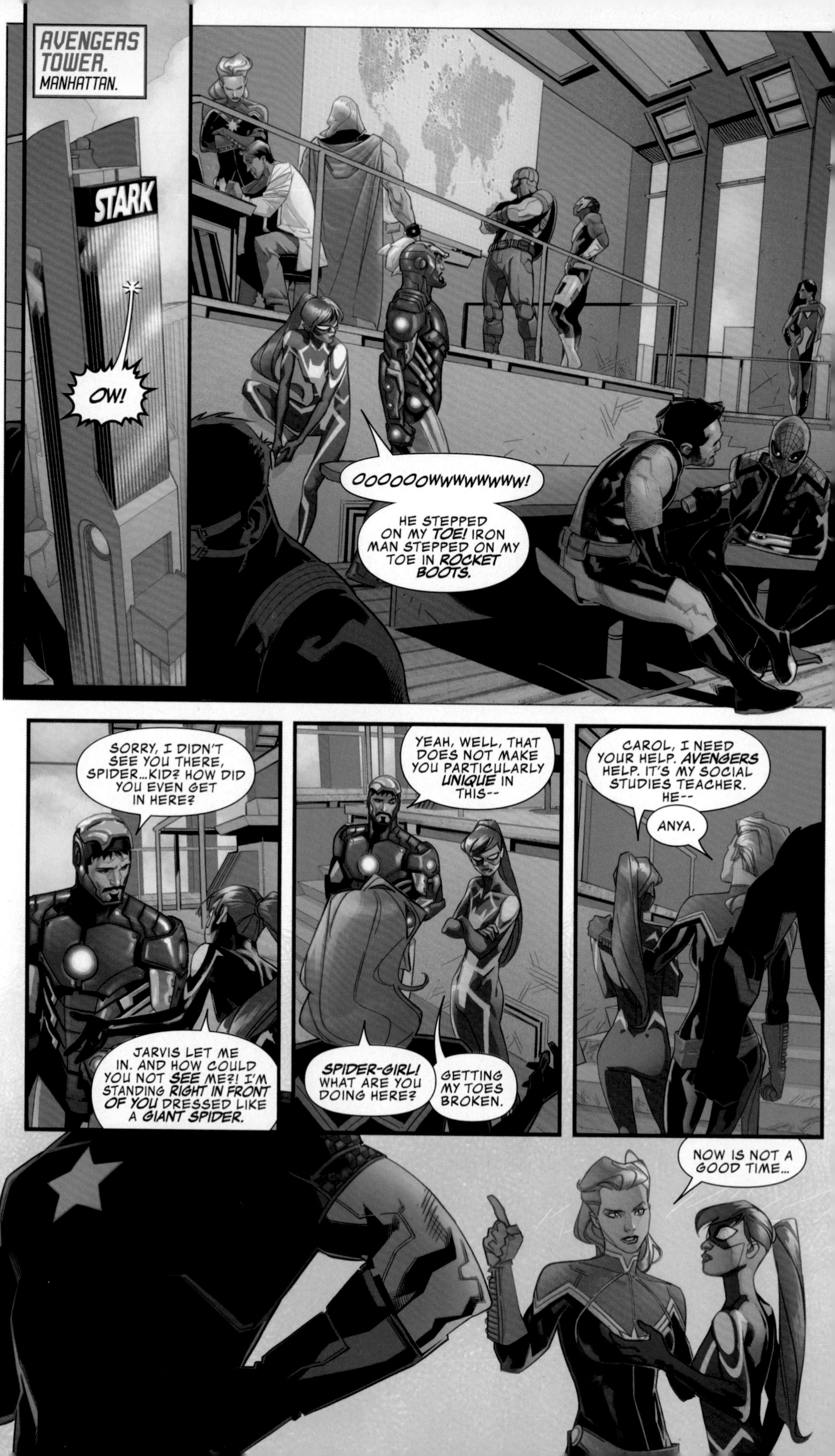

AVENGERS TOWER. MANHATTAN.
STARK
OW!
OOOOOOWWWWWWWW!
HE STEPPED ON MY TOE! IRON MAN STEPPED ON MY TOE IN ROCKET BOOTS.
SORRY, I DIDN'T SEE YOU THERE, SPIDER...KID? HOW DID YOU EVEN GET IN HERE?
JARVIS LET ME IN. AND HOW COULD YOU NOT SEE ME?! I'M STANDING RIGHT IN FRONT OF YOU DRESSED LIKE A GIANT SPIDER.
YEAH, WELL, THAT DOES NOT MAKE YOU PARTICULARLY UNIQUE IN THIS--
SPIDER-GIRL! WHAT ARE YOU DOING HERE?
GETTING MY TOES BROKEN.
CAROL, I NEED YOUR HELP. AVENGERS HELP. IT'S MY SOCIAL STUDIES TEACHER. HE--
ANYA.
NOW IS NOT A GOOD TIME...

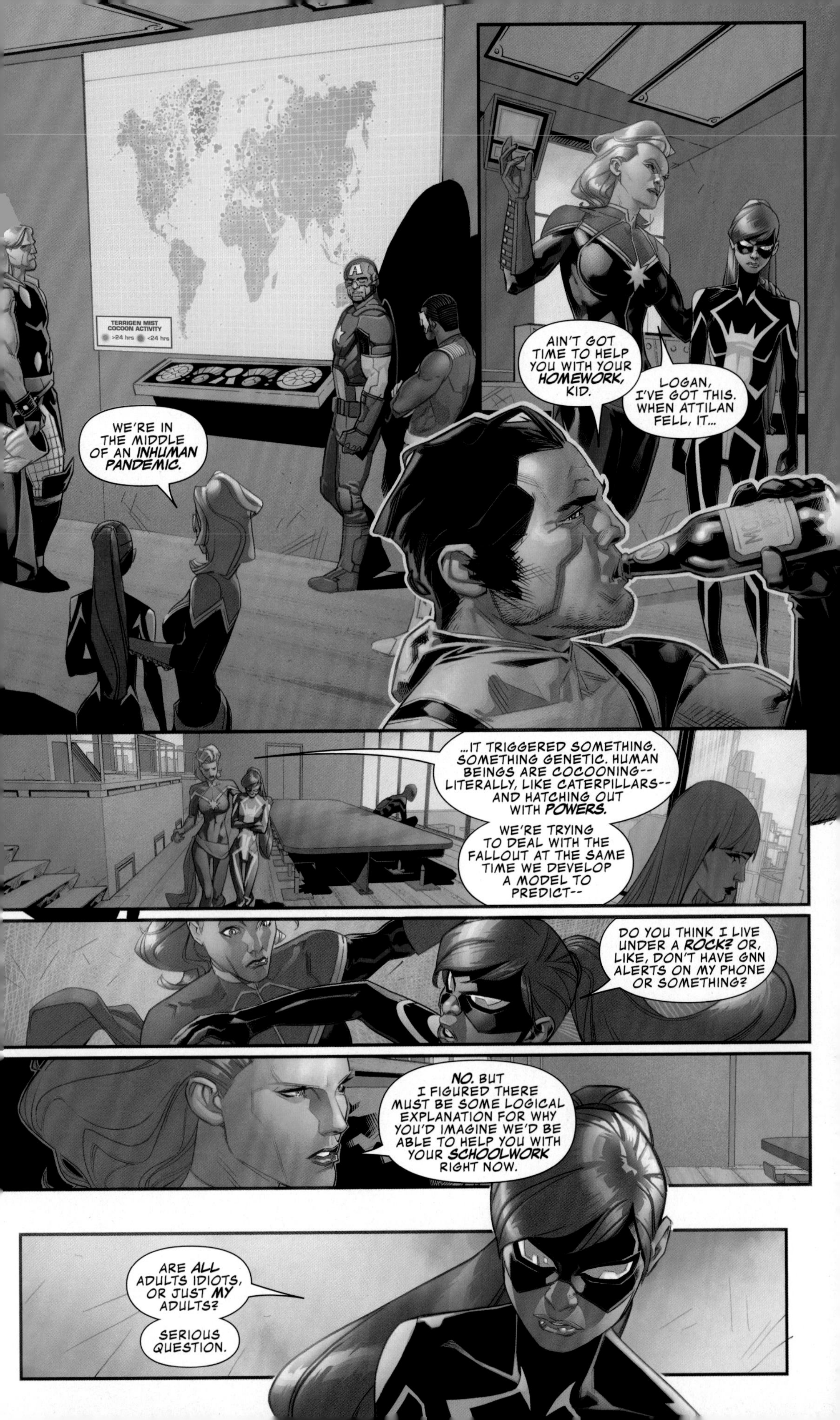
TERRIGEN MIST COCOON ACTIVITY
>24 hrs <24 hrs
WE'RE IN THE MIDDLE OF AN INHUMAN PANDEMIC.
AIN'T GOT TIME TO HELP YOU WITH YOUR HOMEWORK, KID.
LOGAN, I'VE GOT THIS. WHEN ATTILAN FELL, IT...
...IT TRIGGERED SOMETHING. SOMETHING GENETIC. HUMAN BEINGS ARE COCOONING-- LITERALLY, LIKE CATERPILLARS-- AND HATCHING OUT WITH POWERS.
WE'RE TRYING TO DEAL WITH THE FALLOUT AT THE SAME TIME WE DEVELOP A MODEL TO PREDICT--
DO YOU THINK I LIVE UNDER A ROCK? OR, LIKE, DON'T HAVE GNN ALERTS ON MY PHONE OR SOMETHING?
NO. BUT I FIGURED THERE MUST BE SOME LOGICAL EXPLANATION FOR WHY YOU'D IMAGINE WE'D BE ABLE TO HELP YOU WITH YOUR SCHOOLWORK RIGHT NOW.
ARE ALL ADULTS IDIOTS, OR JUST MY ADULTS?
SERIOUS QUESTION.

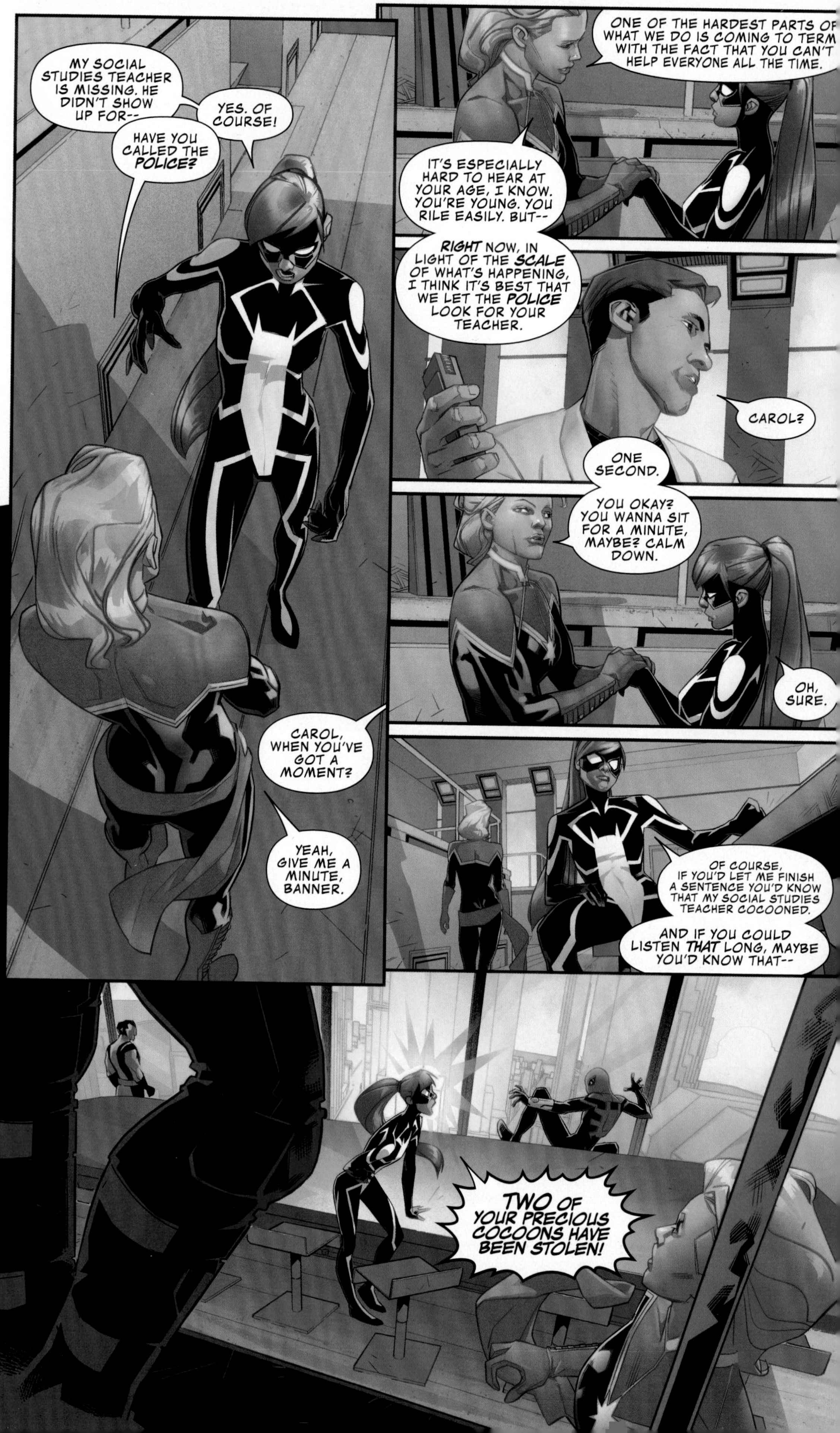
MY SOCIAL STUDIES TEACHER IS MISSING. HE DIDN'T SHOW UP FOR--
YES. OF COURSE!
HAVE YOU CALLED THE POLICE?
CAROL, WHEN YOU'VE GOT A MOMENT?
YEAH, GIVE ME A MINUTE, BANNER.
ONE OF THE HARDEST PARTS OF WHAT WE DO IS COMING TO TERM WITH THE FACT THAT YOU CAN'T HELP EVERYONE ALL THE TIME.
IT'S ESPECIALLY HARD TO HEAR AT YOUR AGE, I KNOW. YOU'RE YOUNG. YOU RILE EASILY. BUT--
RIGHT NOW, IN LIGHT OF THE SCALE OF WHAT'S HAPPENING, I THINK IT'S BEST THAT WE LET THE POLICE LOOK FOR YOUR TEACHER.
CAROL?
ONE SECOND.
YOU OKAY? YOU WANNA SIT FOR A MINUTE, MAYBE? CALM DOWN.
OH, SURE.
OF COURSE, IF YOU'D LET ME FINISH A SENTENCE YOU'D KNOW THAT MY SOCIAL STUDIES TEACHER COCOONED.
AND IF YOU COULD LISTEN THAT LONG, MAYBE YOU'D KNOW THAT--
TWO OF YOUR PRECIOUS COCOONS HAVE BEEN STOLEN!

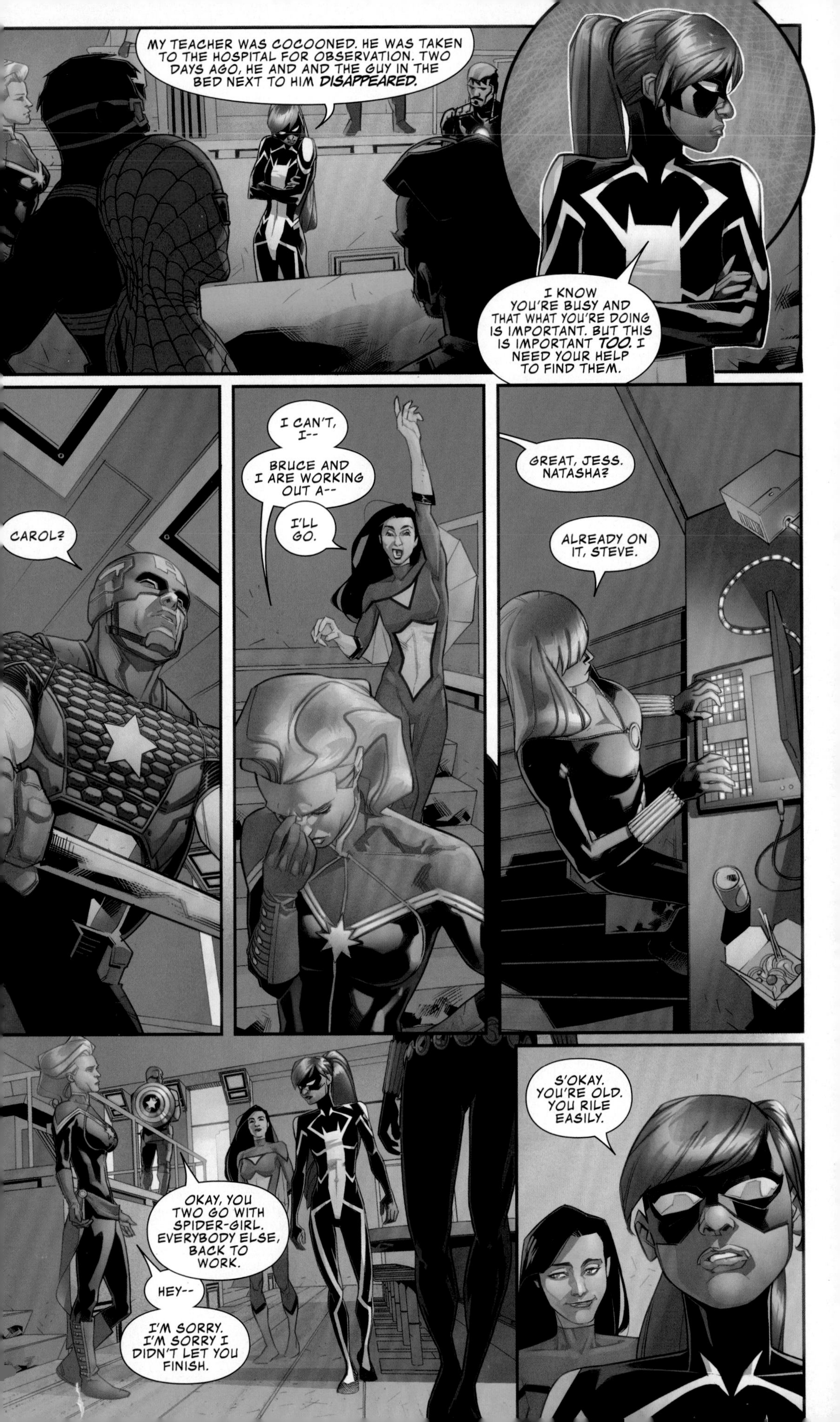

MY TEACHER WAS COCOONED. HE WAS TAKEN TO THE HOSPITAL FOR OBSERVATION. TWO DAYS AGO, HE AND AND THE GUY IN THE BED NEXT TO HIM *DISAPPEARED.*
I KNOW YOU'RE BUSY AND THAT WHAT YOU'RE DOING IS IMPORTANT. BUT THIS IS IMPORTANT *TOO.* I NEED YOUR HELP TO FIND THEM.
CAROL?
I CAN'T, I--
BRUCE AND I ARE WORKING OUT A--
I'LL GO.
GREAT, JESS. NATASHA?
ALREADY ON IT, STEVE.
OKAY, YOU TWO GO WITH SPIDER-GIRL. EVERYBODY ELSE, BACK TO WORK.
HEY--
I'M SORRY. I'M SORRY I DIDN'T LET YOU FINISH.
S'OKAY. YOU'RE OLD. YOU RILE EASILY.

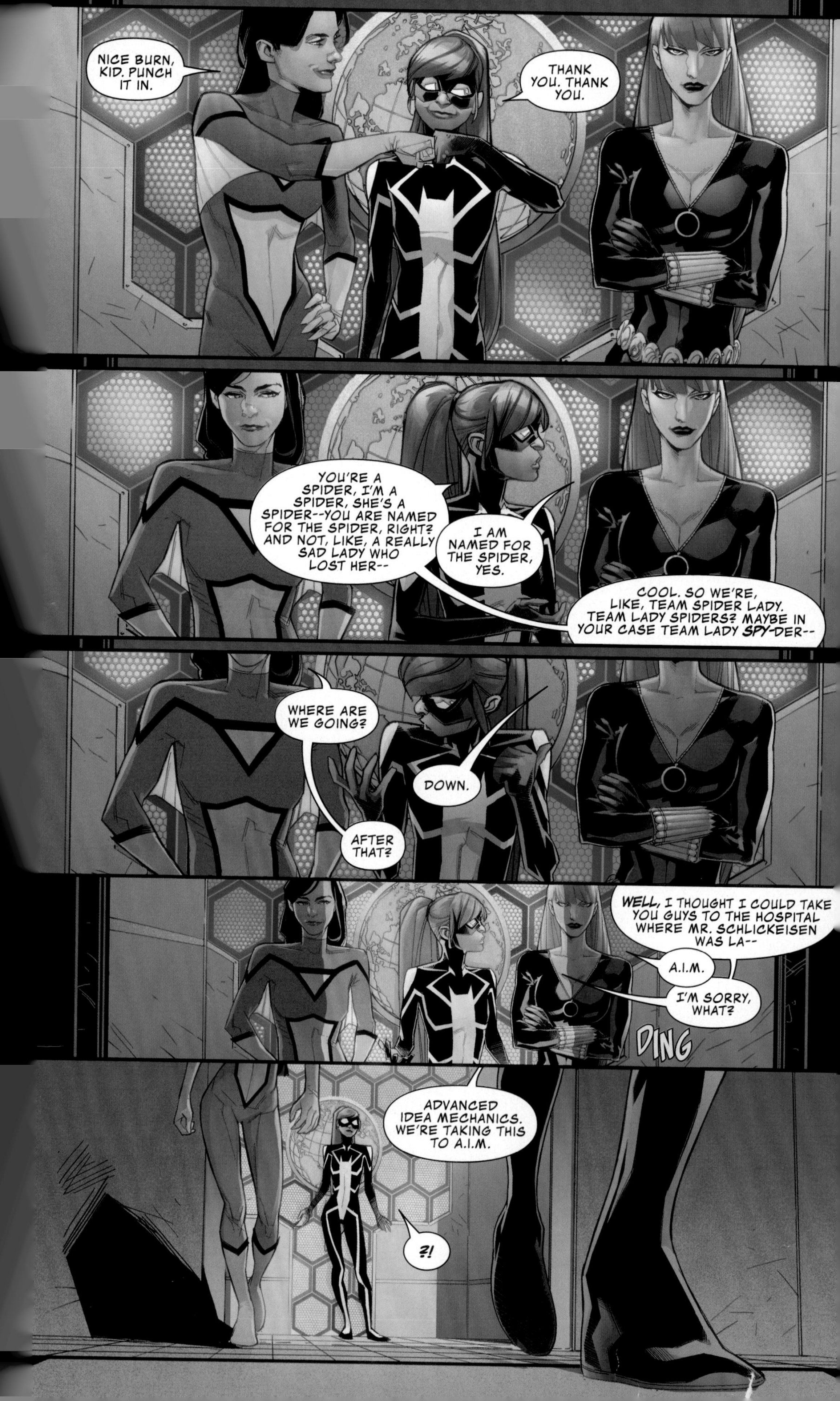

NICE BURN, KID. PUNCH IT IN.
THANK YOU. THANK YOU.
YOU'RE A SPIDER, I'M A SPIDER, SHE'S A SPIDER--YOU ARE NAMED FOR THE SPIDER, RIGHT? AND NOT, LIKE, A REALLY SAD LADY WHO LOST HER--
I AM NAMED FOR THE SPIDER, YES.
COOL. SO WE'RE, LIKE, TEAM SPIDER LADY. TEAM LADY SPIDERS? MAYBE IN YOUR CASE TEAM LADY SPY-DER--
WHERE ARE WE GOING?
DOWN.
AFTER THAT?
WELL, I THOUGHT I COULD TAKE YOU GUYS TO THE HOSPITAL WHERE MR. SCHLICKEISEN WAS LA--
A.I.M.
I'M SORRY, WHAT?
DING
ADVANCED IDEA MECHANICS. WE'RE TAKING THIS TO A.I.M.
?!

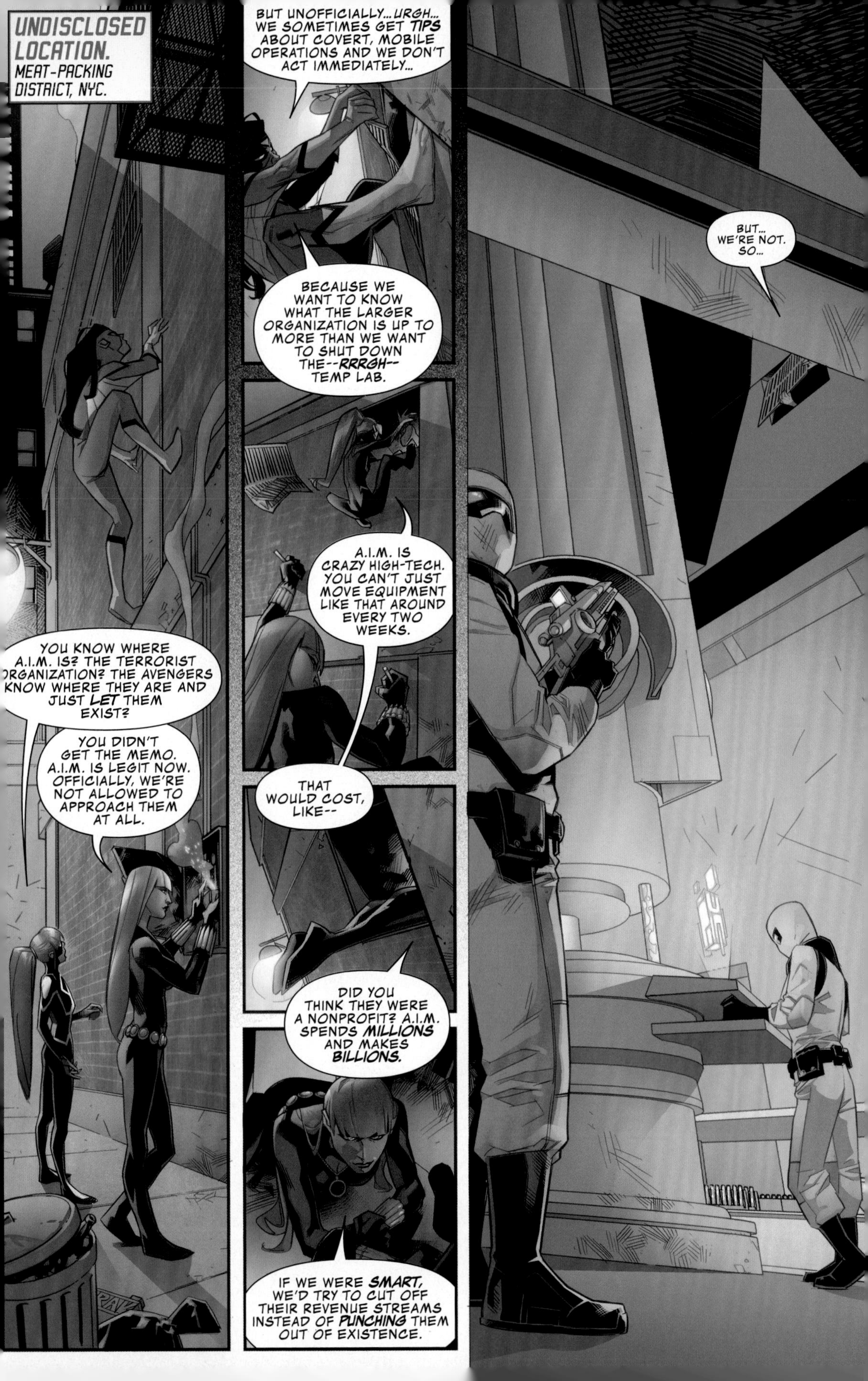
UNDISCLOSED LOCATION.
MEAT-PACKING DISTRICT, NYC.
YOU KNOW WHERE A.I.M. IS? THE TERRORIST ORGANIZATION? THE AVENGERS KNOW WHERE THEY ARE AND JUST LET THEM EXIST?
YOU DIDN'T GET THE MEMO. A.I.M. IS LEGIT NOW. OFFICIALLY, WE'RE NOT ALLOWED TO APPROACH THEM AT ALL.
BUT UNOFFICIALLY... URGH... WE SOMETIMES GET TIPS ABOUT COVERT, MOBILE OPERATIONS AND WE DON'T ACT IMMEDIATELY...
BECAUSE WE WANT TO KNOW WHAT THE LARGER ORGANIZATION IS UP TO MORE THAN WE WANT TO SHUT DOWN THE--RRRGH--TEMP LAB.
A.I.M. IS CRAZY HIGH-TECH. YOU CAN'T JUST MOVE EQUIPMENT LIKE THAT AROUND EVERY TWO WEEKS.
THAT WOULD COST, LIKE--
DID YOU THINK THEY WERE A NONPROFIT? A.I.M. SPENDS MILLIONS AND MAKES BILLIONS.
IF WE WERE SMART, WE'D TRY TO CUT OFF THEIR REVENUE STREAMS INSTEAD OF PUNCHING THEM OUT OF EXISTENCE.
BUT... WE'RE NOT. SO...

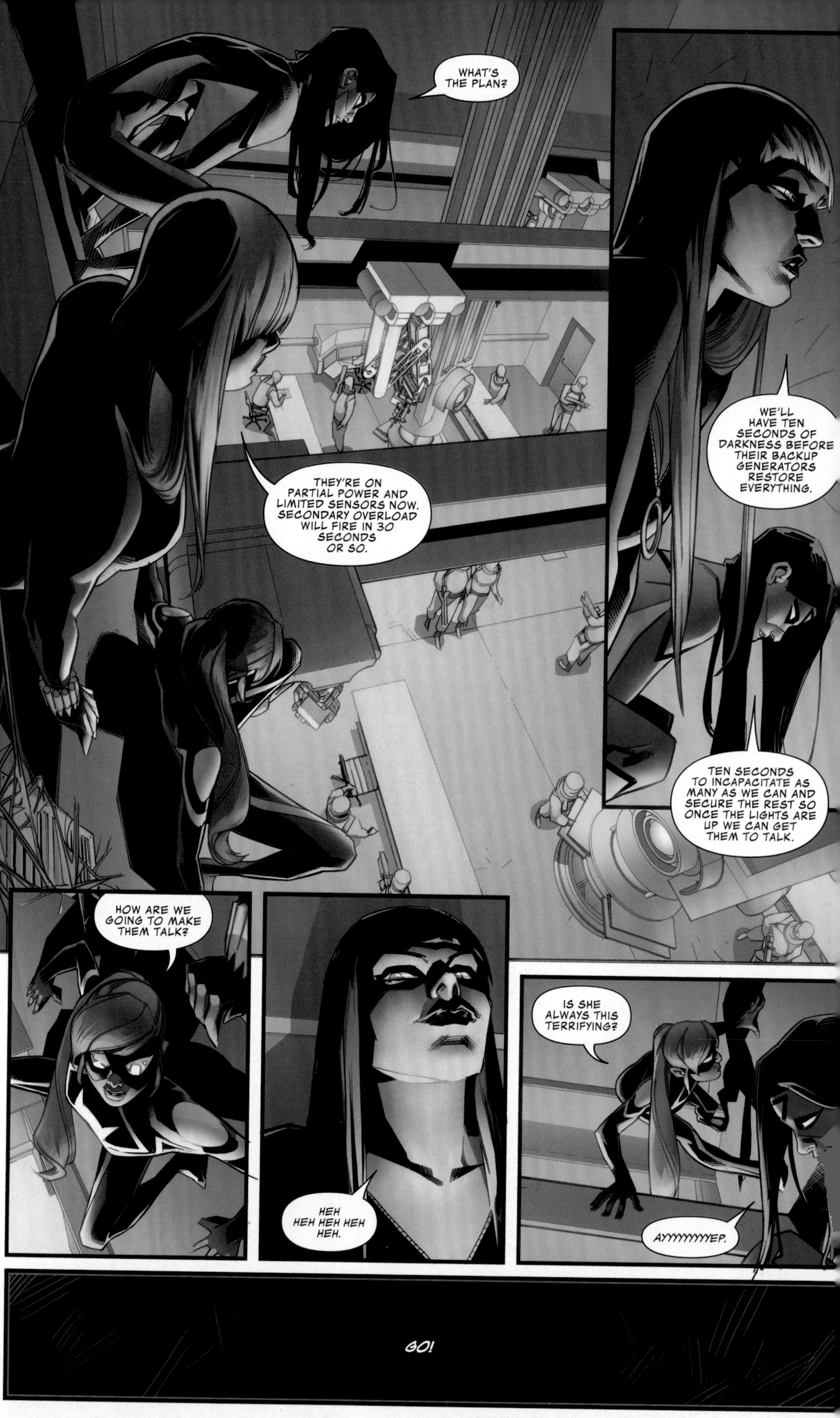
WHAT'S THE PLAN?
THEY'RE ON PARTIAL POWER AND LIMITED SENSORS NOW. SECONDARY OVERLOAD WILL FIRE IN 30 SECONDS OR SO.
WE'LL HAVE TEN SECONDS OF DARKNESS BEFORE THEIR BACKUP GENERATORS RESTORE EVERYTHING.
TEN SECONDS TO INCAPACITATE AS MANY AS WE CAN AND SECURE THE REST SO ONCE THE LIGHTS ARE UP WE CAN GET THEM TO TALK.
HOW ARE WE GOING TO MAKE THEM TALK?
HEH HEH HEH HEH HEH.
IS SHE ALWAYS THIS TERRIFYING?
AYYYYYYYYYEP.
GO!

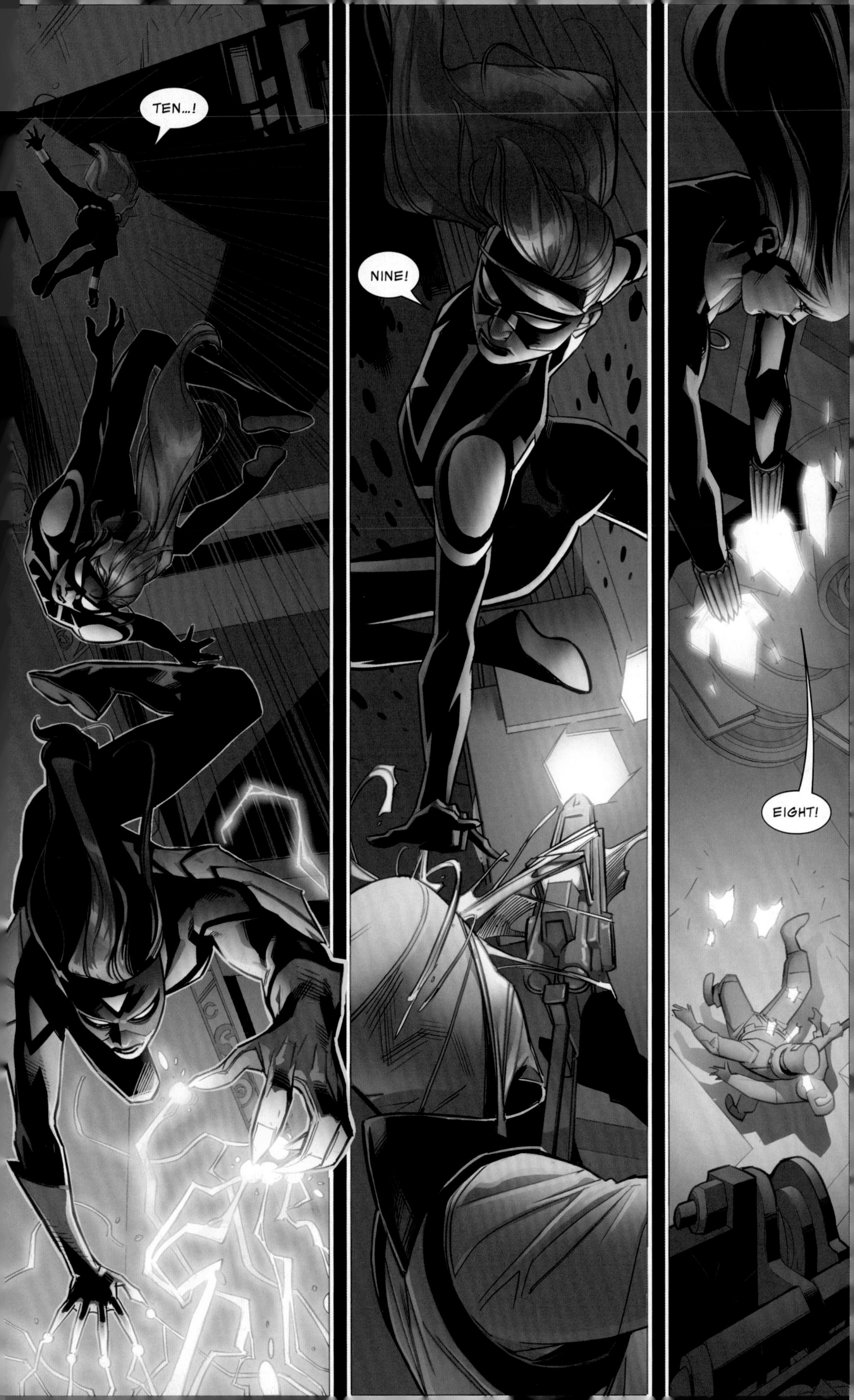
TEN...!
NINE!
EIGHT!

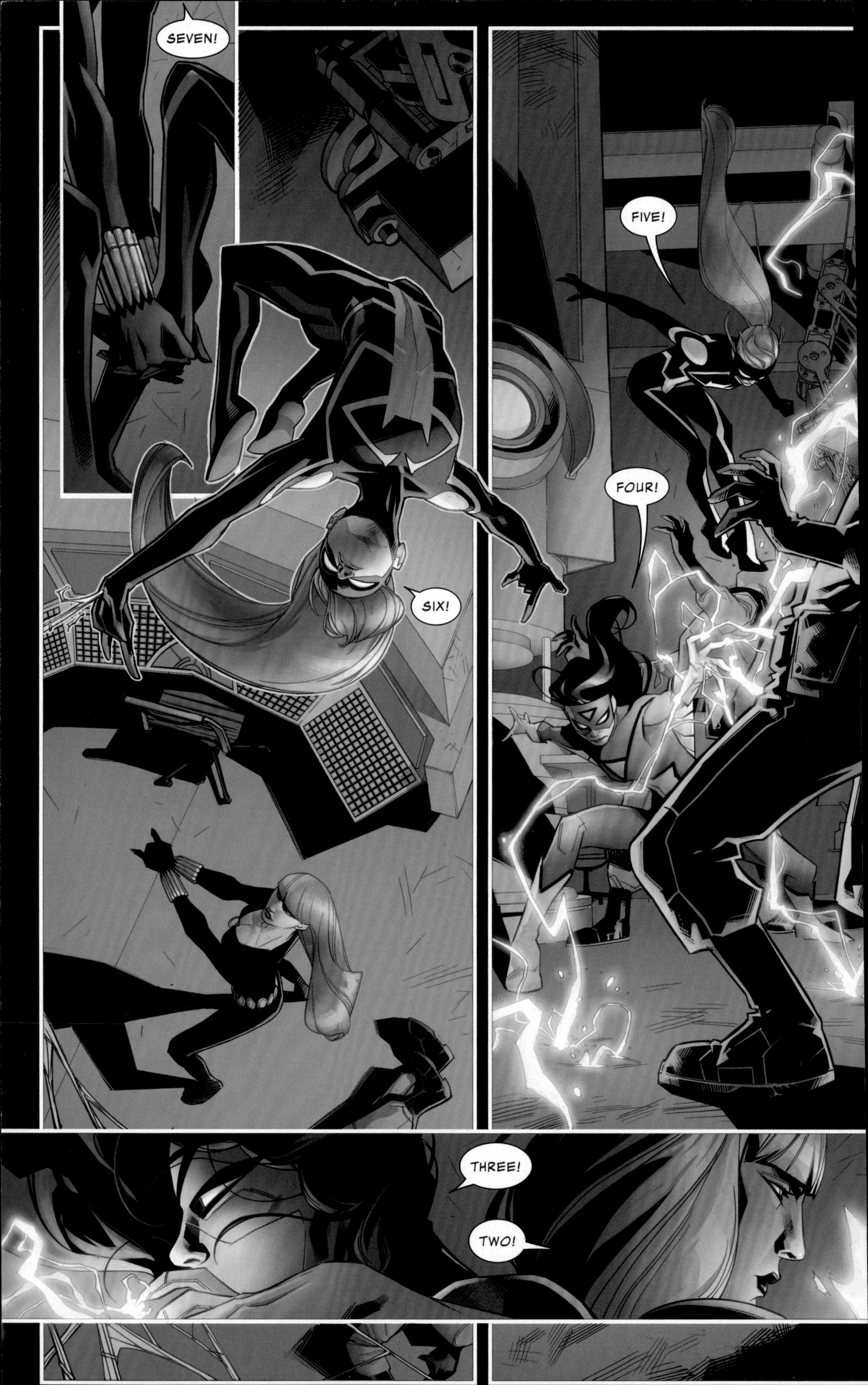
SEVEN!
SIX!
FIVE!
FOUR!
THREE!
TWO!

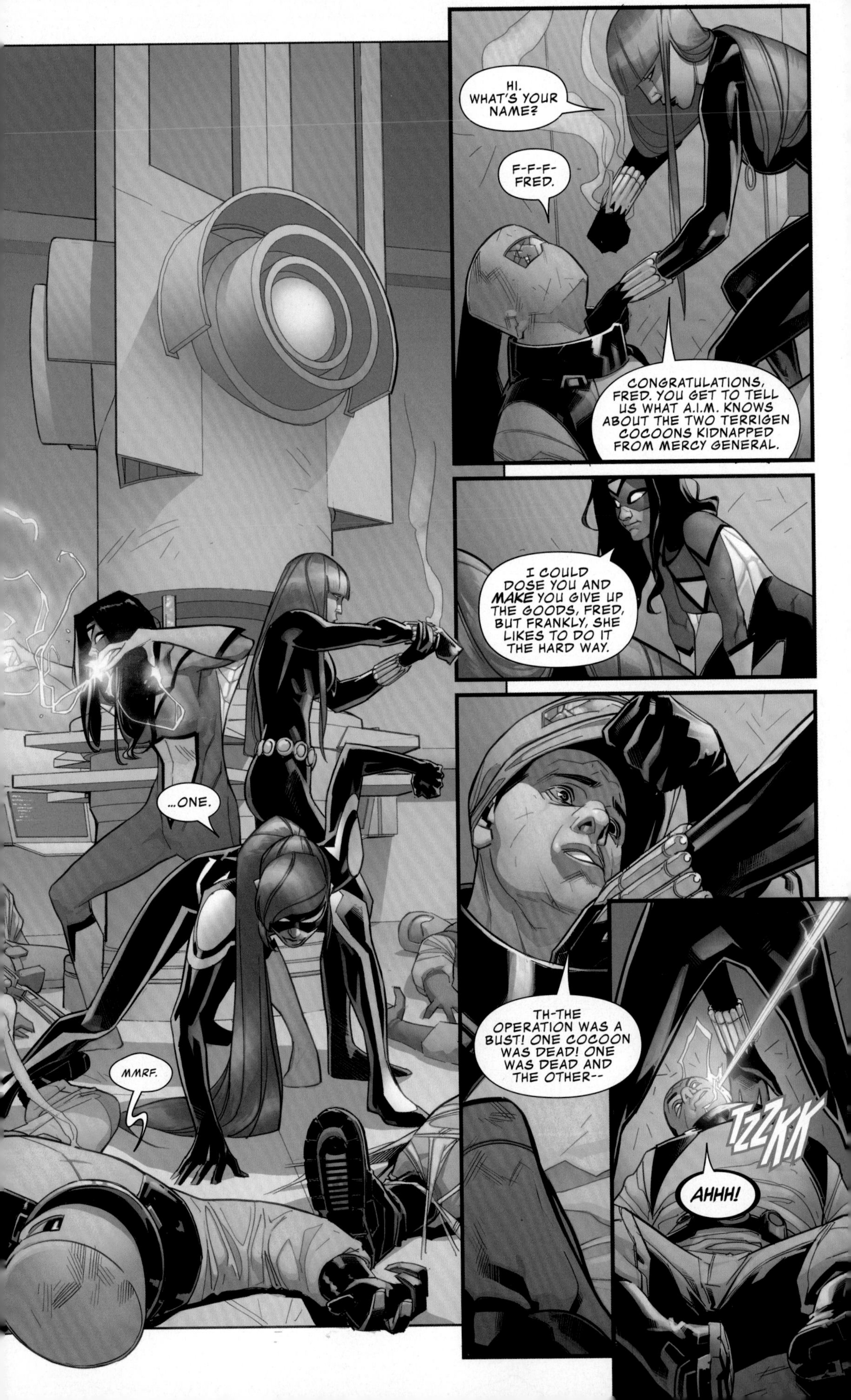

HI. WHAT'S YOUR NAME?
F-F-F-FRED.
CONGRATULATIONS, FRED. YOU GET TO TELL US WHAT A.I.M. KNOWS ABOUT THE TWO TERRIGEN COCOONS KIDNAPPED FROM MERCY GENERAL.
I COULD DOSE YOU AND MAKE YOU GIVE UP THE GOODS, FRED, BUT FRANKLY, SHE LIKES TO DO IT THE HARD WAY.
...ONE.
MMRF.
TH-THE OPERATION WAS A BUST! ONE COCOON WAS DEAD! ONE WAS DEAD AND THE OTHER--
TZZKK
AHHH!

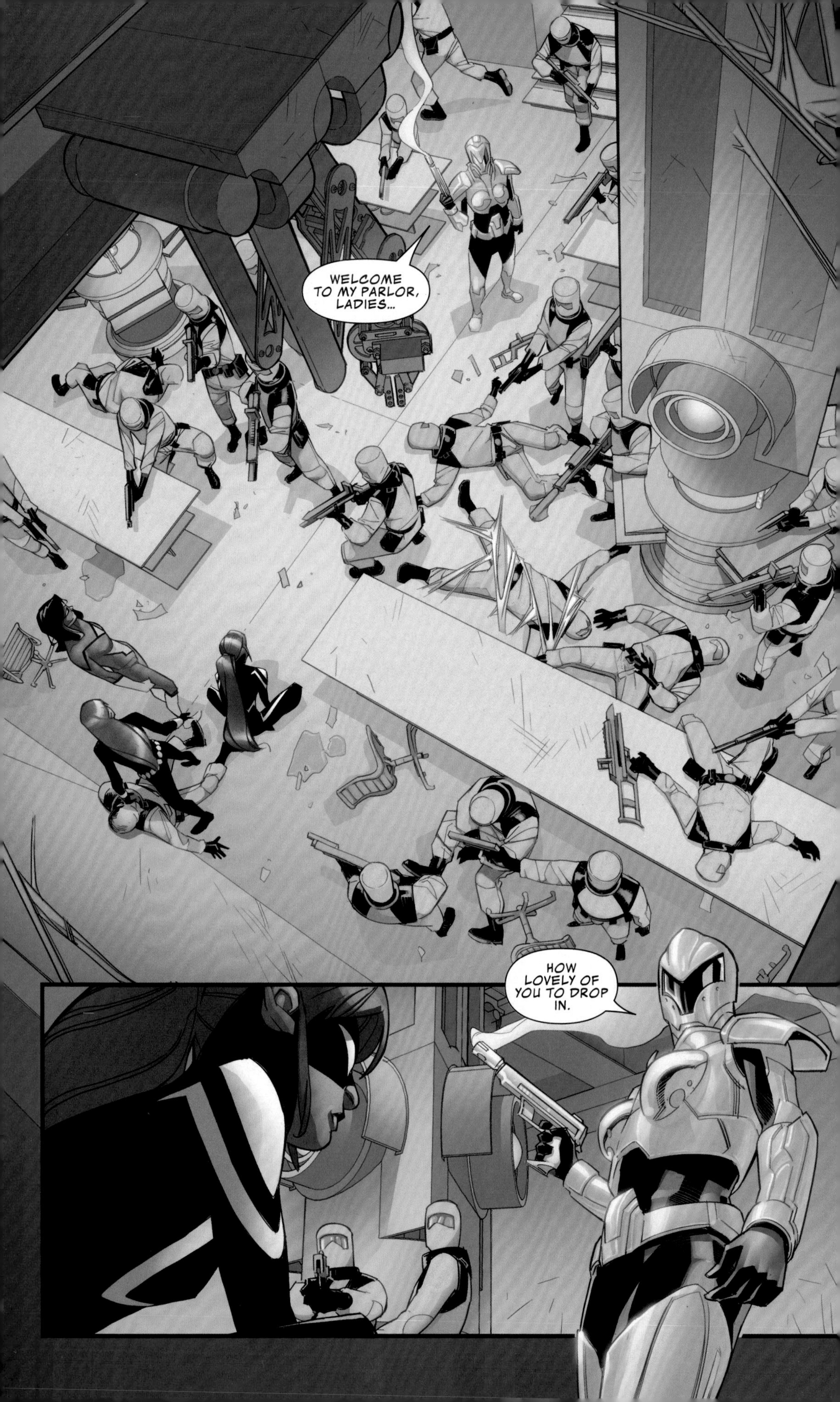

WELCOME TO MY PARLOR, LADIES...
HOW LOVELY OF YOU TO DROP IN.

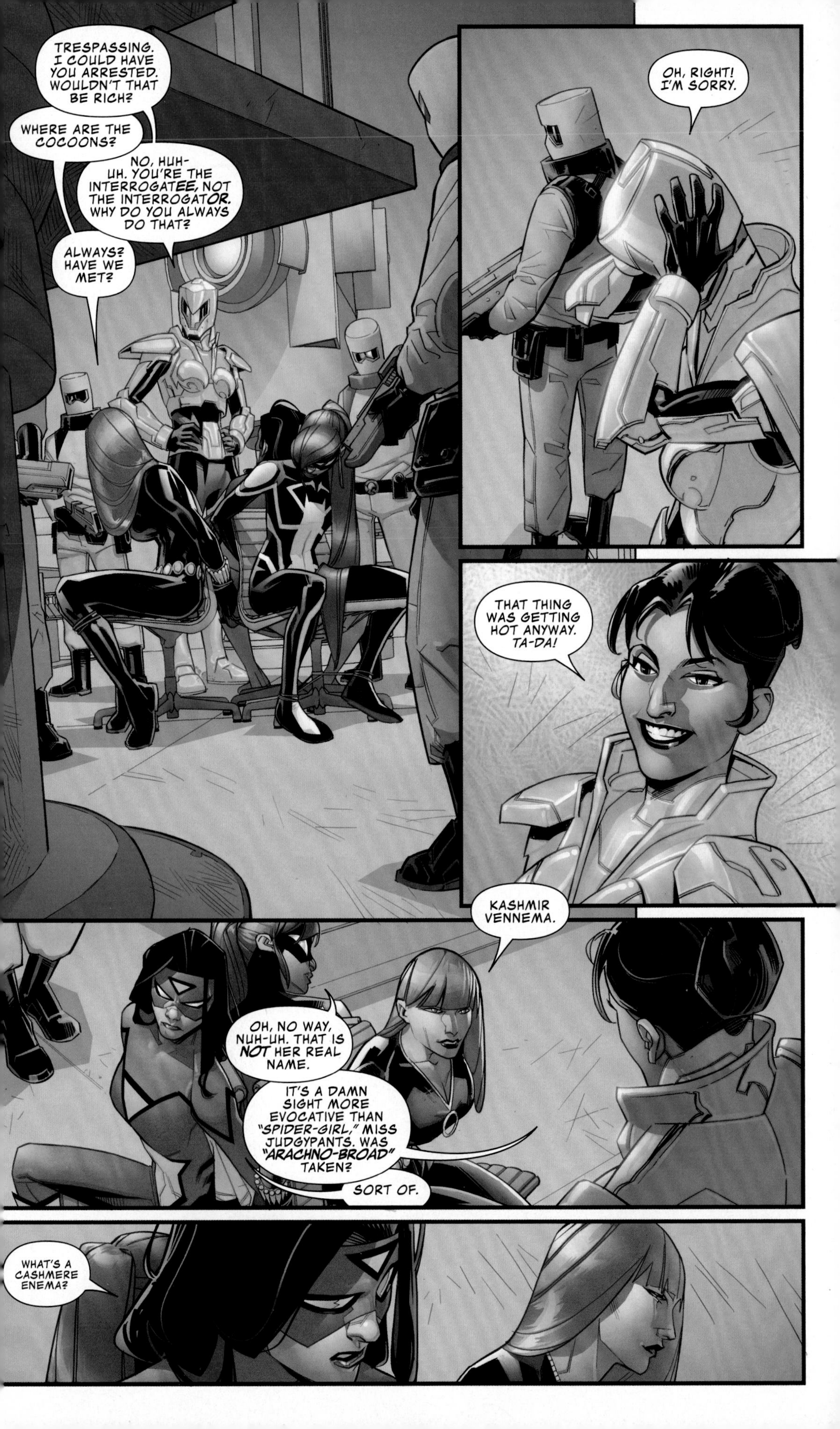

TRESPASSING. I COULD HAVE YOU ARRESTED. WOULDN'T THAT BE RICH?
WHERE ARE THE COCOONS?
NO, HUH-UH. YOU'RE THE INTERROGATEE, NOT THE INTERROGATOR. WHY DO YOU ALWAYS DO THAT?
ALWAYS? HAVE WE MET?
OH, RIGHT! I'M SORRY.
THAT THING WAS GETTING HOT ANYWAY. TA-DA!
KASHMIR VENNEMA.
OH, NO WAY, NUH-UH. THAT IS NOT HER REAL NAME.
IT'S A DAMN SIGHT MORE EVOCATIVE THAN "SPIDER-GIRL," MISS JUDGYPANTS. WAS "ARACHNO-BROAD" TAKEN?
SORT OF.
WHAT'S A CASHMERE ENEMA?

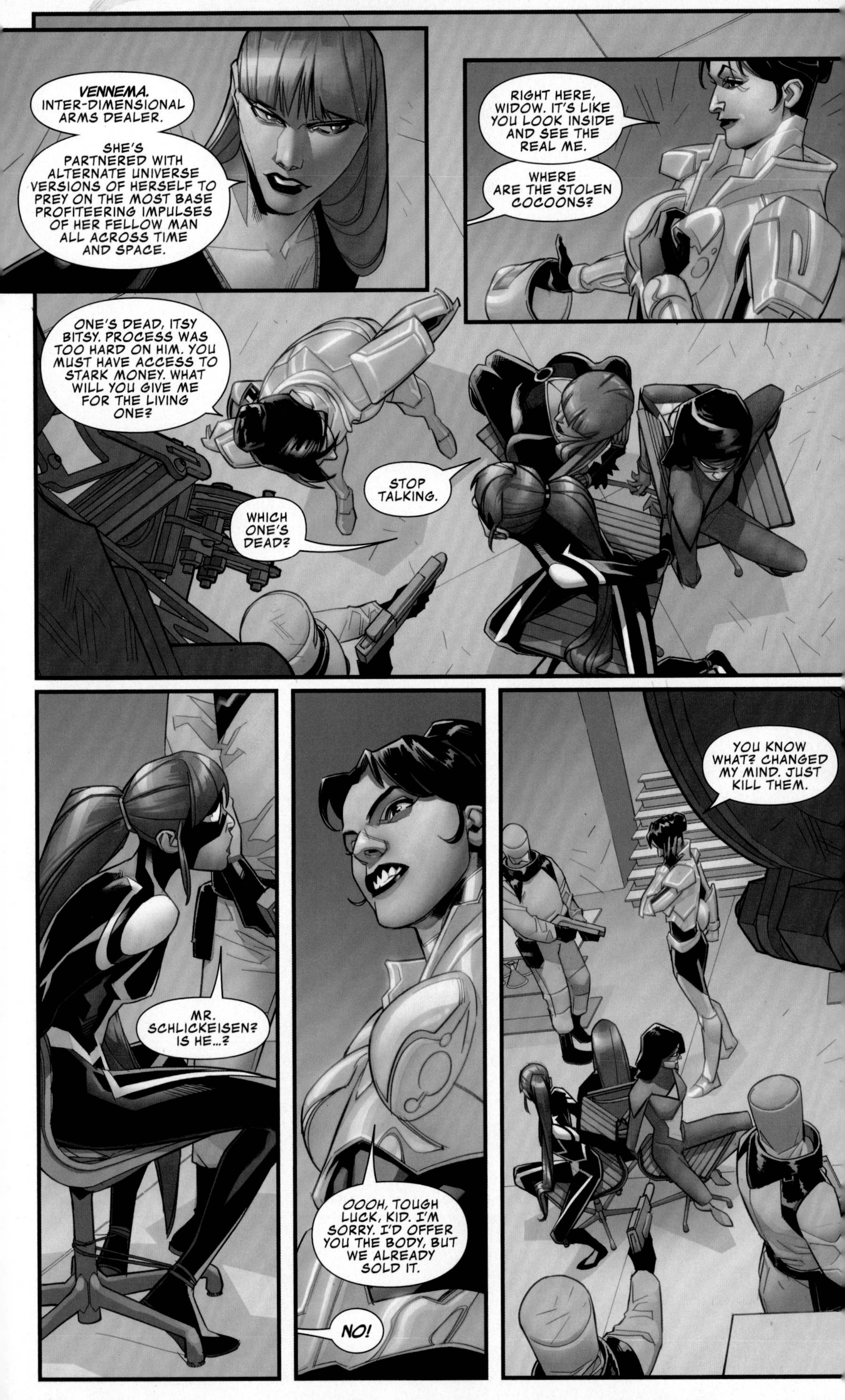
VENNEMA. INTER-DIMENSIONAL ARMS DEALER.
SHE'S PARTNERED WITH ALTERNATE UNIVERSE VERSIONS OF HERSELF TO PREY ON THE MOST BASE PROFITEERING IMPULSES OF HER FELLOW MAN ALL ACROSS TIME AND SPACE.
RIGHT HERE, WIDOW. IT'S LIKE YOU LOOK INSIDE AND SEE THE REAL ME.
WHERE ARE THE STOLEN COCOONS?
ONE'S DEAD, ITSY BITSY. PROCESS WAS TOO HARD ON HIM. YOU MUST HAVE ACCESS TO STARK MONEY. WHAT WILL YOU GIVE ME FOR THE LIVING ONE?
STOP TALKING.
WHICH ONE'S DEAD?
MR. SCHLICKEISEN? IS HE...?
OOOH, TOUGH LUCK, KID. I'M SORRY. I'D OFFER YOU THE BODY, BUT WE ALREADY SOLD IT.
NO!
YOU KNOW WHAT? CHANGED MY MIND. JUST KILL THEM.

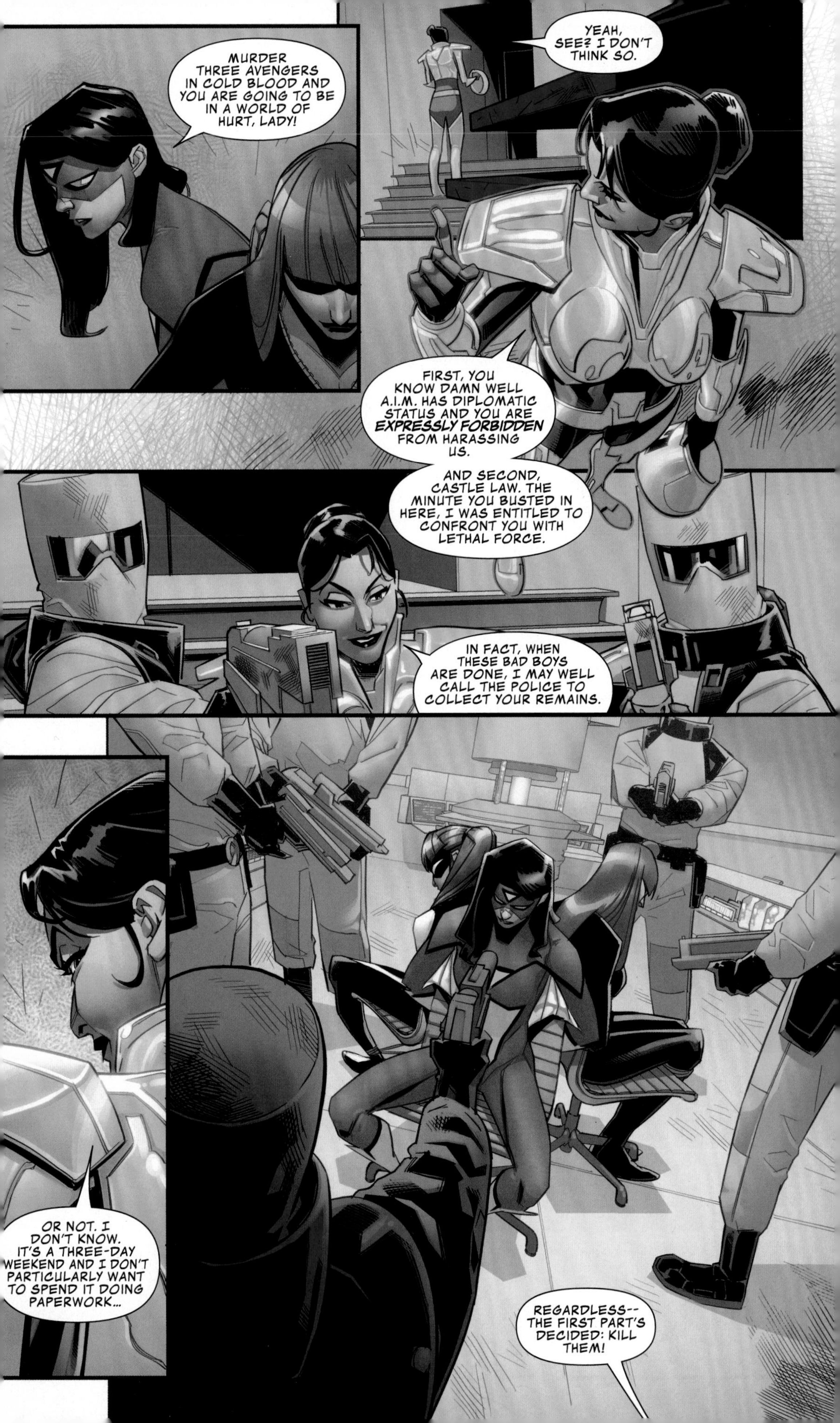
MURDER THREE AVENGERS IN COLD BLOOD AND YOU ARE GOING TO BE IN A WORLD OF HURT, LADY!
YEAH, SEE? I DON'T THINK SO.
FIRST, YOU KNOW DAMN WELL A.I.M. HAS DIPLOMATIC STATUS AND YOU ARE *EXPRESSLY FORBIDDEN* FROM HARASSING US.
AND SECOND, CASTLE LAW. THE MINUTE YOU BUSTED IN HERE, I WAS ENTITLED TO CONFRONT YOU WITH LETHAL FORCE.
IN FACT, WHEN THESE BAD BOYS ARE DONE, I MAY WELL CALL THE POLICE TO COLLECT YOUR REMAINS.
OR NOT. I DON'T KNOW. IT'S A THREE-DAY WEEKEND AND I DON'T PARTICULARLY WANT TO SPEND IT DOING PAPERWORK...
REGARDLESS-- THE FIRST PART'S DECIDED: KILL THEM!

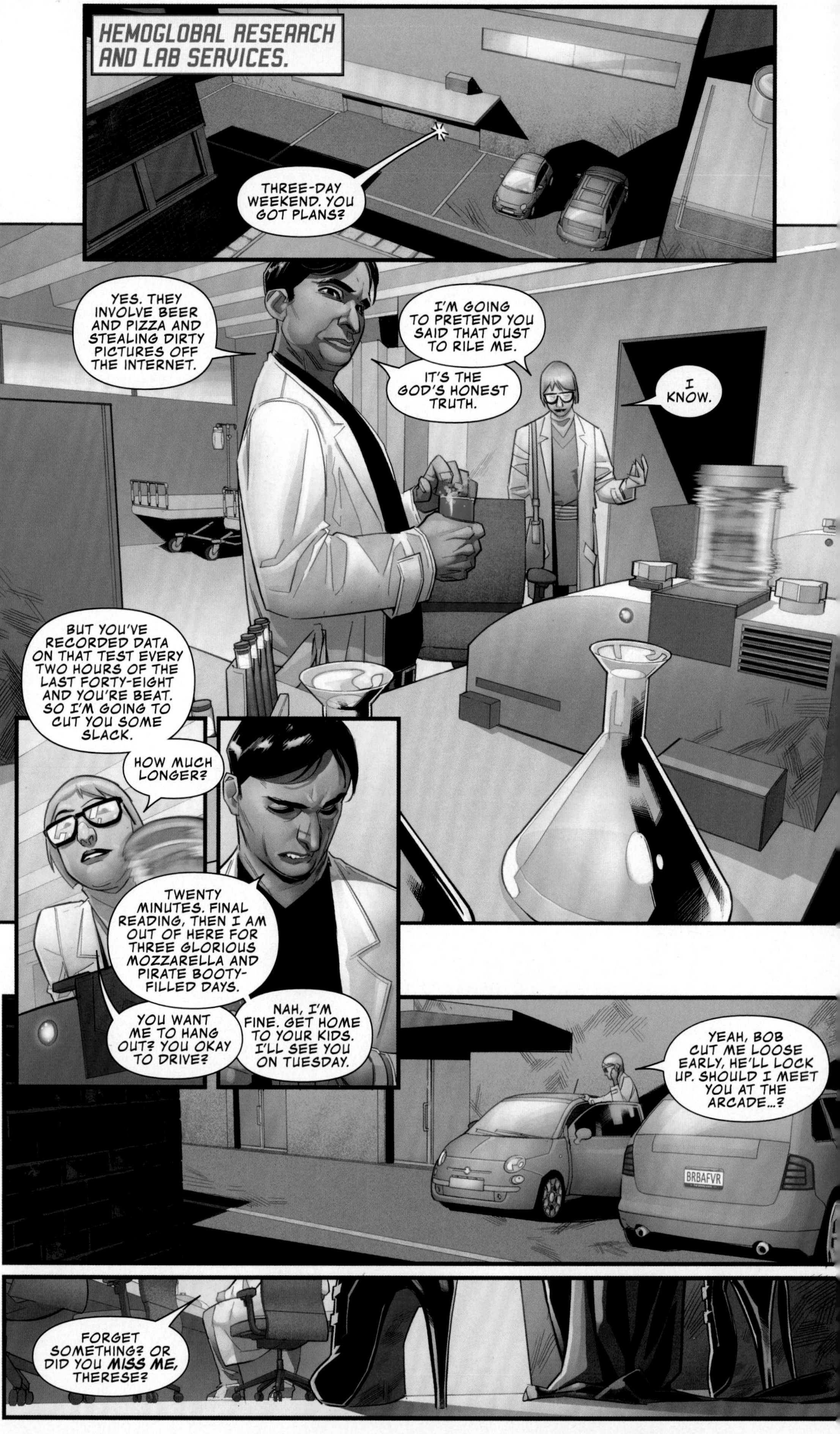
HEMOGLOBAL RESEARCH AND LAB SERVICES.
THREE-DAY WEEKEND. YOU GOT PLANS?
YES. THEY INVOLVE BEER AND PIZZA AND STEALING DIRTY PICTURES OFF THE INTERNET.
I'M GOING TO PRETEND YOU SAID THAT JUST TO RILE ME.
IT'S THE GOD'S HONEST TRUTH.
I KNOW.
BUT YOU'VE RECORDED DATA ON THAT TEST EVERY TWO HOURS OF THE LAST FORTY-EIGHT AND YOU'RE BEAT. SO I'M GOING TO CUT YOU SOME SLACK.
HOW MUCH LONGER?
TWENTY MINUTES. FINAL READING, THEN I AM OUT OF HERE FOR THREE GLORIOUS MOZZARELLA AND PIRATE BOOTY-FILLED DAYS.
YOU WANT ME TO HANG OUT? YOU OKAY TO DRIVE?
NAH, I'M FINE. GET HOME TO YOUR KIDS. I'LL SEE YOU ON TUESDAY.
YEAH, BOB CUT ME LOOSE EARLY, HE'LL LOCK UP. SHOULD I MEET YOU AT THE ARCADE...?
BRBAFVR
FORGET SOMETHING? OR DID YOU *MISS ME*, THERESE?

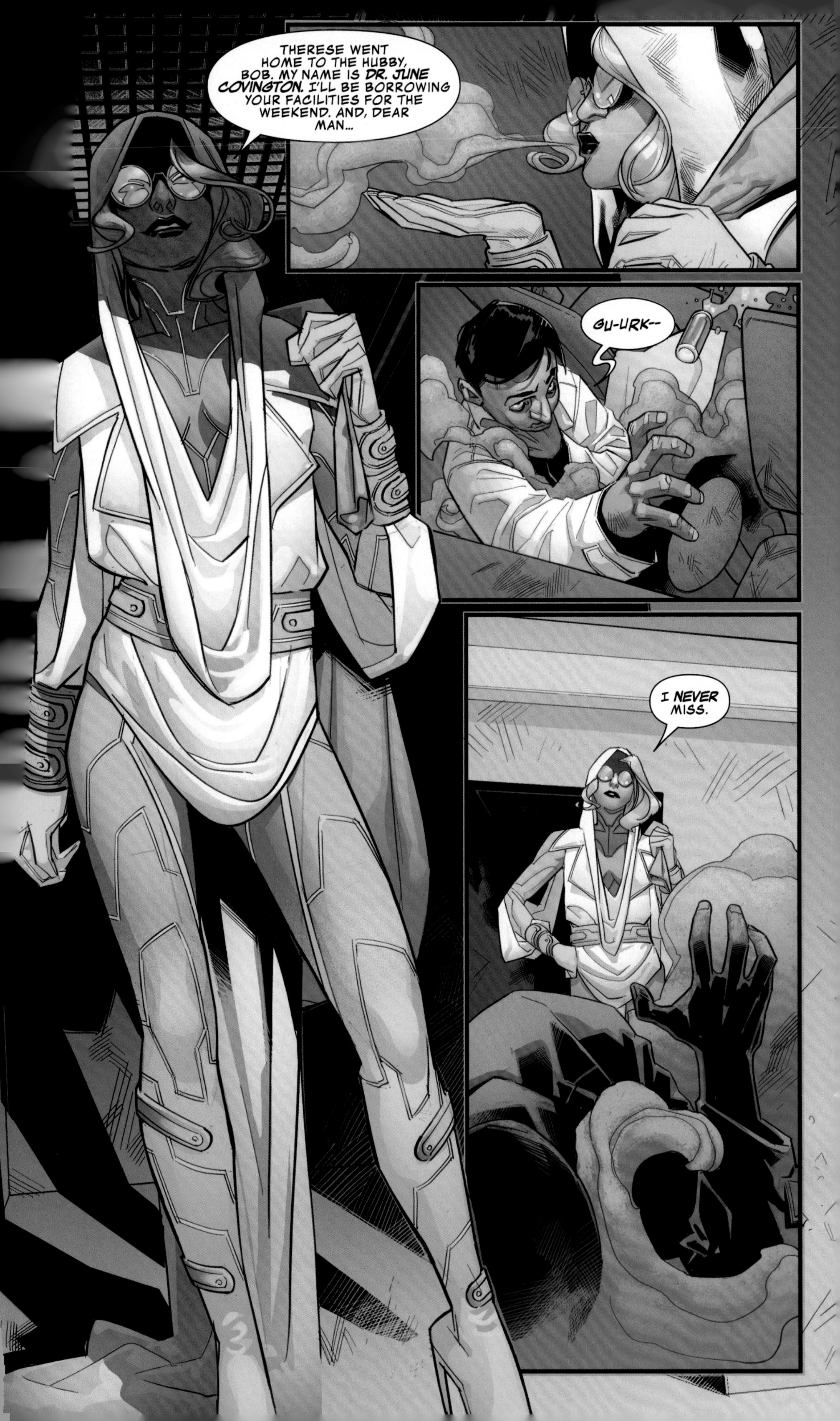
THERESE WENT HOME TO THE HUBBY, BOB. MY NAME IS DR. JUNE COVINGTON. I'LL BE BORROWING YOUR FACILITIES FOR THE WEEKEND. AND, DEAR MAN...
GU-URK--
I NEVER MISS.

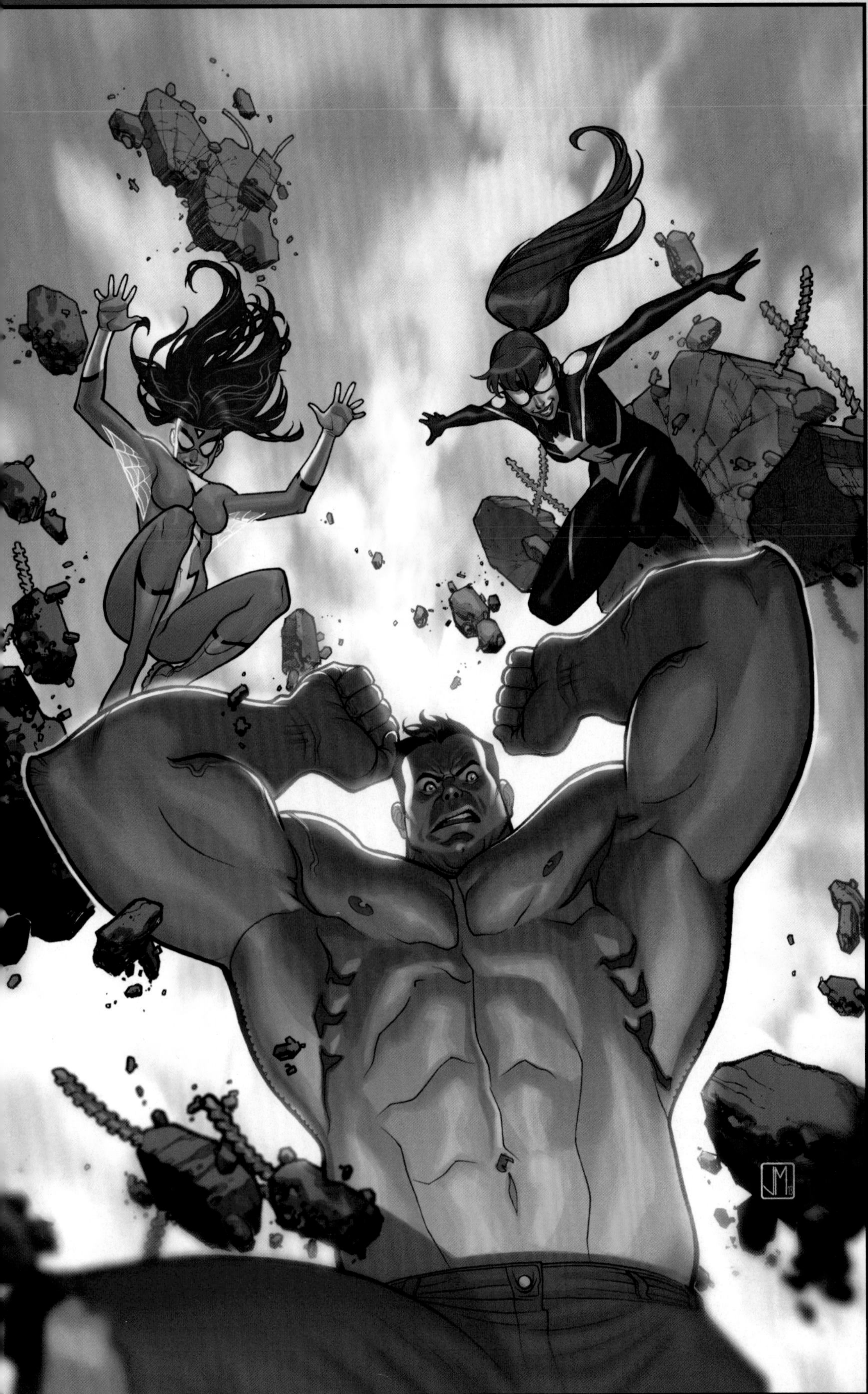

TWENTY-TWO

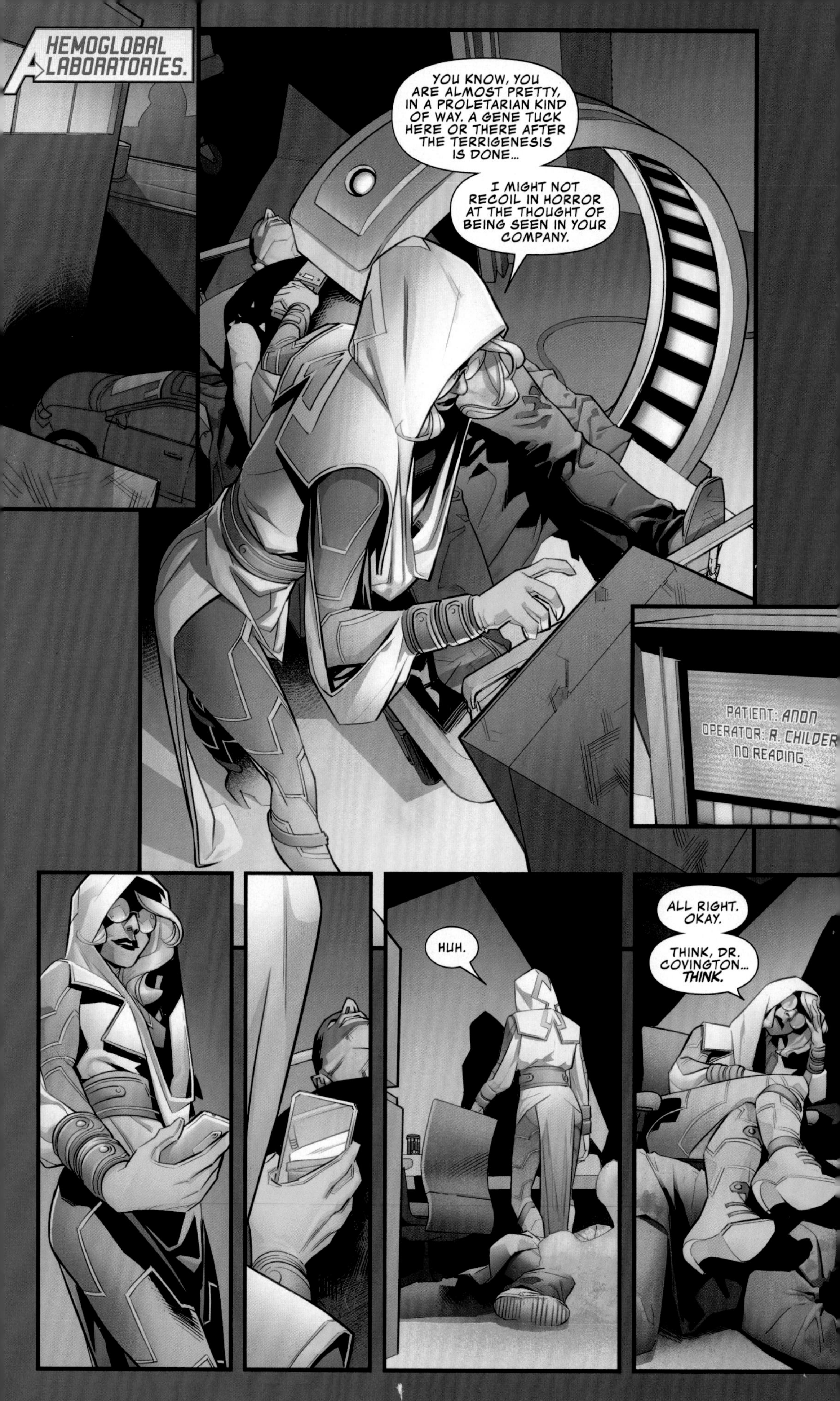
HEMOGLOBAL LABORATORIES.
YOU KNOW, YOU ARE ALMOST PRETTY, IN A PROLETARIAN KIND OF WAY. A GENE TUCK HERE OR THERE AFTER THE TERRIGENESIS IS DONE...
I MIGHT NOT RECOIL IN HORROR AT THE THOUGHT OF BEING SEEN IN YOUR COMPANY.
PATIENT: ANON
OPERATOR: R. CHILDER
NO READING_
HUH.
ALL RIGHT. OKAY.
THINK, DR. COVINGTON... THINK.

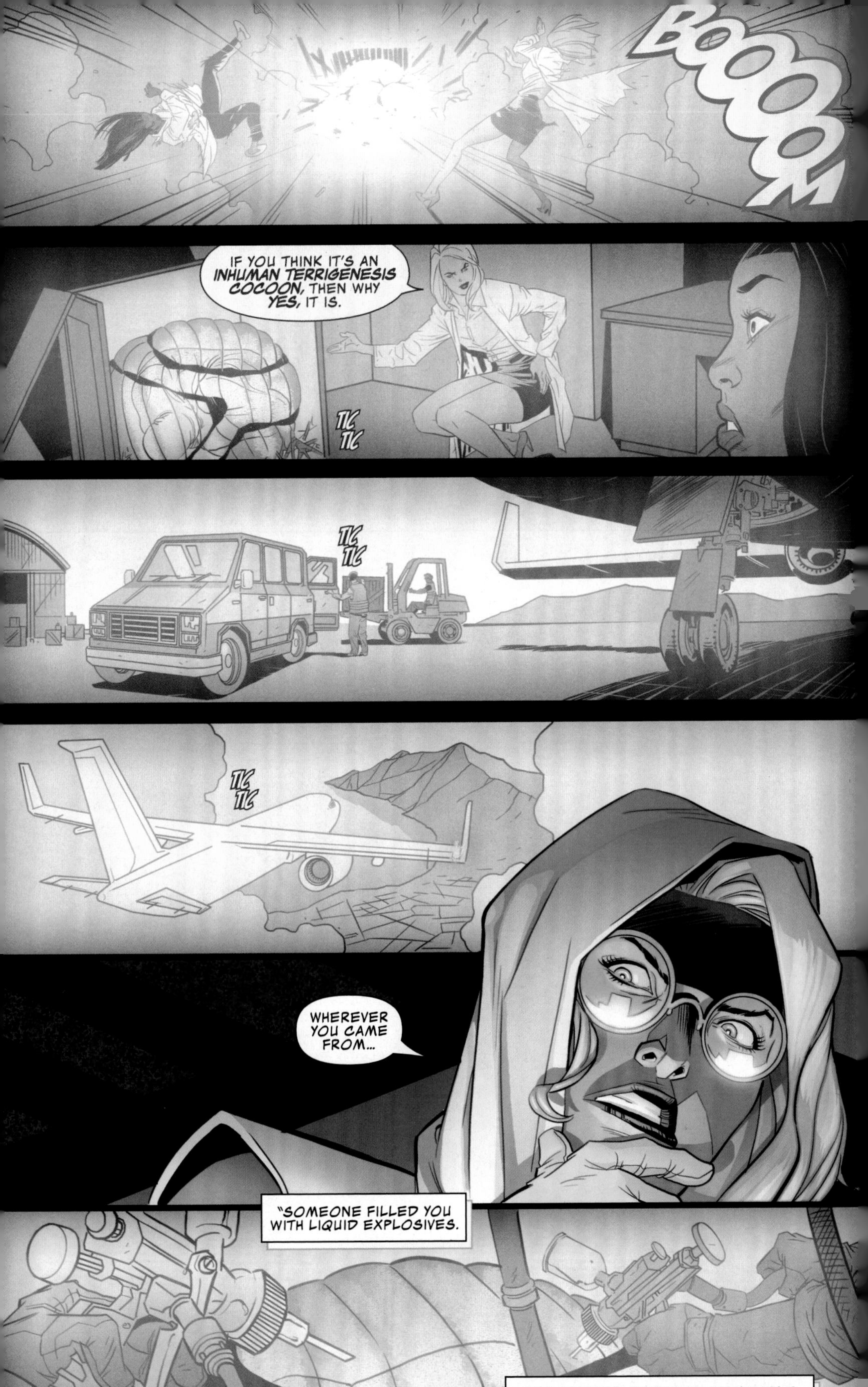
BOOOOM
IF YOU THINK IT'S AN INHUMAN TERRIGENESIS COCOON, THEN WHY YES, IT IS.
TIC TIC
TIC TIC
TIC TIC
WHEREVER YOU CAME FROM...
"SOMEONE FILLED YOU WITH LIQUID EXPLOSIVES.
"WHO WOULD WASTE AN INVALUABLE TERRIGEN COCOON JUST TO KILL ME? WITH A LIVE INHUMAN INSIDE?"

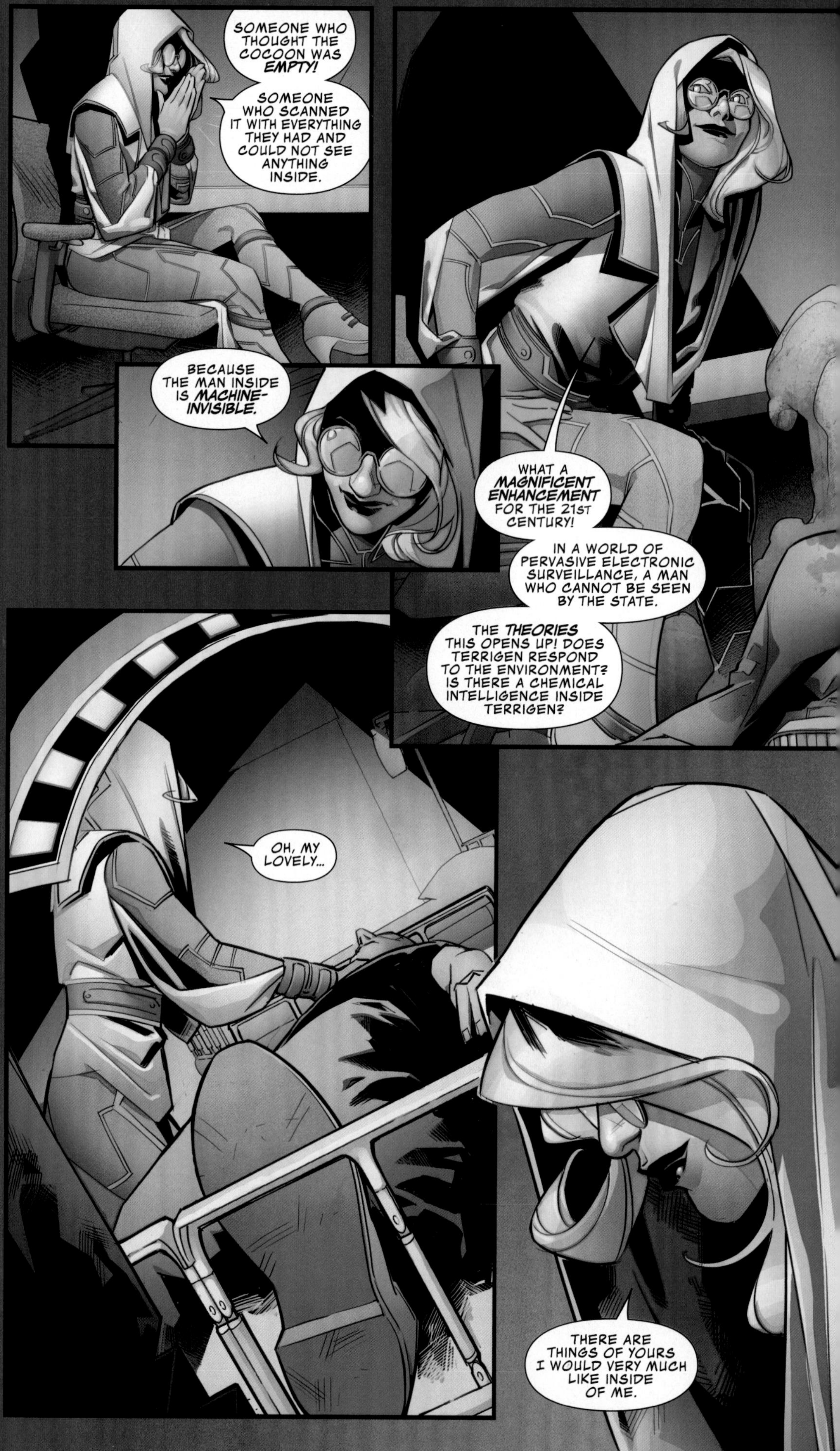
SOMEONE WHO THOUGHT THE COCOON WAS EMPTY!
SOMEONE WHO SCANNED IT WITH EVERYTHING THEY HAD AND COULD NOT SEE ANYTHING INSIDE.
BECAUSE THE MAN INSIDE IS MACHINE-INVISIBLE.
WHAT A MAGNIFICENT ENHANCEMENT FOR THE 21ST CENTURY!
IN A WORLD OF PERVASIVE ELECTRONIC SURVEILLANCE, A MAN WHO CANNOT BE SEEN BY THE STATE.
THE THEORIES THIS OPENS UP! DOES TERRIGEN RESPOND TO THE ENVIRONMENT? IS THERE A CHEMICAL INTELLIGENCE INSIDE TERRIGEN?
OH, MY LOVELY...
THERE ARE THINGS OF YOURS I WOULD VERY MUCH LIKE INSIDE OF ME.

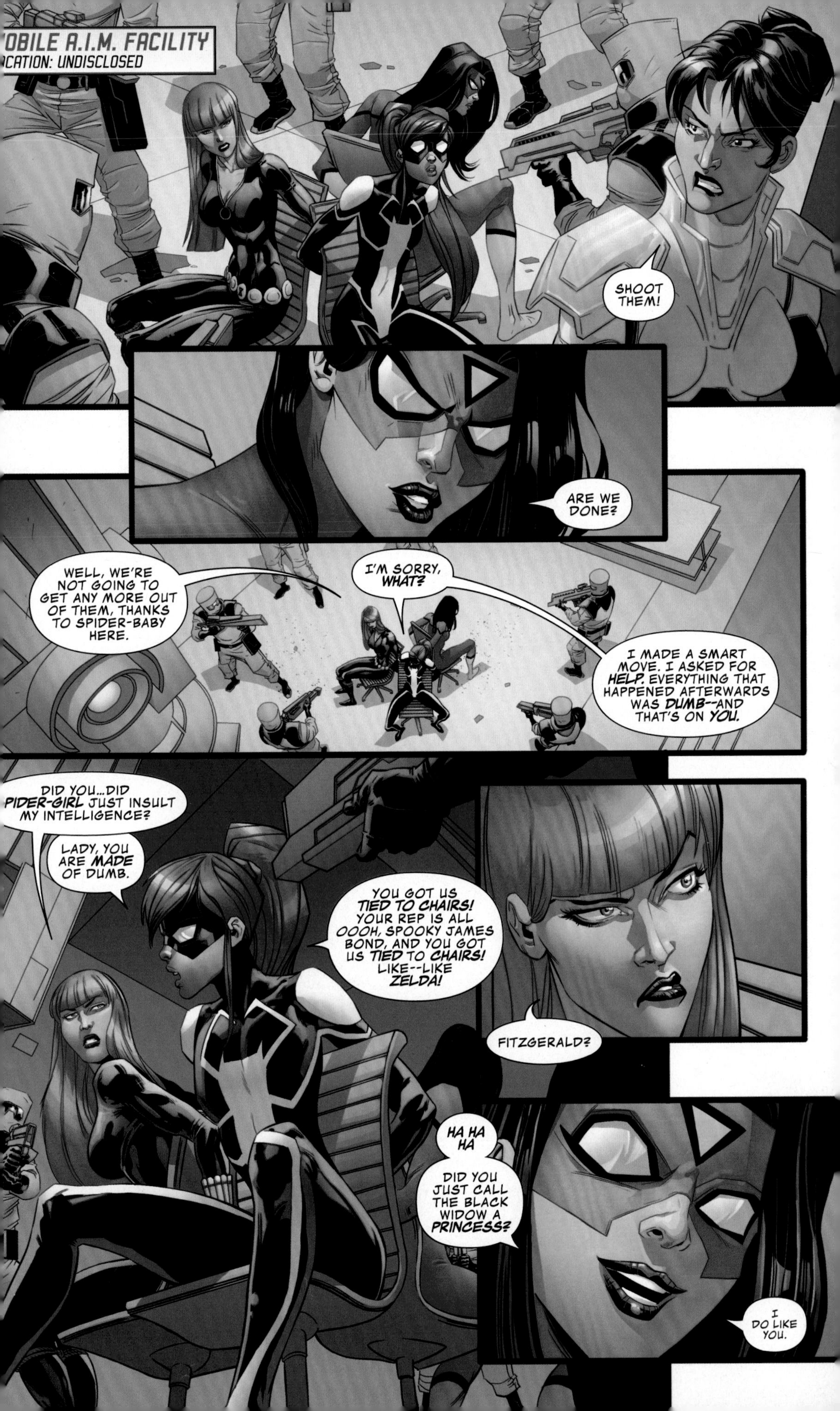

OBILE A.I.M. FACILITY
CATION: UNDISCLOSED
SHOOT THEM!
ARE WE DONE?
WELL, WE'RE NOT GOING TO GET ANY MORE OUT OF THEM, THANKS TO SPIDER-BABY HERE.
I'M SORRY, WHAT?
I MADE A SMART MOVE. I ASKED FOR HELP. EVERYTHING THAT HAPPENED AFTERWARDS WAS DUMB--AND THAT'S ON YOU.
DID YOU...DID PIDER-GIRL JUST INSULT MY INTELLIGENCE?
LADY, YOU ARE MADE OF DUMB.
YOU GOT US TIED TO CHAIRS! YOUR REP IS ALL OOOH, SPOOKY JAMES BOND, AND YOU GOT US TIED TO CHAIRS! LIKE--LIKE ZELDA!
FITZGERALD?
HA HA HA
DID YOU JUST CALL THE BLACK WIDOW A PRINCESS?
I DO LIKE YOU.

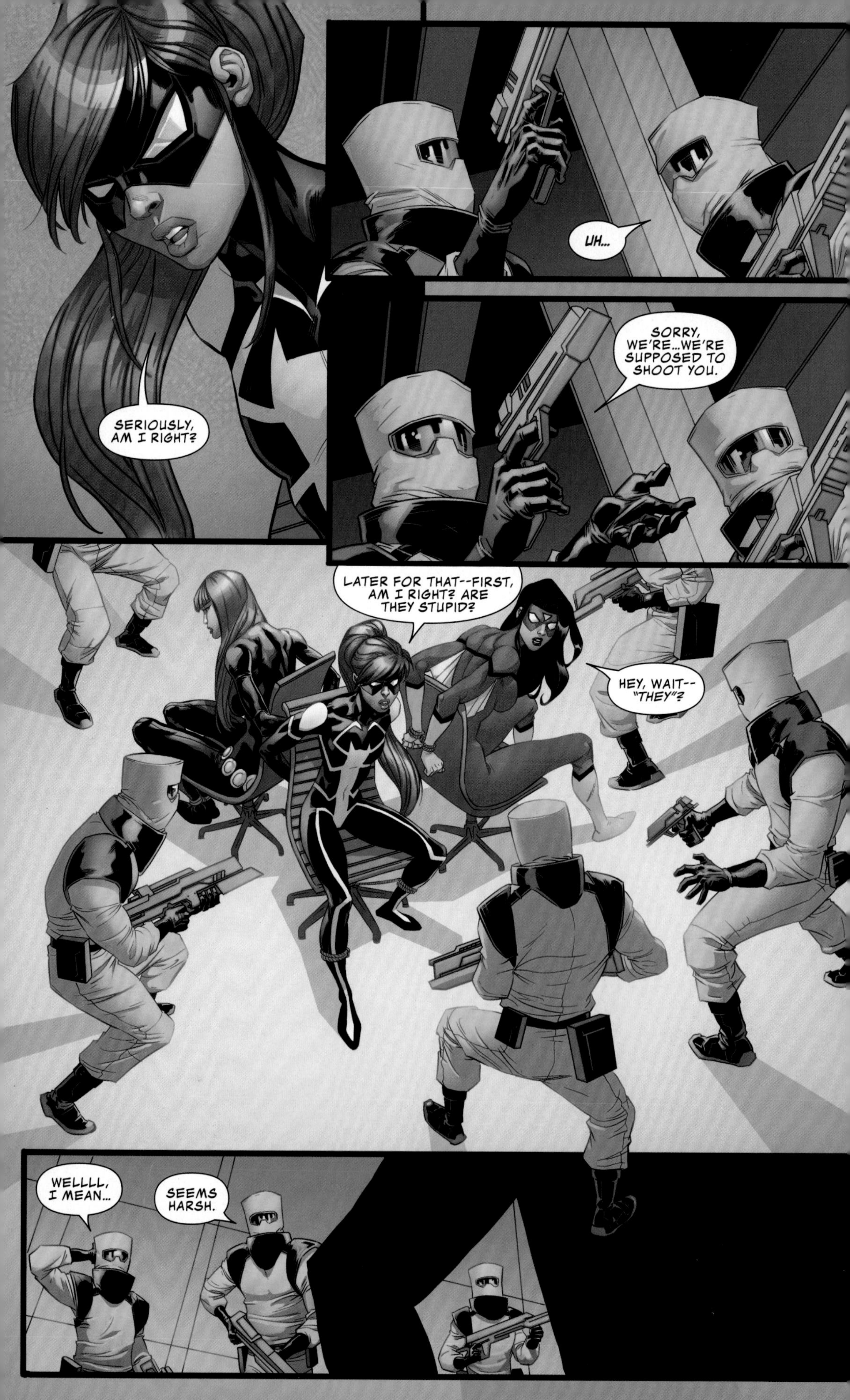
SERIOUSLY, AM I RIGHT?
UH...
SORRY, WE'RE...WE'RE SUPPOSED TO SHOOT YOU.
LATER FOR THAT--FIRST, AM I RIGHT? ARE THEY STUPID?
HEY, WAIT-- "THEY"?
WELLLL, I MEAN...
SEEMS HARSH.

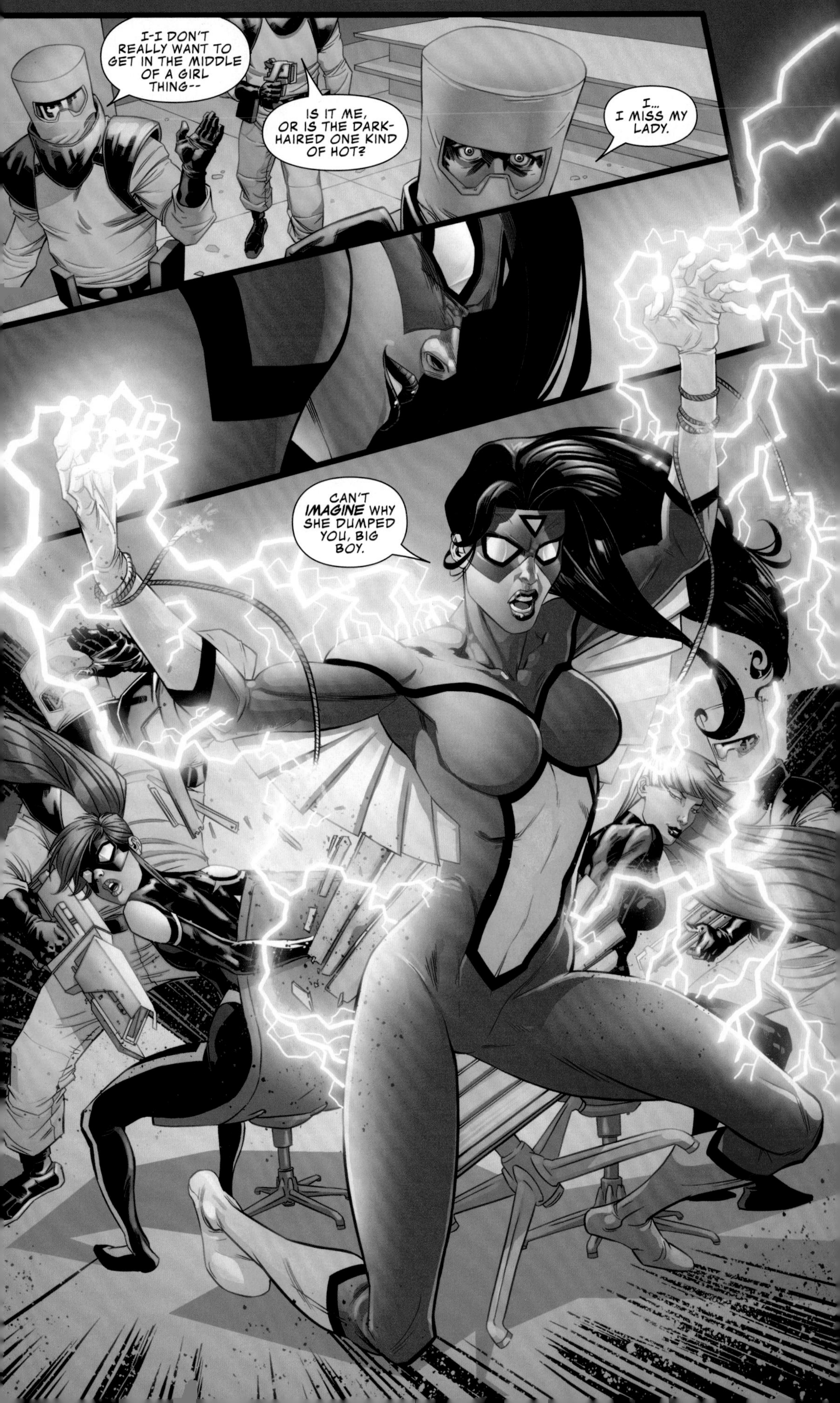
I-I DON'T REALLY WANT TO GET IN THE MIDDLE OF A GIRL THING--
IS IT ME, OR IS THE DARK-HAIRED ONE KIND OF HOT?
I... I MISS MY LADY.
CAN'T *IMAGINE* WHY SHE DUMPED YOU, BIG BOY.

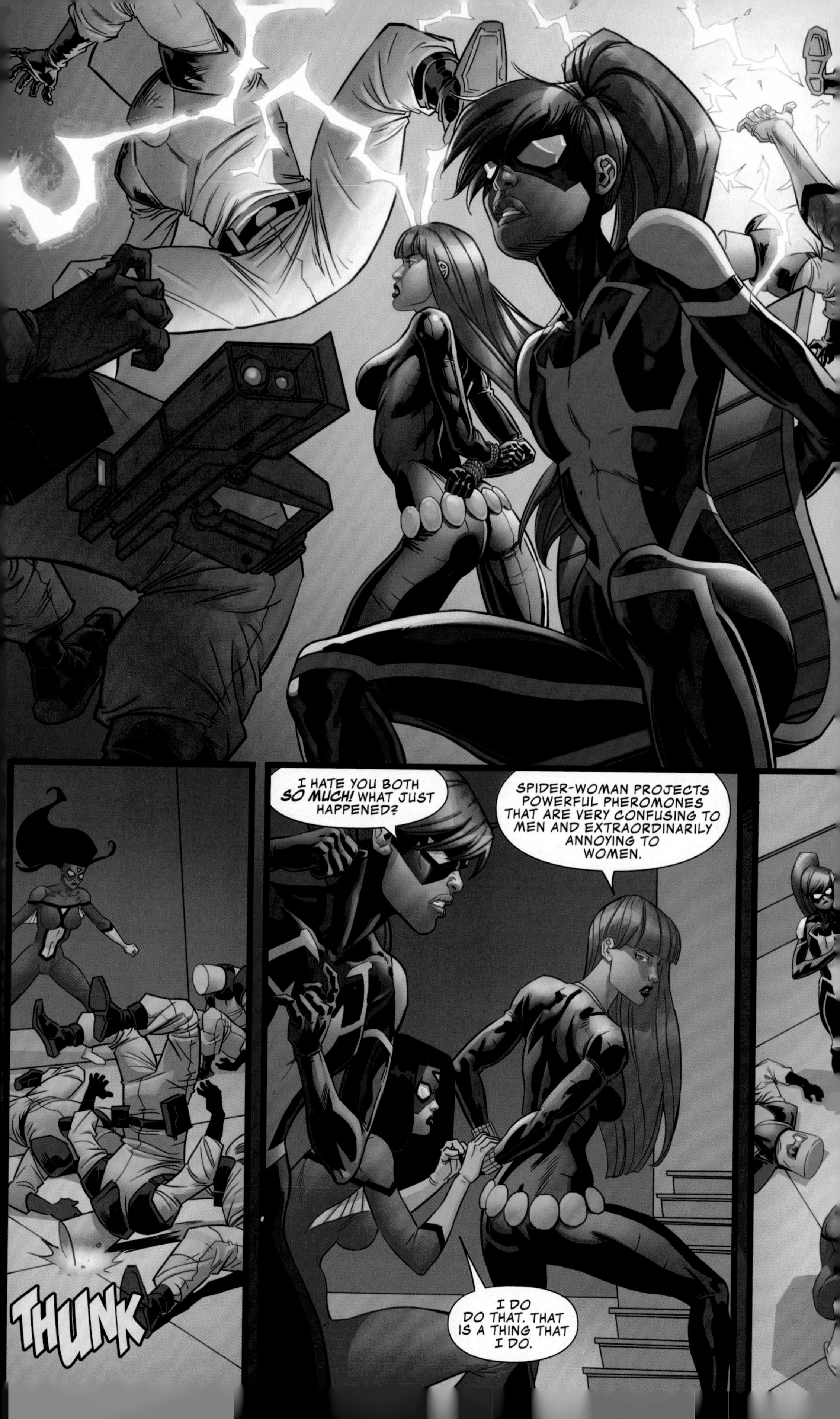
THUNK
I HATE YOU BOTH SO MUCH! WHAT JUST HAPPENED?
SPIDER-WOMAN PROJECTS POWERFUL PHEROMONES THAT ARE VERY CONFUSING TO MEN AND EXTRAORDINARILY ANNOYING TO WOMEN.
I DO DO THAT. THAT IS A THING THAT I DO.

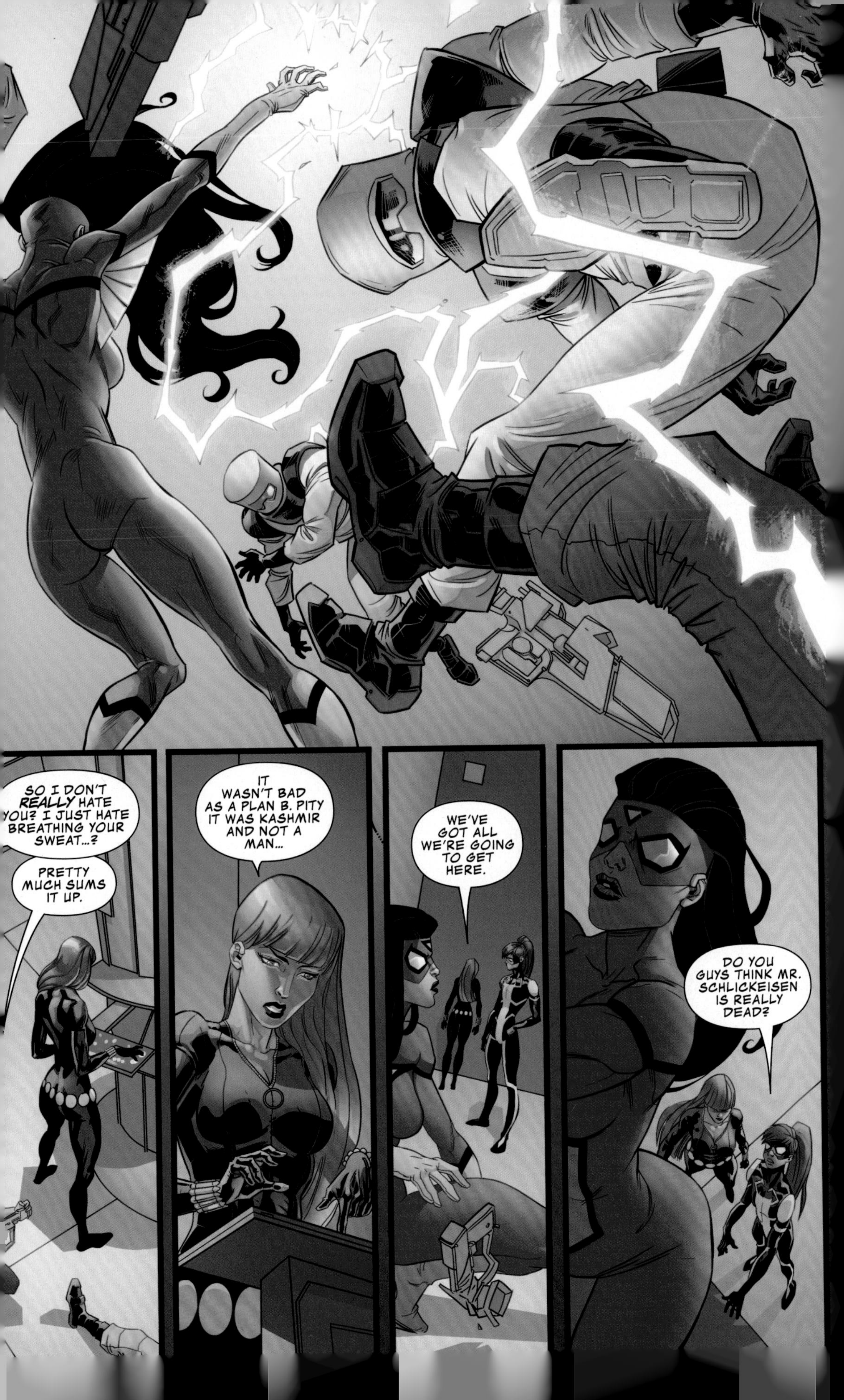
SO I DON'T REALLY HATE YOU? I JUST HATE BREATHING YOUR SWEAT...?
PRETTY MUCH SUMS IT UP.
IT WASN'T BAD AS A PLAN B. PITY IT WAS KASHMIR AND NOT A MAN...
WE'VE GOT ALL WE'RE GOING TO GET HERE.
DO YOU GUYS THINK MR. SCHLICKEISEN IS REALLY DEAD?

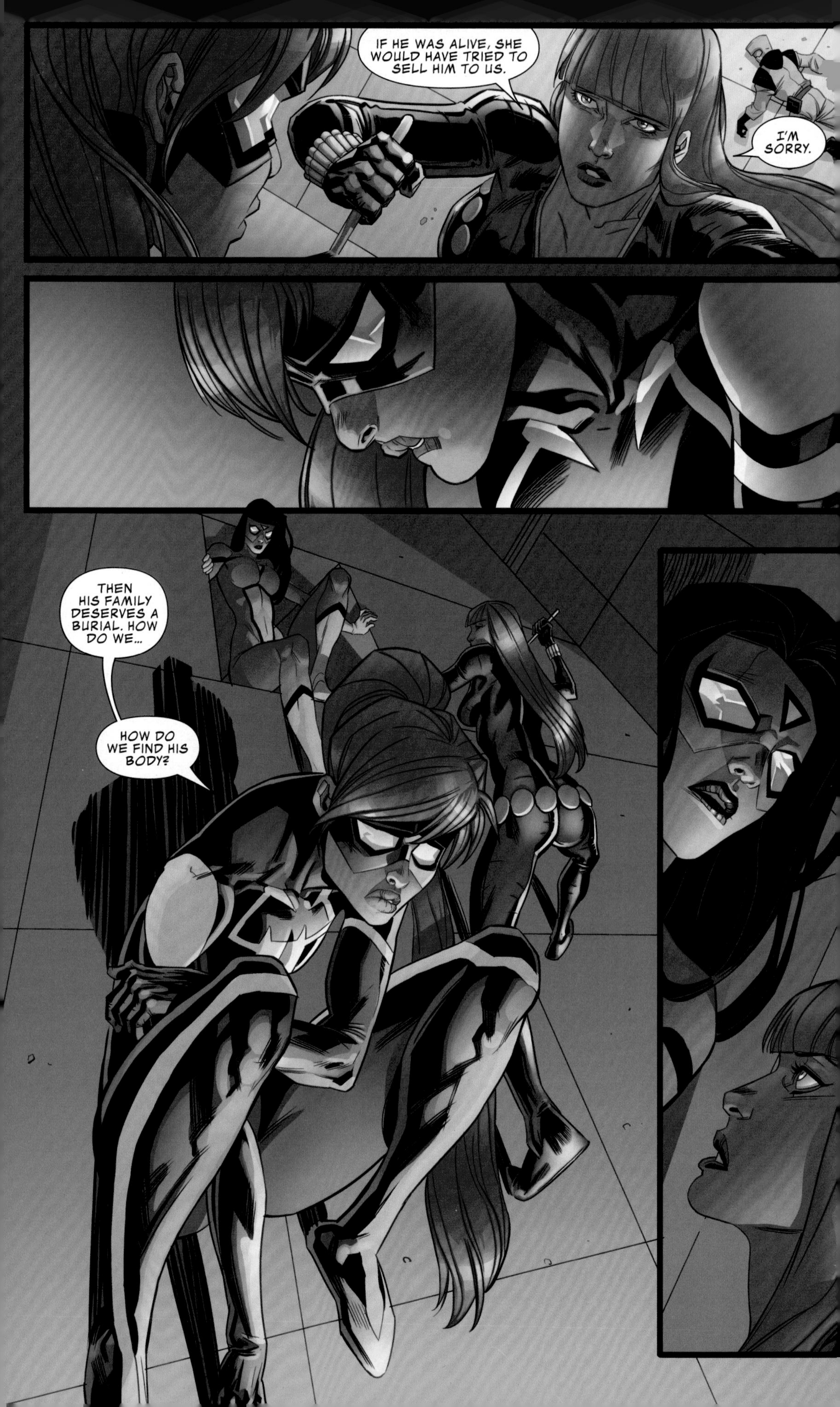
IF HE WAS ALIVE, SHE WOULD HAVE TRIED TO SELL HIM TO US.
I'M SORRY.
THEN HIS FAMILY DESERVES A BURIAL. HOW DO WE...
HOW DO WE FIND HIS BODY?

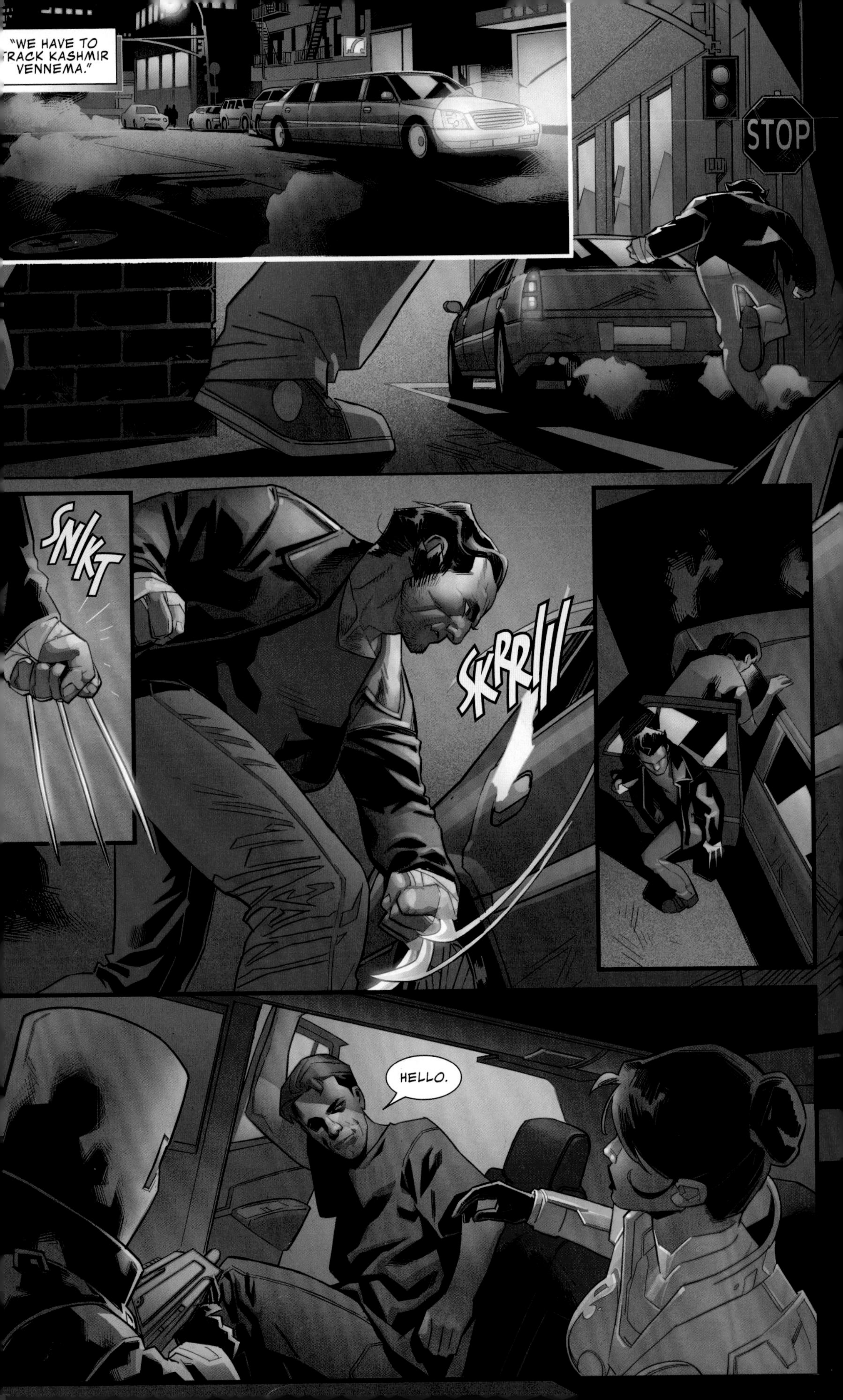
"WE HAVE TO TRACK KASHMIR VENNEMA."
SNIKT
SKRRIII
HELLO.

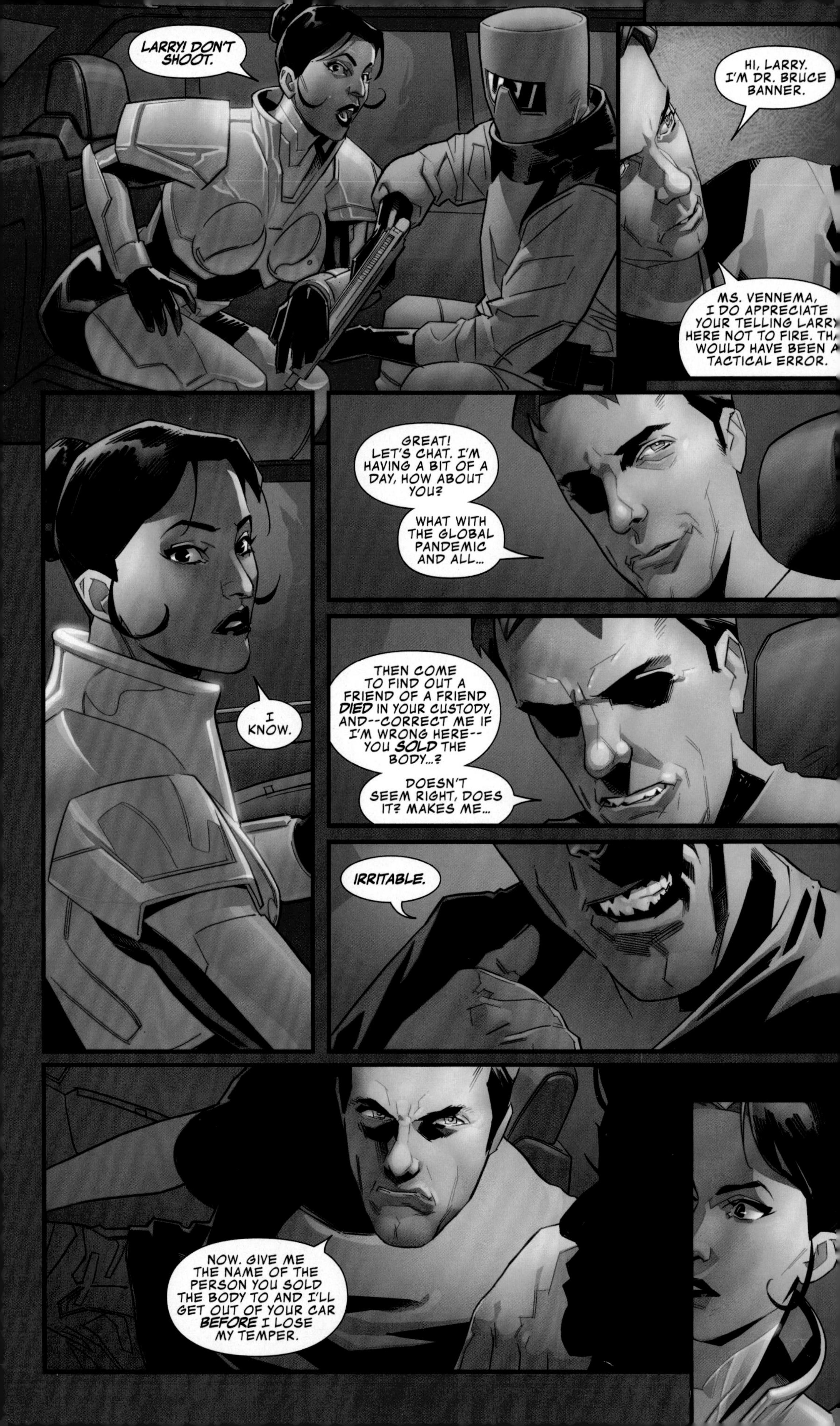
LARRY! DON'T SHOOT.
HI, LARRY. I'M DR. BRUCE BANNER.
MS. VENNEMA, I DO APPRECIATE YOUR TELLING LARRY HERE NOT TO FIRE. THAT WOULD HAVE BEEN A TACTICAL ERROR.
GREAT! LET'S CHAT. I'M HAVING A BIT OF A DAY, HOW ABOUT YOU?
WHAT WITH THE GLOBAL PANDEMIC AND ALL...
I KNOW.
THEN COME TO FIND OUT A FRIEND OF A FRIEND DIED IN YOUR CUSTODY, AND--CORRECT ME IF I'M WRONG HERE--YOU SOLD THE BODY...?
DOESN'T SEEM RIGHT, DOES IT? MAKES ME...
IRRITABLE.
NOW. GIVE ME THE NAME OF THE PERSON YOU SOLD THE BODY TO AND I'LL GET OUT OF YOUR CAR BEFORE I LOSE MY TEMPER.

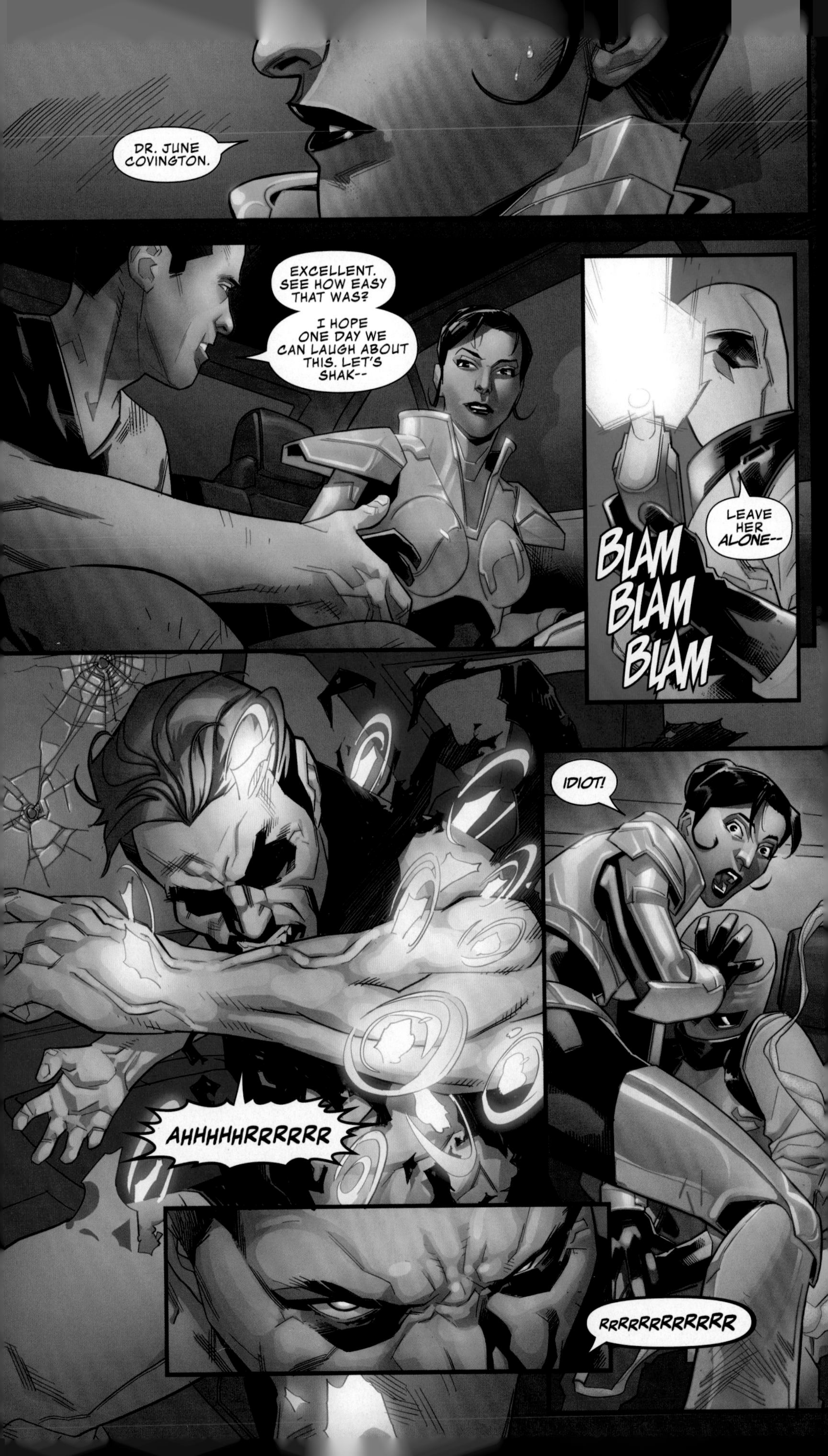
DR. JUNE COVINGTON.
EXCELLENT. SEE HOW EASY THAT WAS?
I HOPE ONE DAY WE CAN LAUGH ABOUT THIS. LET'S SHAK--
LEAVE HER ALONE--
BLAM BLAM BLAM
IDIOT!
AHHHHHRRRRRR
RRRRRRRRRRR

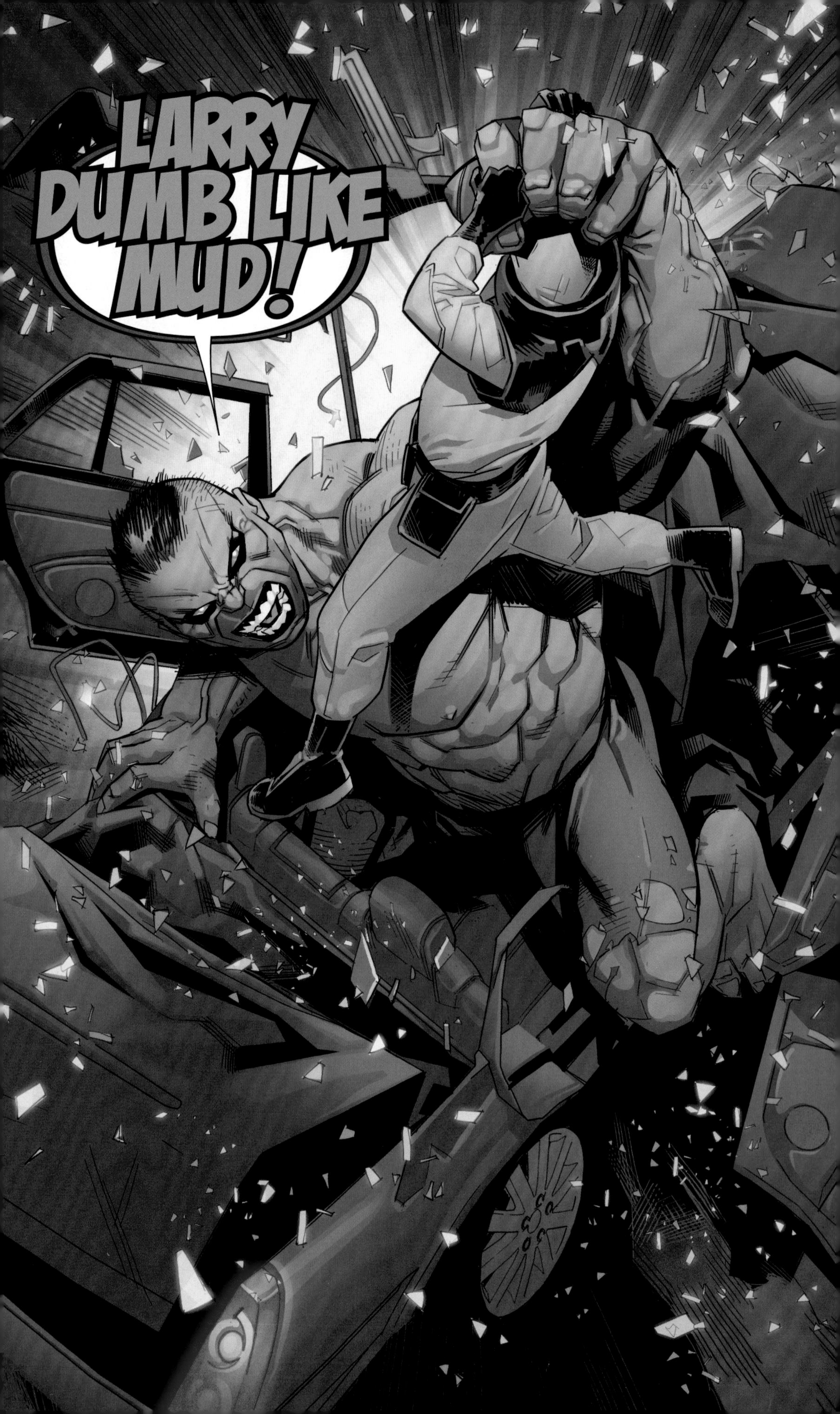
LARRY DUMB LIKE MUD!

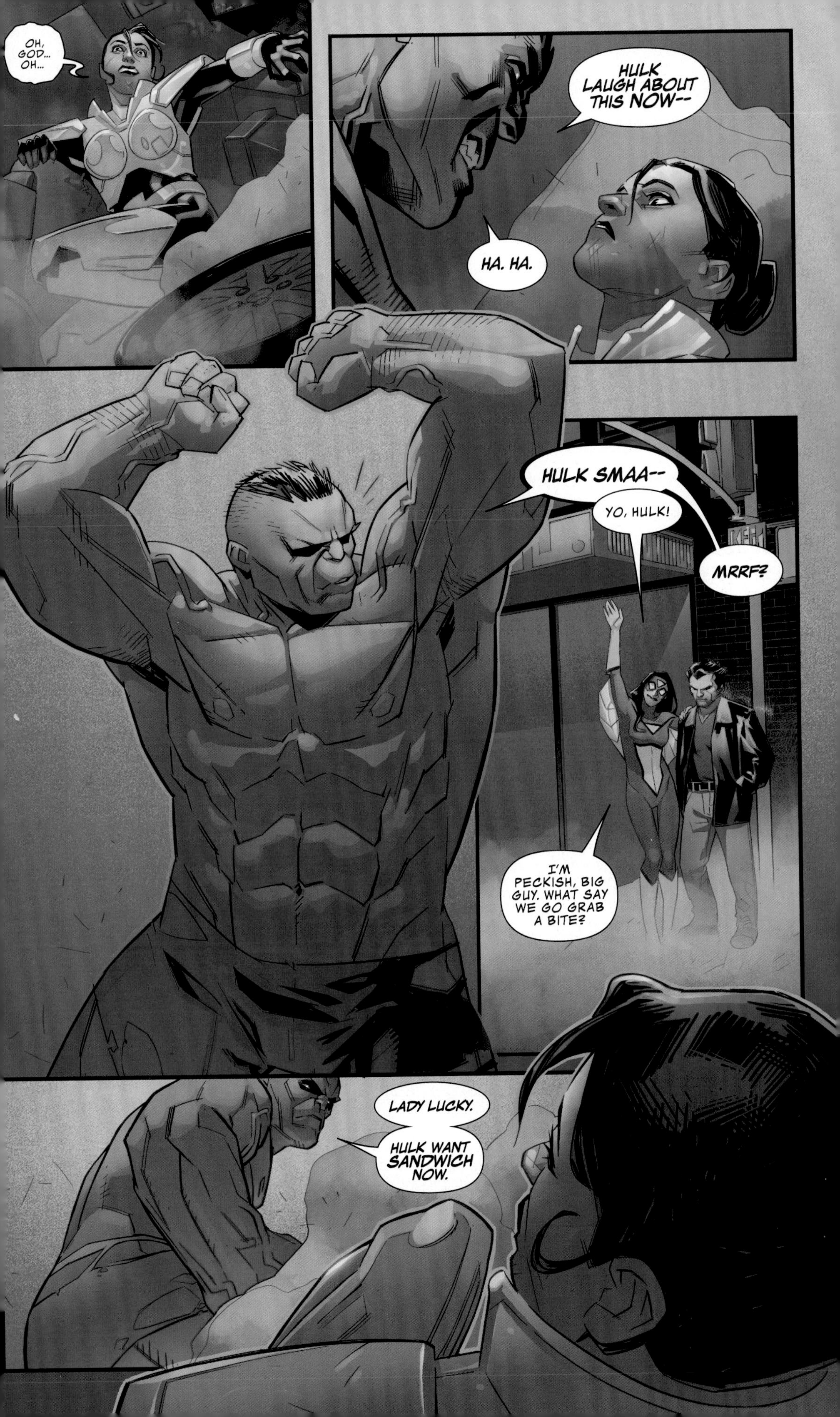
OH, GOD... OH...
HULK LAUGH ABOUT THIS NOW--
HA. HA.
HULK SMAA--
YO, HULK!
MRRF?
I'M PECKISH, BIG GUY. WHAT SAY WE GO GRAB A BITE?
LADY LUCKY.
HULK WANT SANDWICH NOW.

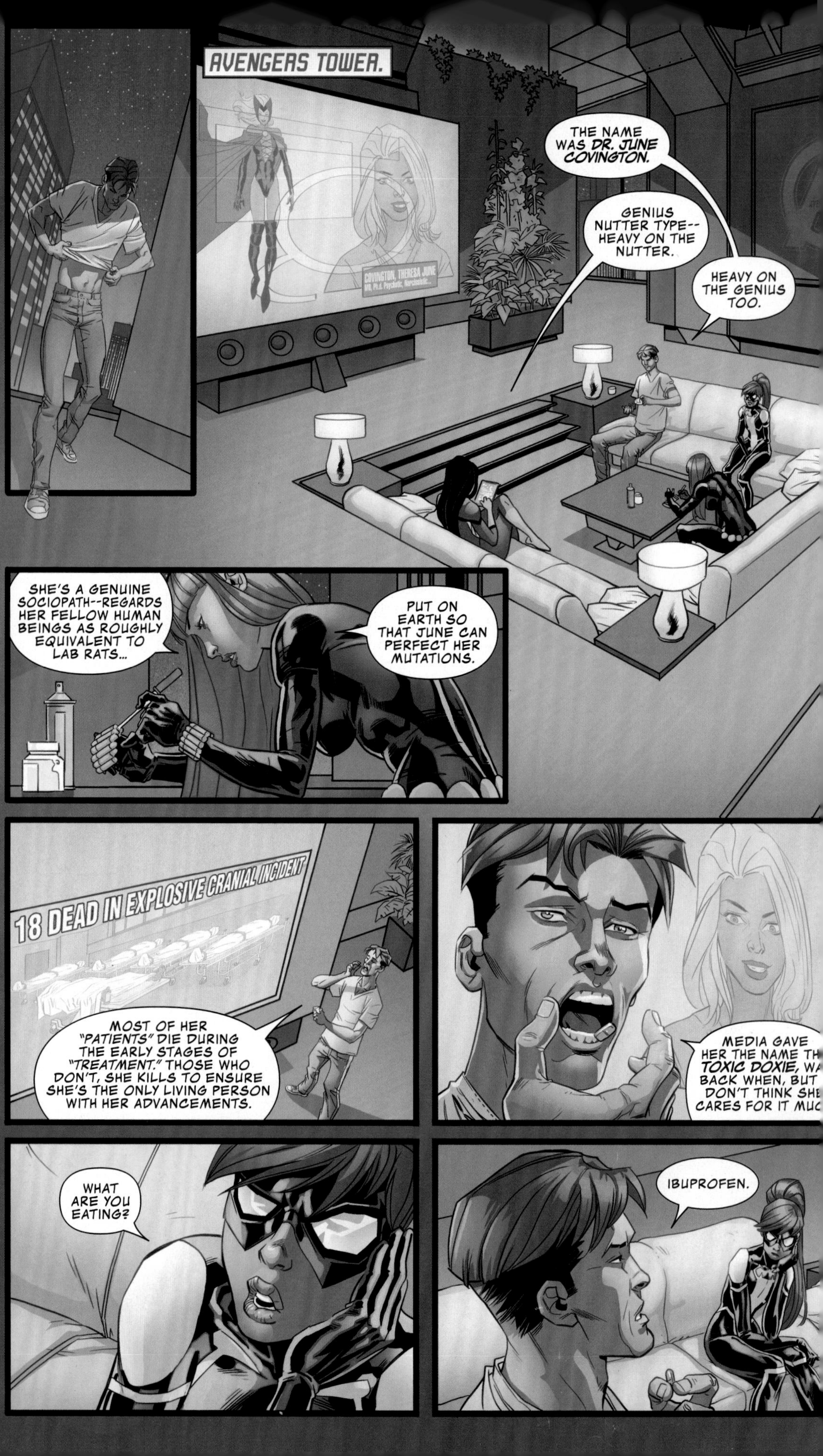

AVENGERS TOWER.
COVINGTON, THERESA JUNE
THE NAME WAS DR. JUNE COVINGTON.
GENIUS NUTTER TYPE--HEAVY ON THE NUTTER.
HEAVY ON THE GENIUS TOO.
SHE'S A GENUINE SOCIOPATH--REGARDS HER FELLOW HUMAN BEINGS AS ROUGHLY EQUIVALENT TO LAB RATS...
PUT ON EARTH SO THAT JUNE CAN PERFECT HER MUTATIONS.
18 DEAD IN EXPLOSIVE CRANIAL INCIDENT
MOST OF HER "PATIENTS" DIE DURING THE EARLY STAGES OF "TREATMENT." THOSE WHO DON'T, SHE KILLS TO ENSURE SHE'S THE ONLY LIVING PERSON WITH HER ADVANCEMENTS.
MEDIA GAVE HER THE NAME TH TOXIC DOXIE, WA BACK WHEN, BUT DON'T THINK SHE CARES FOR IT MUC
WHAT ARE YOU EATING?
IBUPROFEN.

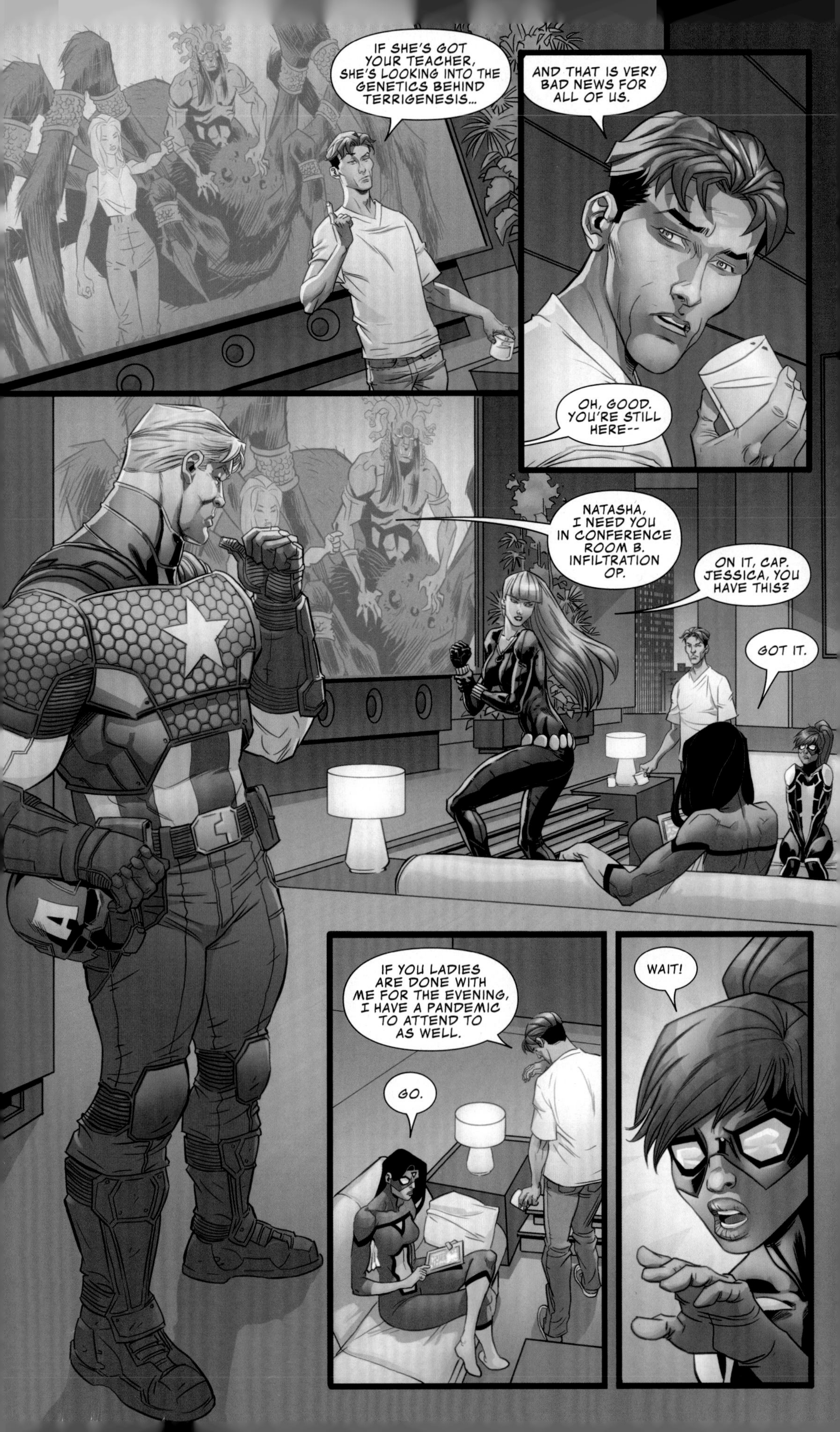
IF SHE'S GOT YOUR TEACHER, SHE'S LOOKING INTO THE GENETICS BEHIND TERRIGENESIS...
AND THAT IS VERY BAD NEWS FOR ALL OF US.
OH, GOOD. YOU'RE STILL HERE--
NATASHA, I NEED YOU IN CONFERENCE ROOM B. INFILTRATION OP.
ON IT, CAP. JESSICA, YOU HAVE THIS?
GOT IT.
IF YOU LADIES ARE DONE WITH ME FOR THE EVENING, I HAVE A PANDEMIC TO ATTEND TO AS WELL.
GO.
WAIT!

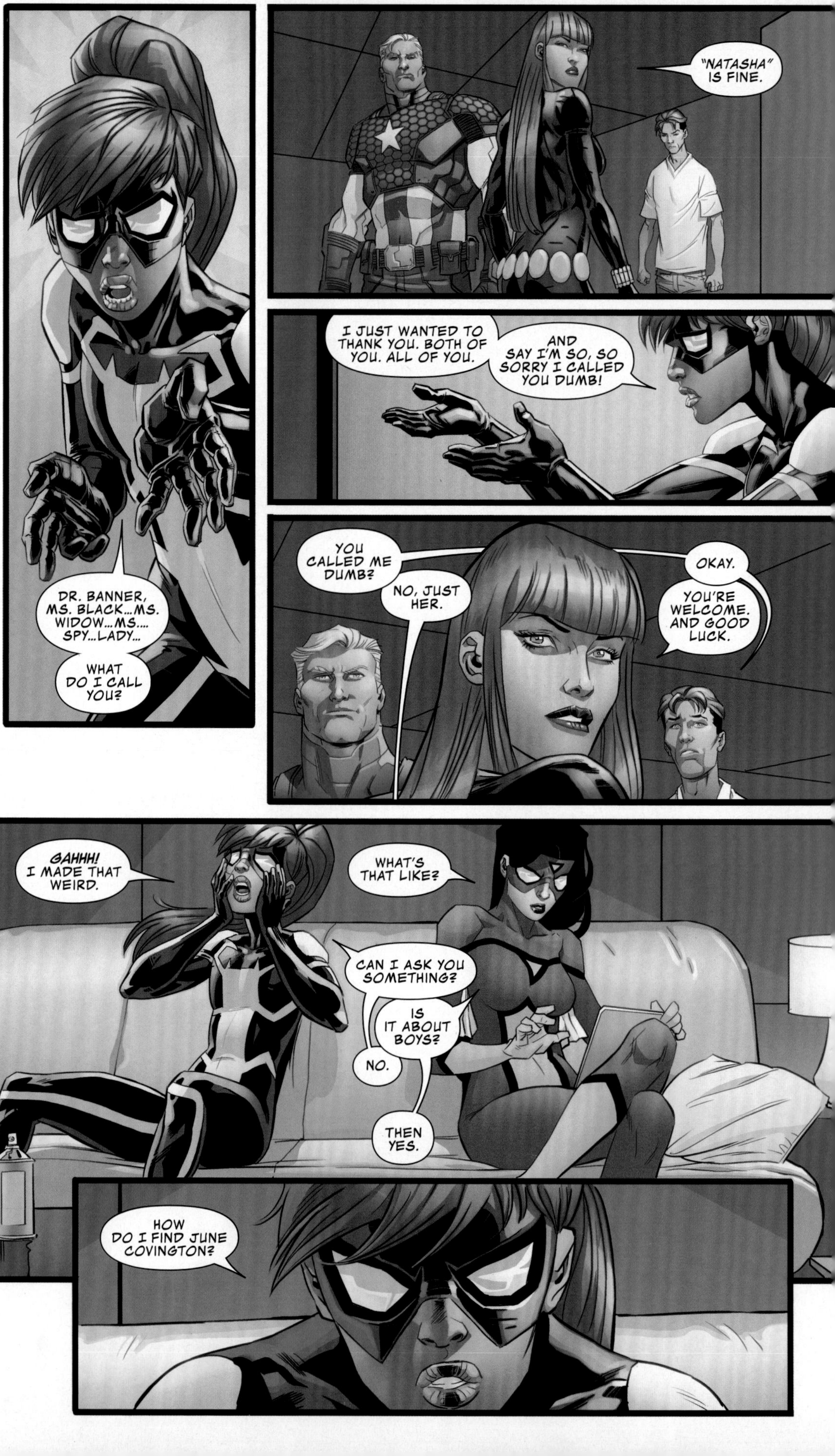
DR. BANNER, MS. BLACK...MS. WIDOW...MS.... SPY...LADY...
WHAT DO I CALL YOU?
"NATASHA" IS FINE.
I JUST WANTED TO THANK YOU. BOTH OF YOU. ALL OF YOU.
AND SAY I'M SO, SO SORRY I CALLED YOU DUMB!
YOU CALLED ME DUMB?
NO, JUST HER.
OKAY.
YOU'RE WELCOME. AND GOOD LUCK.
GAHHH! I MADE THAT WEIRD.
WHAT'S THAT LIKE?
CAN I ASK YOU SOMETHING?
IS IT ABOUT BOYS?
NO.
THEN YES.
HOW DO I FIND JUNE COVINGTON?

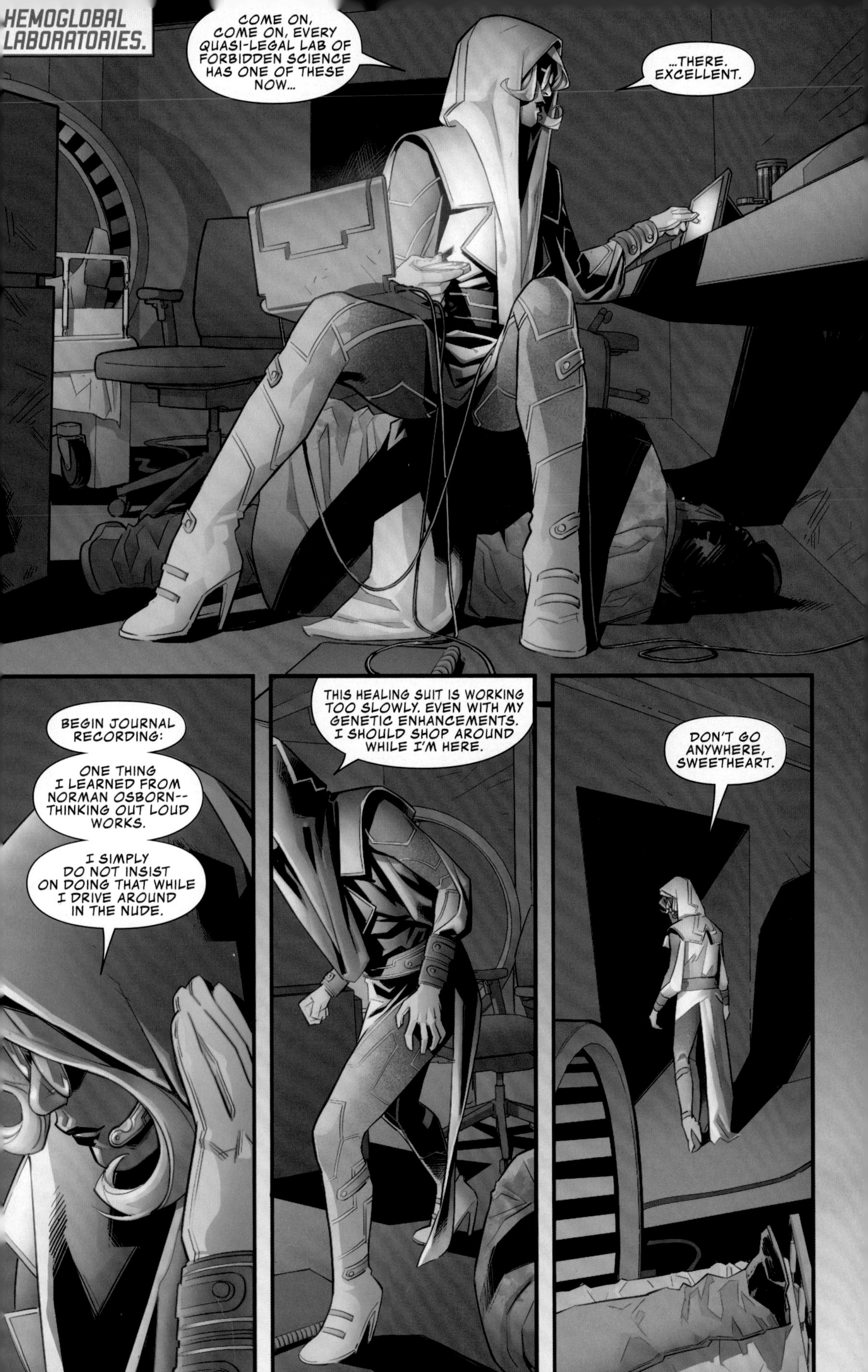
HEMOGLOBAL LABORATORIES.
COME ON, COME ON, EVERY QUASI-LEGAL LAB OF FORBIDDEN SCIENCE HAS ONE OF THESE NOW...
...THERE. EXCELLENT.
BEGIN JOURNAL RECORDING:
ONE THING I LEARNED FROM NORMAN OSBORN-- THINKING OUT LOUD WORKS.
I SIMPLY DO NOT INSIST ON DOING THAT WHILE I DRIVE AROUND IN THE NUDE.
THIS HEALING SUIT IS WORKING TOO SLOWLY. EVEN WITH MY GENETIC ENHANCEMENTS. I SHOULD SHOP AROUND WHILE I'M HERE.
DON'T GO ANYWHERE, SWEETHEART.

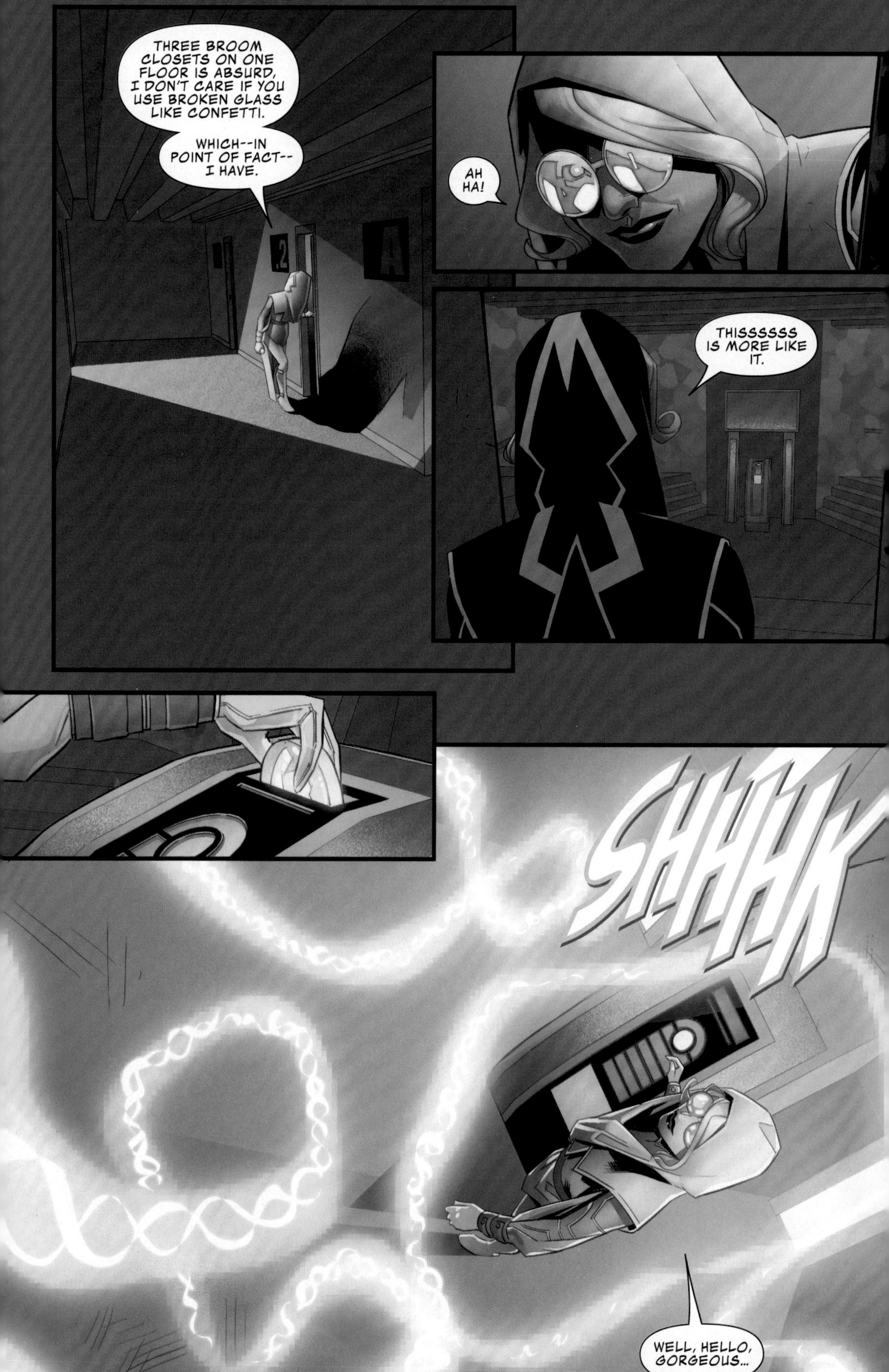
THREE BROOM CLOSETS ON ONE FLOOR IS ABSURD, I DON'T CARE IF YOU USE BROKEN GLASS LIKE CONFETTI.
WHICH--IN POINT OF FACT--I HAVE.
AH HA!
THISSSSSS IS MORE LIKE IT.
SHHHK
WELL, HELLO, GORGEOUS...

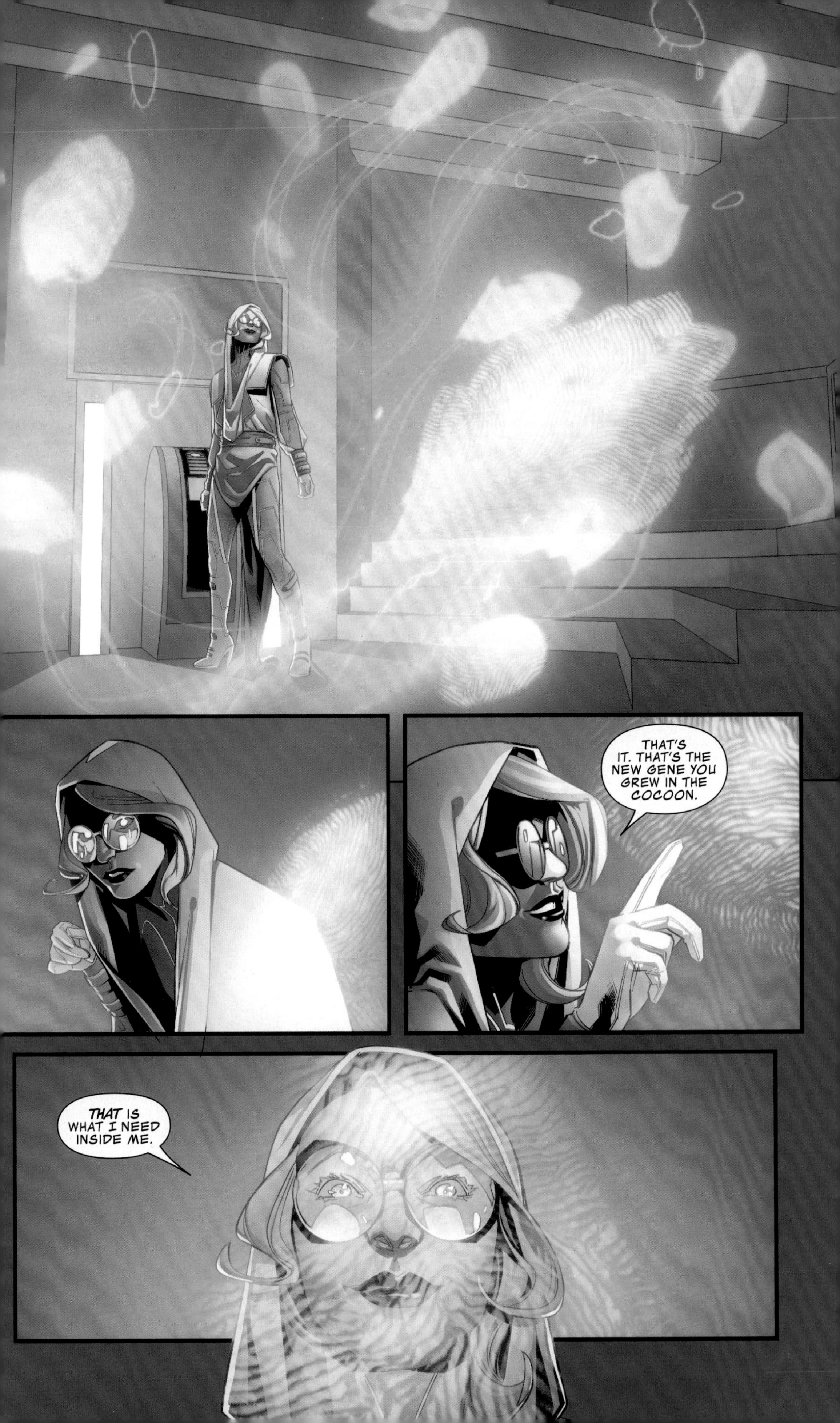
THAT'S IT. THAT'S THE NEW GENE YOU GREW IN THE COCOON.
THAT IS WHAT I NEED INSIDE ME.

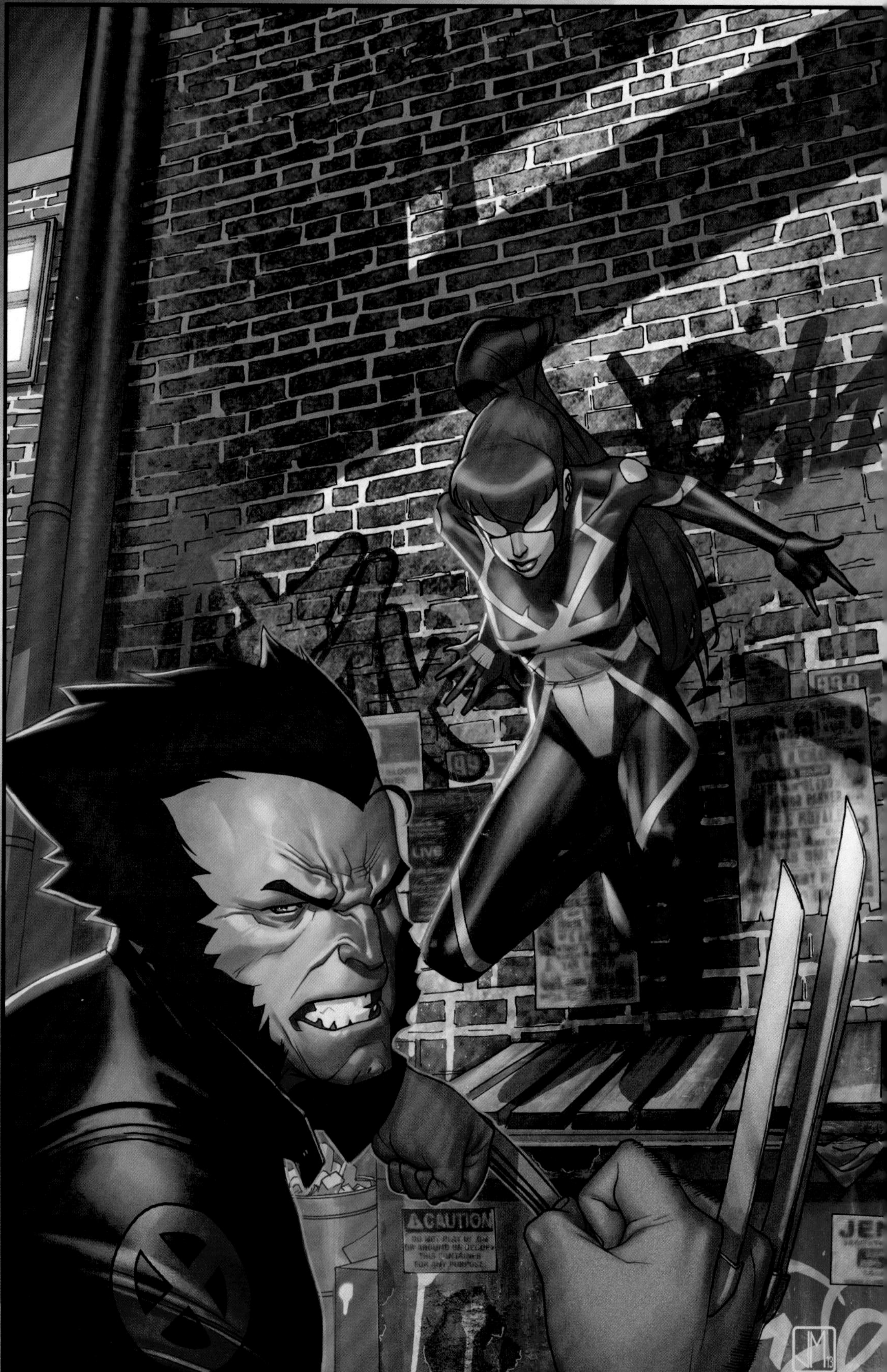
CAUTION

TWENTY-THREE

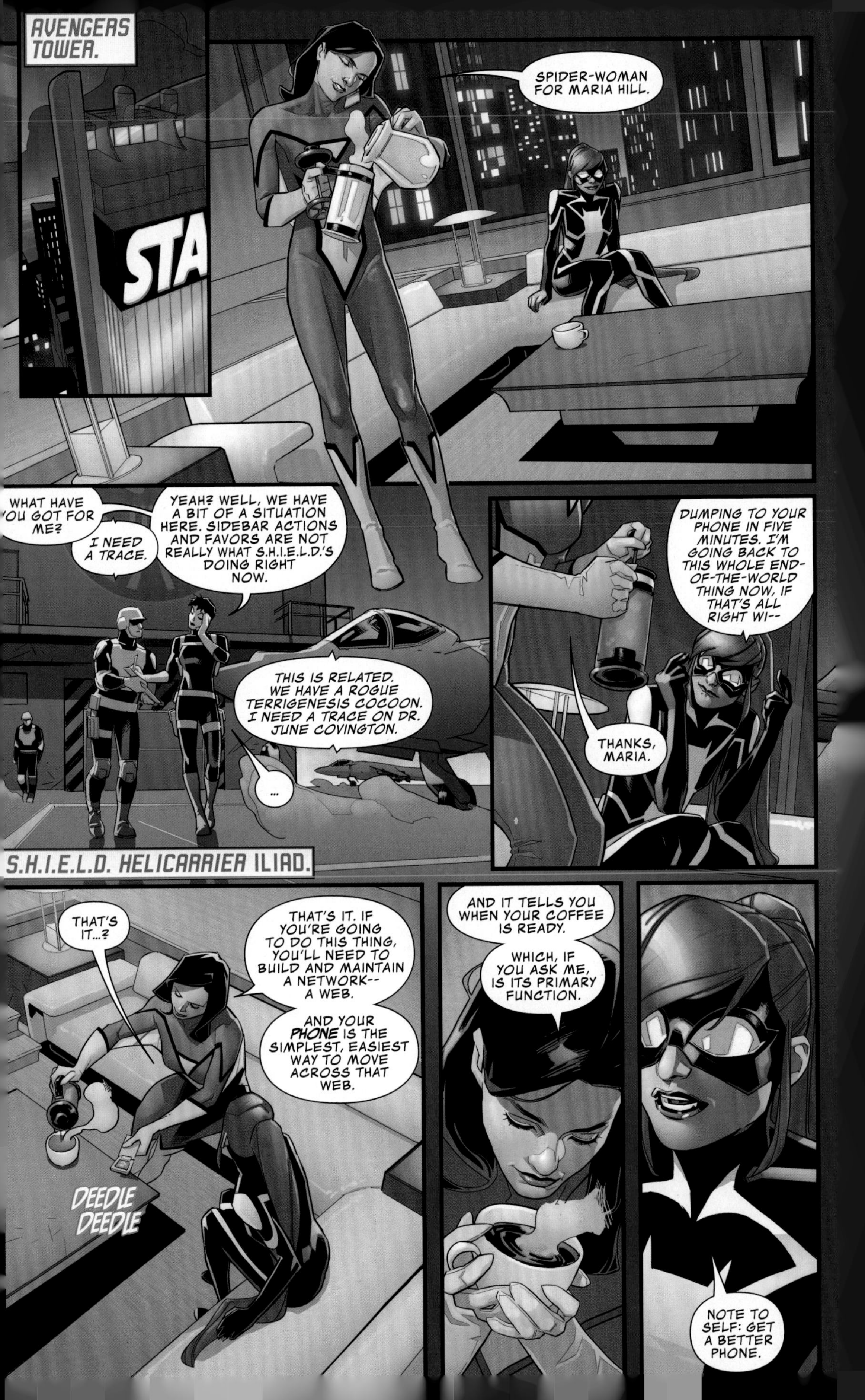
AVENGERS TOWER.
SPIDER-WOMAN FOR MARIA HILL.
WHAT HAVE YOU GOT FOR ME?
I NEED A TRACE.
YEAH? WELL, WE HAVE A BIT OF A SITUATION HERE. SIDEBAR ACTIONS AND FAVORS ARE NOT REALLY WHAT S.H.I.E.L.D.'S DOING RIGHT NOW.
THIS IS RELATED. WE HAVE A ROGUE TERRIGENESIS COCOON. I NEED A TRACE ON DR. JUNE COVINGTON.
...
S.H.I.E.L.D. HELICARRIER ILIAD.
DUMPING TO YOUR PHONE IN FIVE MINUTES. I'M GOING BACK TO THIS WHOLE END-OF-THE-WORLD THING NOW, IF THAT'S ALL RIGHT WI--
THANKS, MARIA.
THAT'S IT...?
THAT'S IT. IF YOU'RE GOING TO DO THIS THING, YOU'LL NEED TO BUILD AND MAINTAIN A NETWORK-- A WEB.
AND YOUR PHONE IS THE SIMPLEST, EASIEST WAY TO MOVE ACROSS THAT WEB.
DEEDLE DEEDLE
AND IT TELLS YOU WHEN YOUR COFFEE IS READY.
WHICH, IF YOU ASK ME, IS ITS PRIMARY FUNCTION.
NOTE TO SELF: GET A BETTER PHONE.

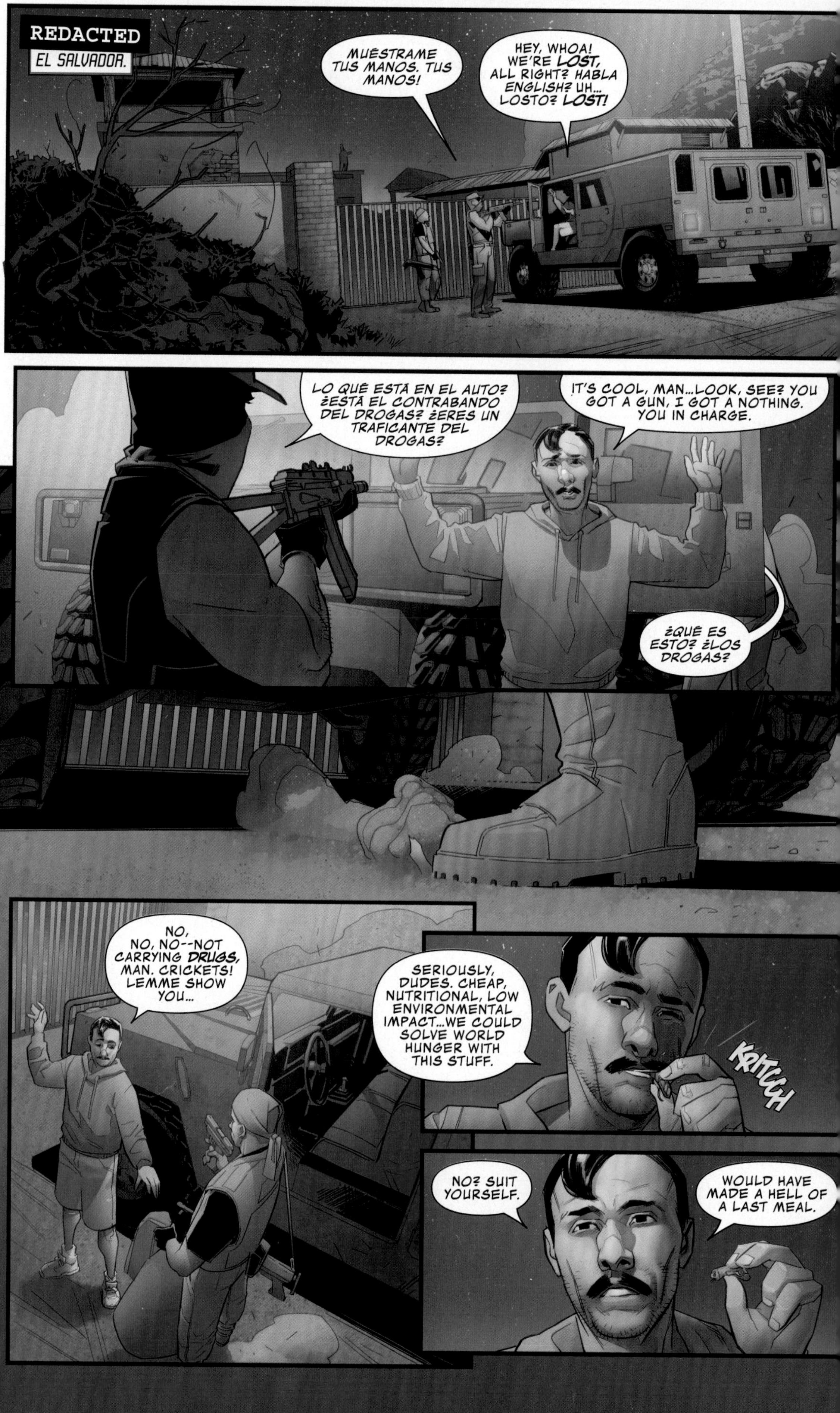
REDACTED
EL SALVADOR.
MUESTRAME TUS MANOS. TUS MANOS!
HEY, WHOA! WE'RE LOST, ALL RIGHT? HABLA ENGLISH? UH... LOSTO? LOST!
LO QUÉ ESTÁ EN EL AUTO? ¿ESTÁ EL CONTRABANDO DEL DROGAS? ¿ERES UN TRAFICANTE DEL DROGAS?
IT'S COOL, MAN...LOOK, SEE? YOU GOT A GUN, I GOT A NOTHING. YOU IN CHARGE.
¿QUÉ ES ESTO? ¿LOS DROGAS?
NO, NO, NO--NOT CARRYING DRUGS, MAN. CRICKETS! LEMME SHOW YOU...
SERIOUSLY, DUDES. CHEAP, NUTRITIONAL, LOW ENVIRONMENTAL IMPACT...WE COULD SOLVE WORLD HUNGER WITH THIS STUFF.
KRITCH
NO? SUIT YOURSELF.
WOULD HAVE MADE A HELL OF A LAST MEAL.

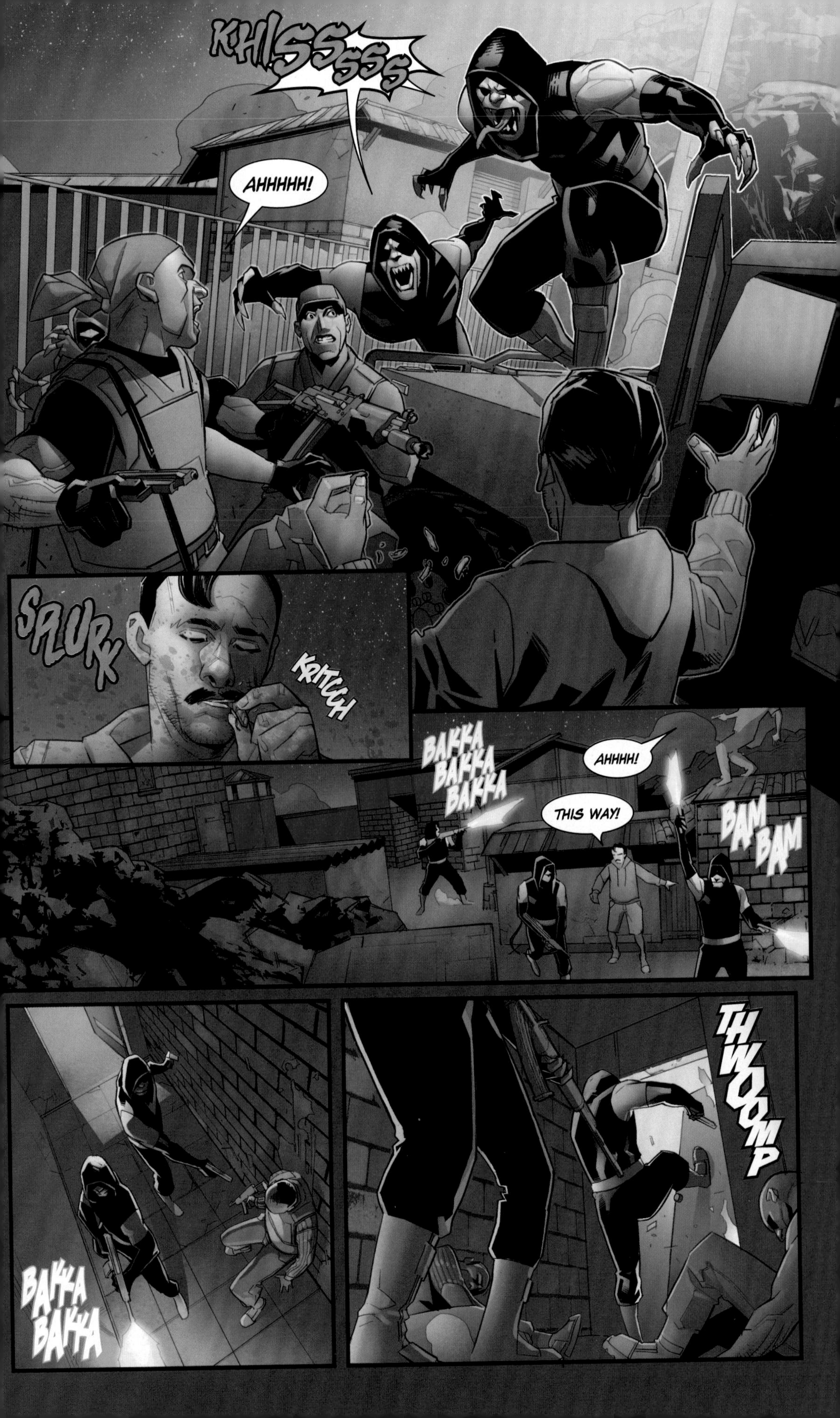
KHISSSSS
AHHHHH!
SPLURK
KRITCH
BAKKA BAKKA BAKKA
AHHHH!
THIS WAY!
BAM BAM
BAKKA BAKKA
THWOOMP

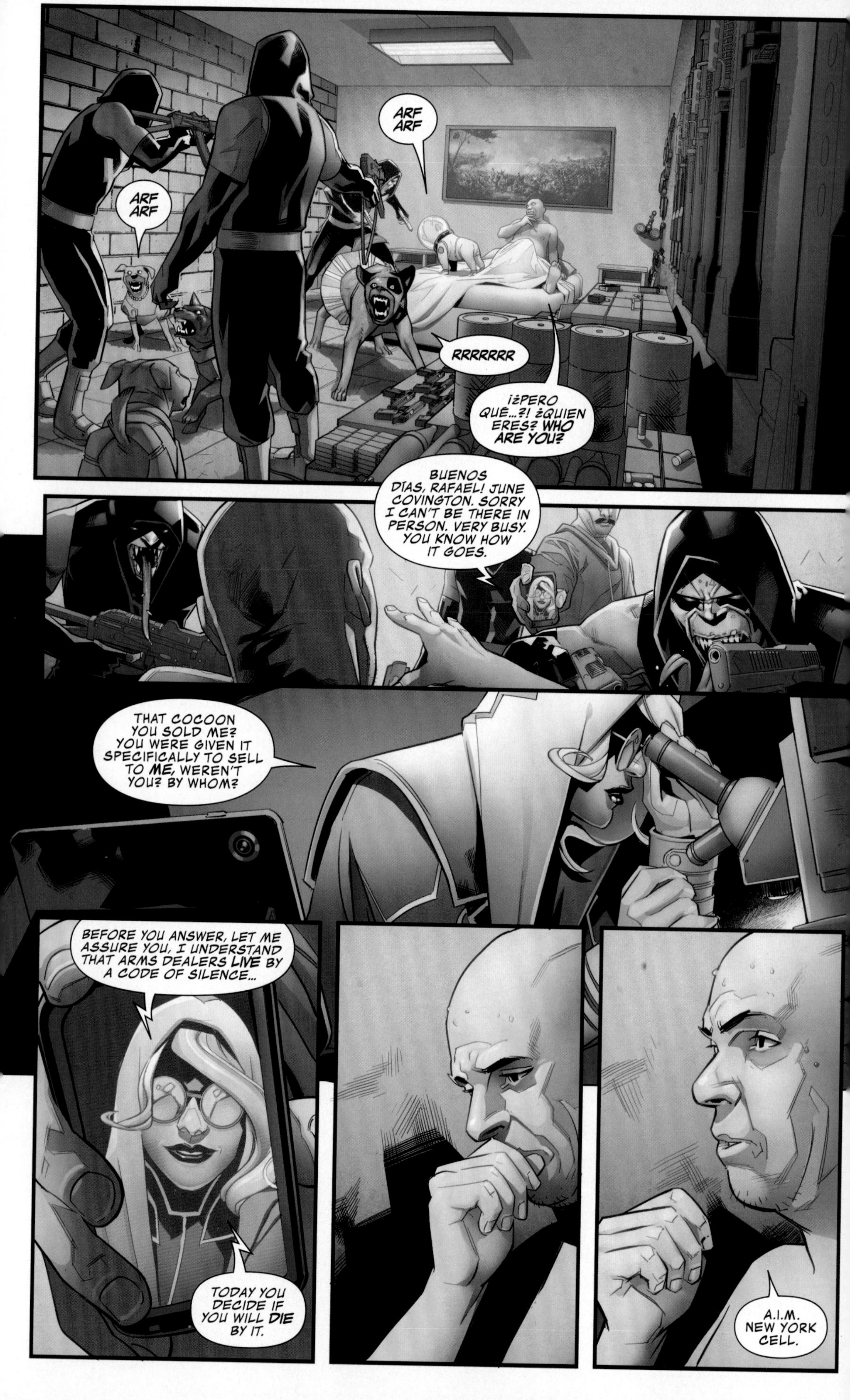

ARF ARF
ARF ARF
RRRRRRR
¡¿PERO QUÉ...?! ¿QUIEN ERES? WHO ARE YOU?
BUENOS DÍAS, RAFAEL! JUNE COVINGTON. SORRY I CAN'T BE THERE IN PERSON. VERY BUSY. YOU KNOW HOW IT GOES.
THAT COCOON YOU SOLD ME? YOU WERE GIVEN IT SPECIFICALLY TO SELL TO ME, WEREN'T YOU? BY WHOM?
BEFORE YOU ANSWER, LET ME ASSURE YOU, I UNDERSTAND THAT ARMS DEALERS LIVE BY A CODE OF SILENCE...
TODAY YOU DECIDE IF YOU WILL DIE BY IT.
A.I.M. NEW YORK CELL.

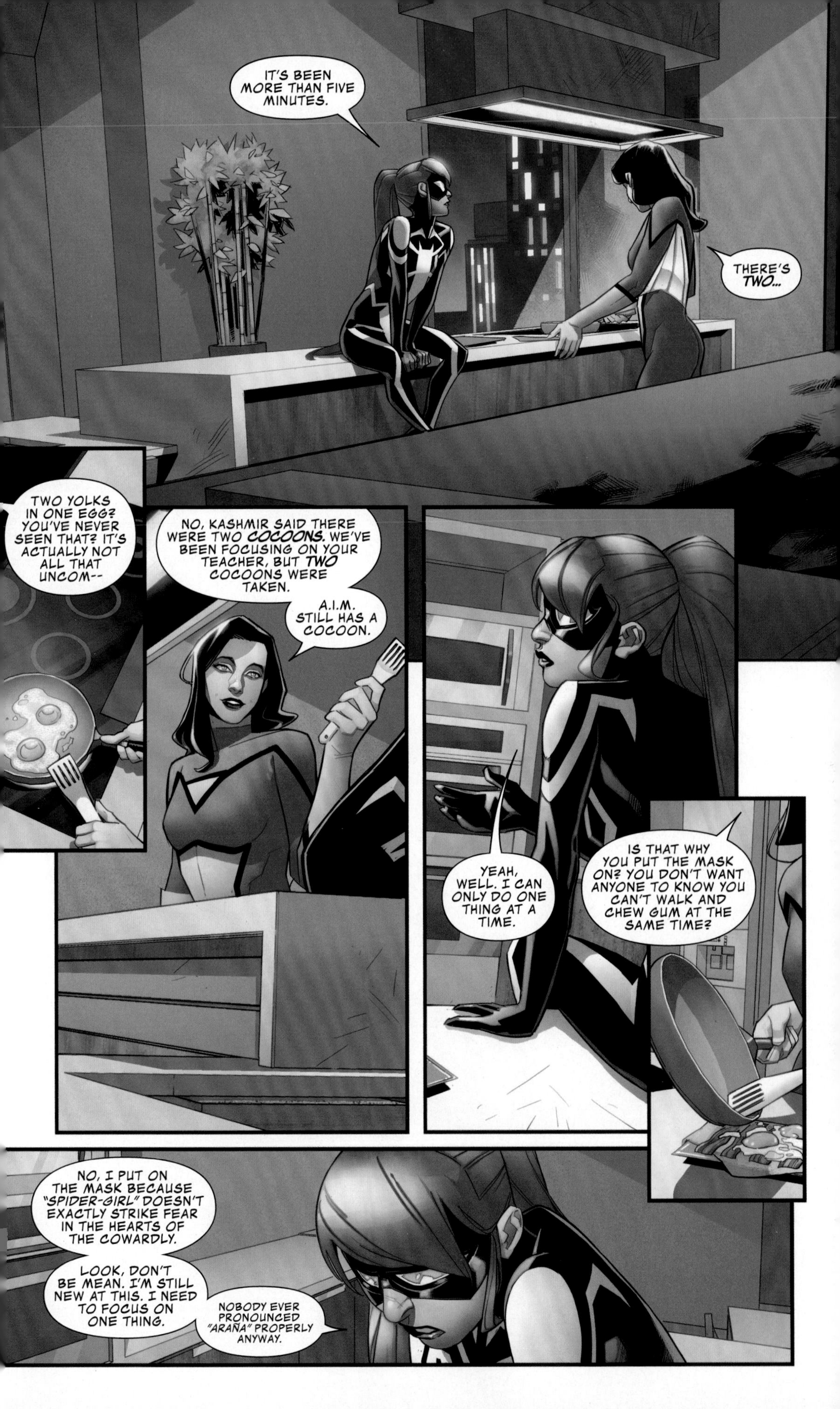
IT'S BEEN MORE THAN FIVE MINUTES.
THERE'S TWO...
TWO YOLKS IN ONE EGG? YOU'VE NEVER SEEN THAT? IT'S ACTUALLY NOT ALL THAT UNCOM--
NO, KASHMIR SAID THERE WERE TWO COCOONS. WE'VE BEEN FOCUSING ON YOUR TEACHER, BUT TWO COCOONS WERE TAKEN.
A.I.M. STILL HAS A COCOON.
YEAH, WELL. I CAN ONLY DO ONE THING AT A TIME.
IS THAT WHY YOU PUT THE MASK ON? YOU DON'T WANT ANYONE TO KNOW YOU CAN'T WALK AND CHEW GUM AT THE SAME TIME?
NO, I PUT ON THE MASK BECAUSE "SPIDER-GIRL" DOESN'T EXACTLY STRIKE FEAR IN THE HEARTS OF THE COWARDLY.
LOOK, DON'T BE MEAN. I'M STILL NEW AT THIS. I NEED TO FOCUS ON ONE THING.
NOBODY EVER PRONOUNCED "ARAÑA" PROPERLY ANYWAY.

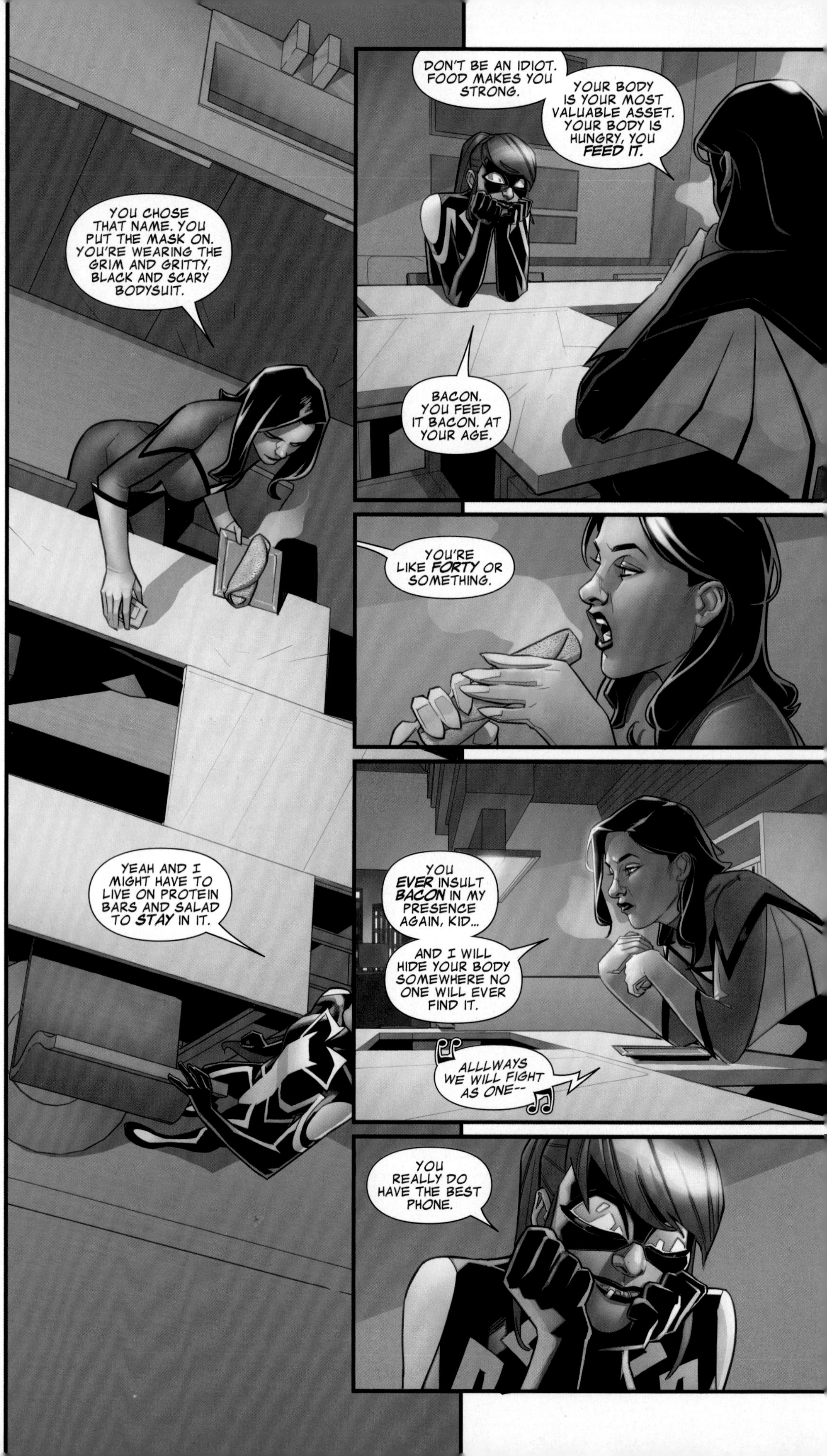
YOU CHOSE THAT NAME. YOU PUT THE MASK ON. YOU'RE WEARING THE GRIM AND GRITTY, BLACK AND SCARY BODYSUIT.
YEAH AND I MIGHT HAVE TO LIVE ON PROTEIN BARS AND SALAD TO *STAY* IN IT.
DON'T BE AN IDIOT. FOOD MAKES YOU STRONG.
YOUR BODY IS YOUR MOST VALUABLE ASSET. YOUR BODY IS HUNGRY, YOU *FEED IT.*
BACON. YOU FEED IT BACON. AT YOUR AGE.
YOU'RE LIKE *FORTY* OR SOMETHING.
YOU *EVER* INSULT *BACON* IN MY PRESENCE AGAIN, KID...
AND I WILL HIDE YOUR BODY SOMEWHERE NO ONE WILL EVER FIND IT.
ALLLWAYS WE WILL FIGHT AS ONE--
YOU REALLY DO HAVE THE BEST PHONE.

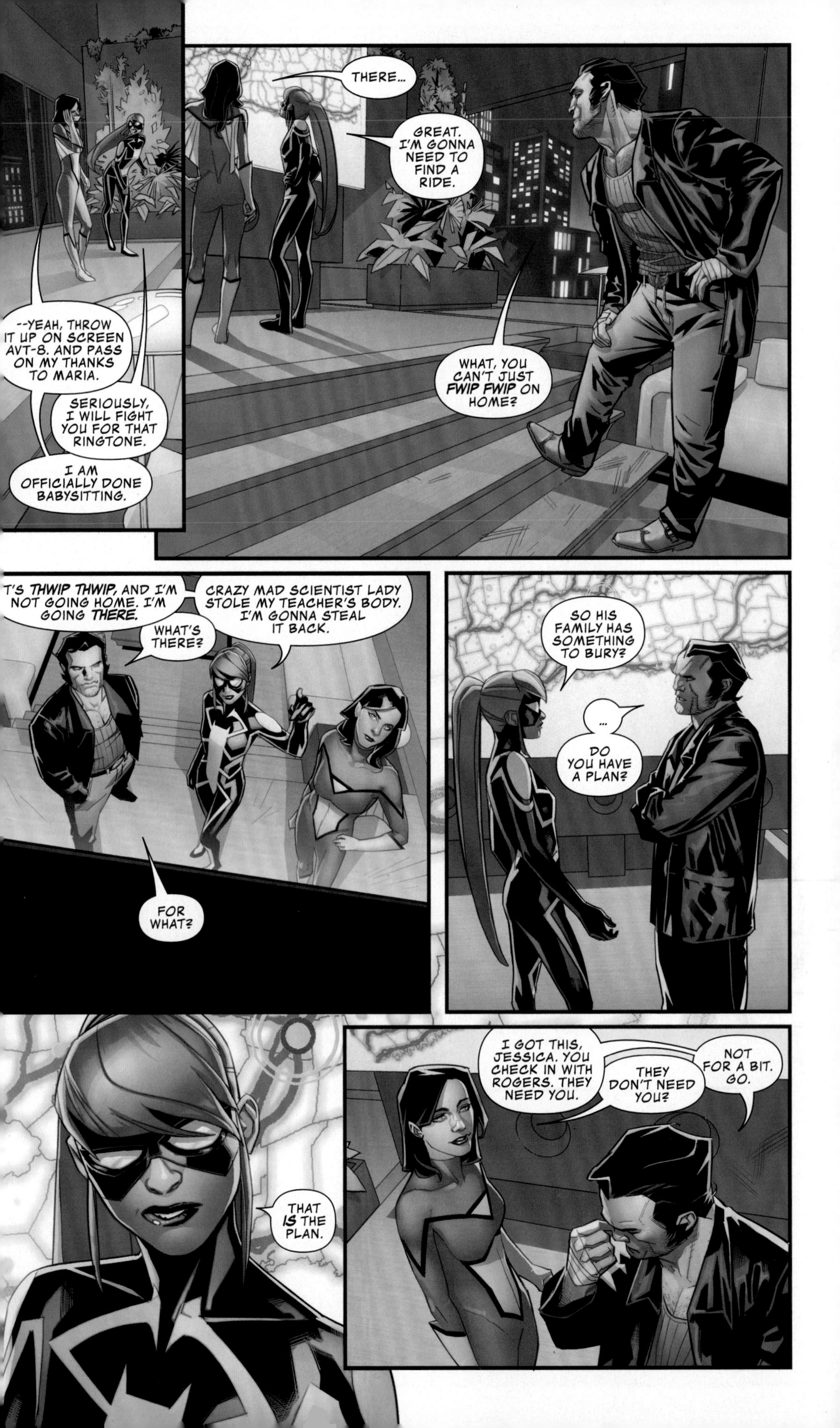
--YEAH, THROW IT UP ON SCREEN AVT-8. AND PASS ON MY THANKS TO MARIA.
SERIOUSLY, I WILL FIGHT YOU FOR THAT RINGTONE.
I AM OFFICIALLY DONE BABYSITTING.
THERE...
GREAT. I'M GONNA NEED TO FIND A RIDE.
WHAT, YOU CAN'T JUST FWIP FWIP ON HOME?
T'S THWIP THWIP, AND I'M NOT GOING HOME. I'M GOING THERE.
WHAT'S THERE?
CRAZY MAD SCIENTIST LADY STOLE MY TEACHER'S BODY. I'M GONNA STEAL IT BACK.
FOR WHAT?
SO HIS FAMILY HAS SOMETHING TO BURY?
...
DO YOU HAVE A PLAN?
THAT IS THE PLAN.
I GOT THIS, JESSICA. YOU CHECK IN WITH ROGERS. THEY NEED YOU.
THEY DON'T NEED YOU?
NOT FOR A BIT. GO.

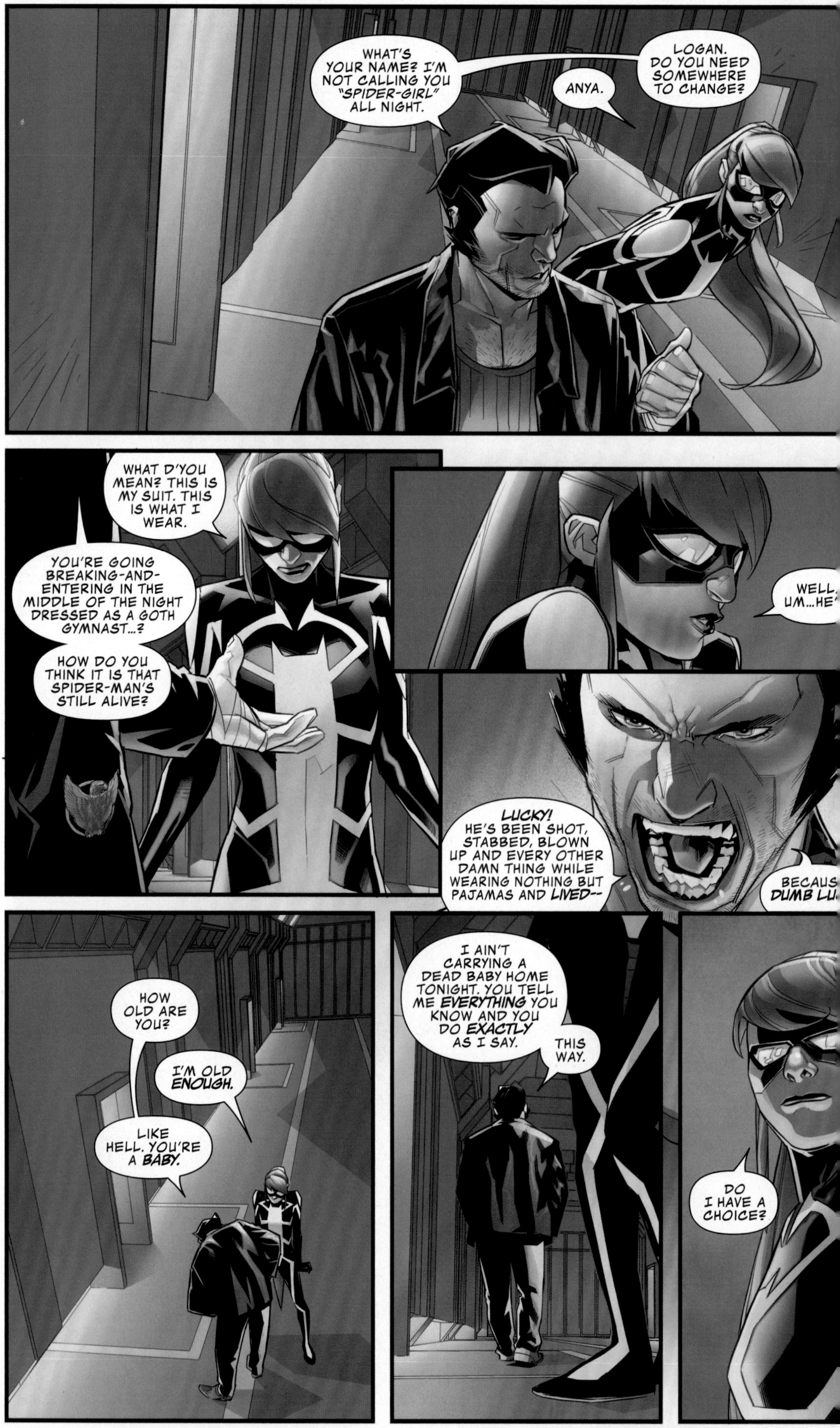

WHAT'S YOUR NAME? I'M NOT CALLING YOU "SPIDER-GIRL" ALL NIGHT.
ANYA.
LOGAN. DO YOU NEED SOMEWHERE TO CHANGE?
WHAT D'YOU MEAN? THIS IS MY SUIT. THIS IS WHAT I WEAR.
YOU'RE GOING BREAKING-AND-ENTERING IN THE MIDDLE OF THE NIGHT DRESSED AS A GOTH GYMNAST...?
HOW DO YOU THINK IT IS THAT SPIDER-MAN'S STILL ALIVE?
WELL, UM...HE'
LUCKY! HE'S BEEN SHOT, STABBED, BLOWN UP AND EVERY OTHER DAMN THING WHILE WEARING NOTHING BUT PAJAMAS AND LIVED--
BECAUS DUMB LU
HOW OLD ARE YOU?
I'M OLD ENOUGH.
LIKE HELL. YOU'RE A BABY.
I AIN'T CARRYING A DEAD BABY HOME TONIGHT. YOU TELL ME EVERYTHING YOU KNOW AND YOU DO EXACTLY AS I SAY.
THIS WAY.
DO I HAVE A CHOICE?

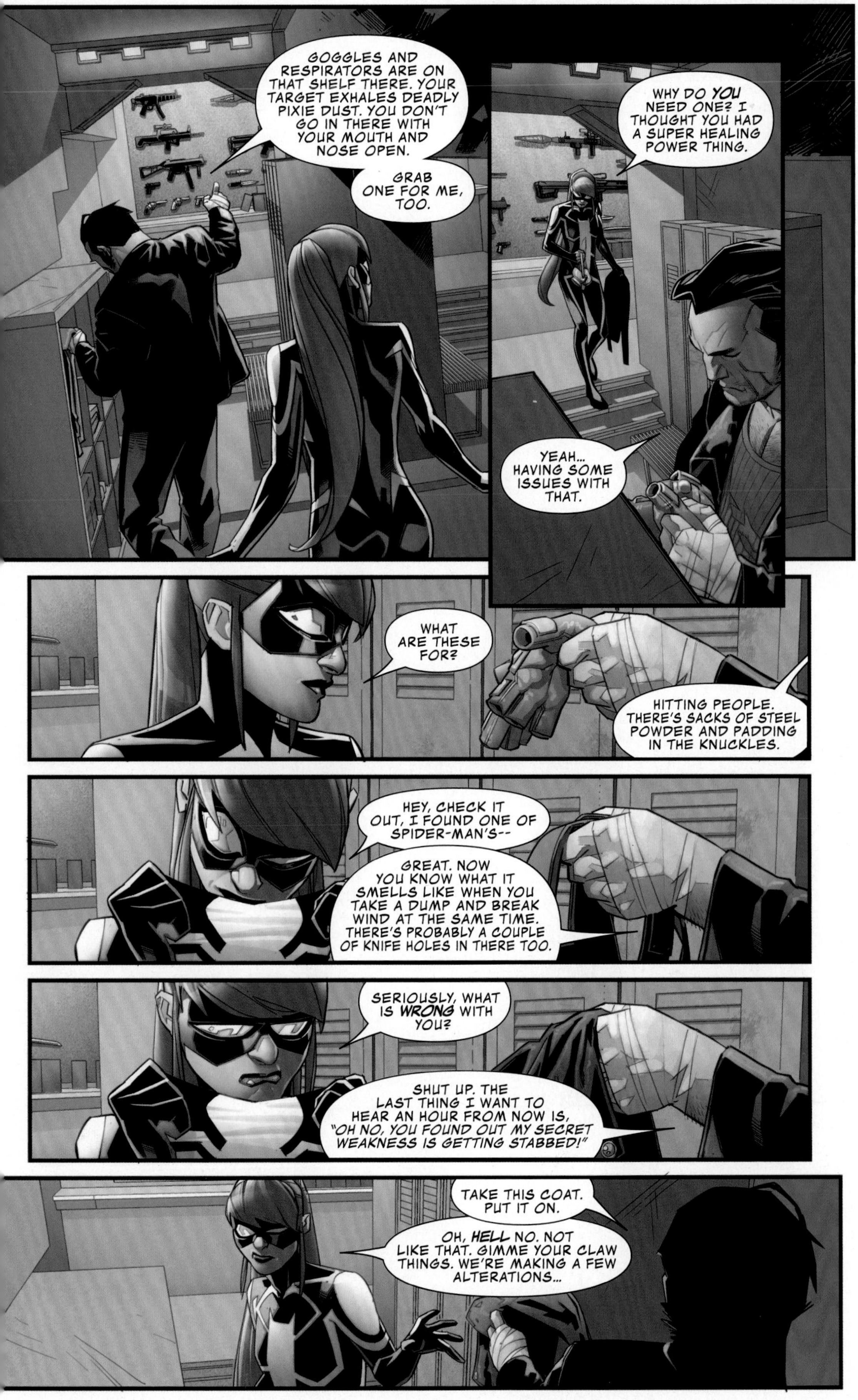
GOGGLES AND RESPIRATORS ARE ON THAT SHELF THERE. YOUR TARGET EXHALES DEADLY PIXIE DUST. YOU DON'T GO IN THERE WITH YOUR MOUTH AND NOSE OPEN.
GRAB ONE FOR ME, TOO.
WHY DO *YOU* NEED ONE? I THOUGHT YOU HAD A SUPER HEALING POWER THING.
YEAH... HAVING SOME ISSUES WITH THAT.
WHAT ARE THESE FOR?
HITTING PEOPLE. THERE'S SACKS OF STEEL POWDER AND PADDING IN THE KNUCKLES.
HEY, CHECK IT OUT, I FOUND ONE OF SPIDER-MAN'S--
GREAT. NOW YOU KNOW WHAT IT SMELLS LIKE WHEN YOU TAKE A DUMP AND BREAK WIND AT THE SAME TIME. THERE'S PROBABLY A COUPLE OF KNIFE HOLES IN THERE TOO.
SERIOUSLY, WHAT IS ***WRONG*** WITH YOU?
SHUT UP. THE LAST THING I WANT TO HEAR AN HOUR FROM NOW IS, *"OH NO, YOU FOUND OUT MY SECRET WEAKNESS IS GETTING STABBED!"*
TAKE THIS COAT. PUT IT ON.
OH, ***HELL*** NO. NOT LIKE THAT. GIMME YOUR CLAW THINGS. WE'RE MAKING A FEW ALTERATIONS...

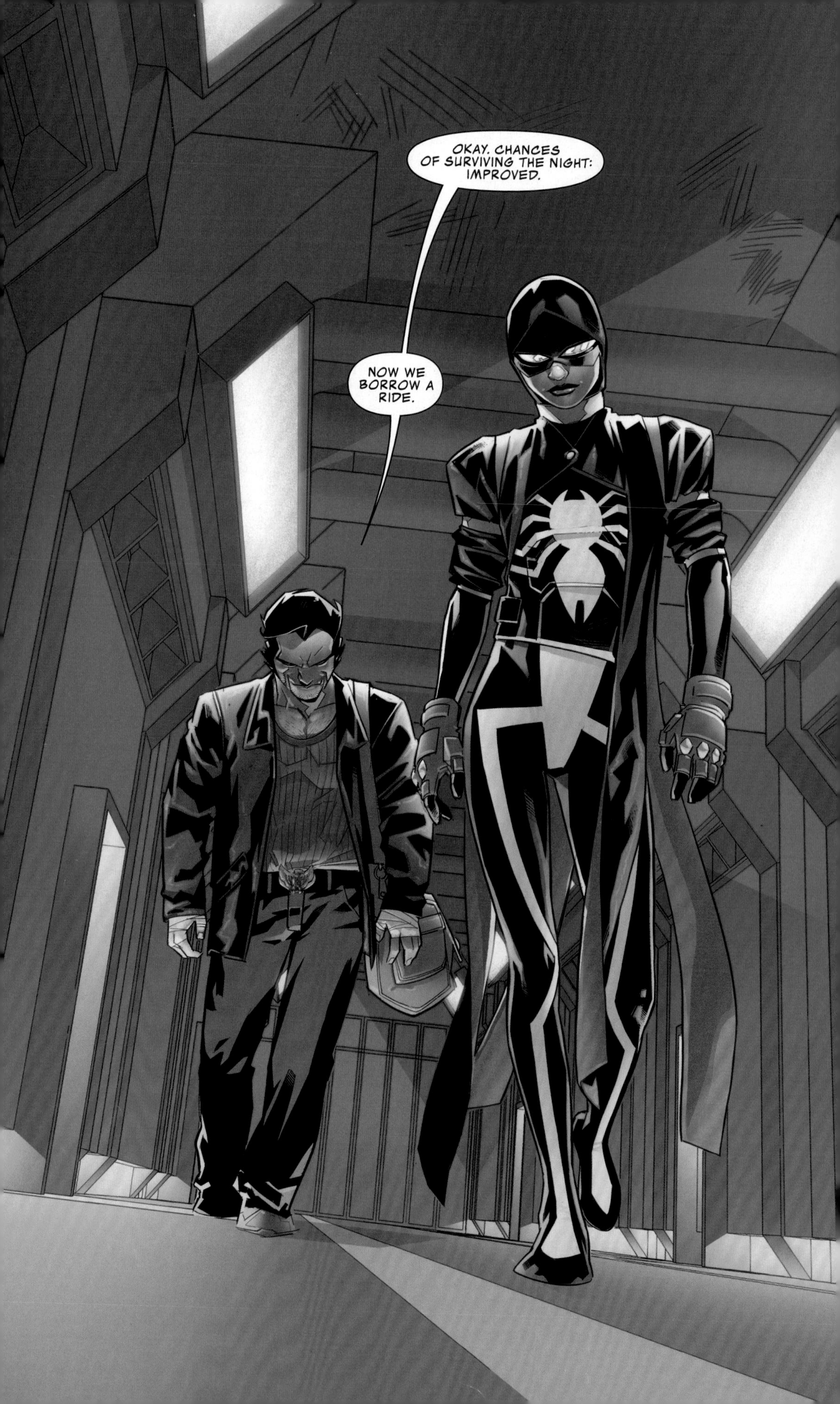
OKAY. CHANCES OF SURVIVING THE NIGHT: IMPROVED.
NOW WE BORROW A RIDE.

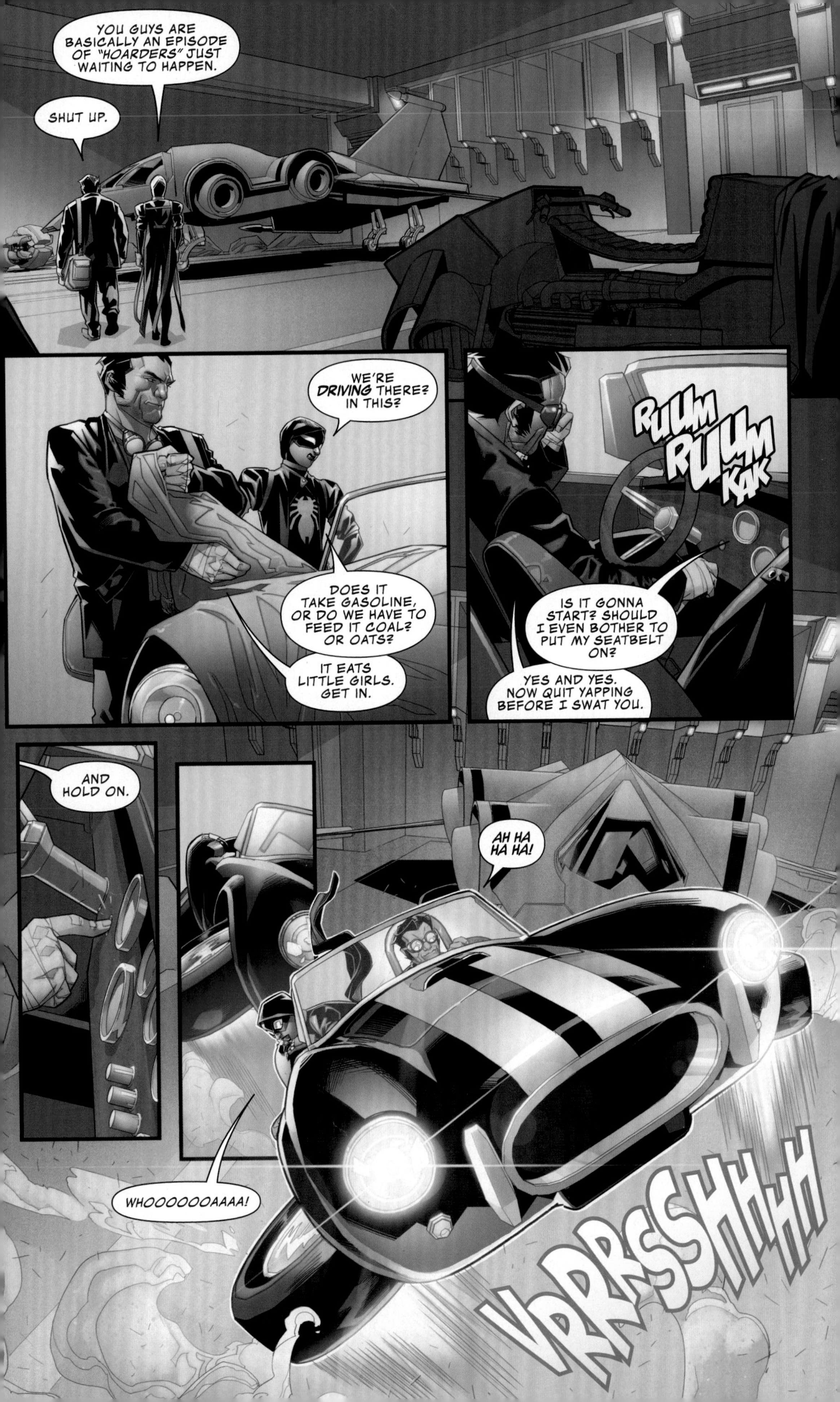

YOU GUYS ARE BASICALLY AN EPISODE OF "HOARDERS" JUST WAITING TO HAPPEN.
SHUT UP.
WE'RE *DRIVING* THERE? IN THIS?
DOES IT TAKE GASOLINE, OR DO WE HAVE TO FEED IT COAL? OR OATS?
IT EATS LITTLE GIRLS. GET IN.
RUUM RUUM KAK
IS IT GONNA START? SHOULD I EVEN BOTHER TO PUT MY SEATBELT ON?
YES AND YES. NOW QUIT YAPPING BEFORE I SWAT YOU.
AND HOLD ON.
AH HA HA HA!
WHOOOOOOAAAA!
VRRRSSHHHH

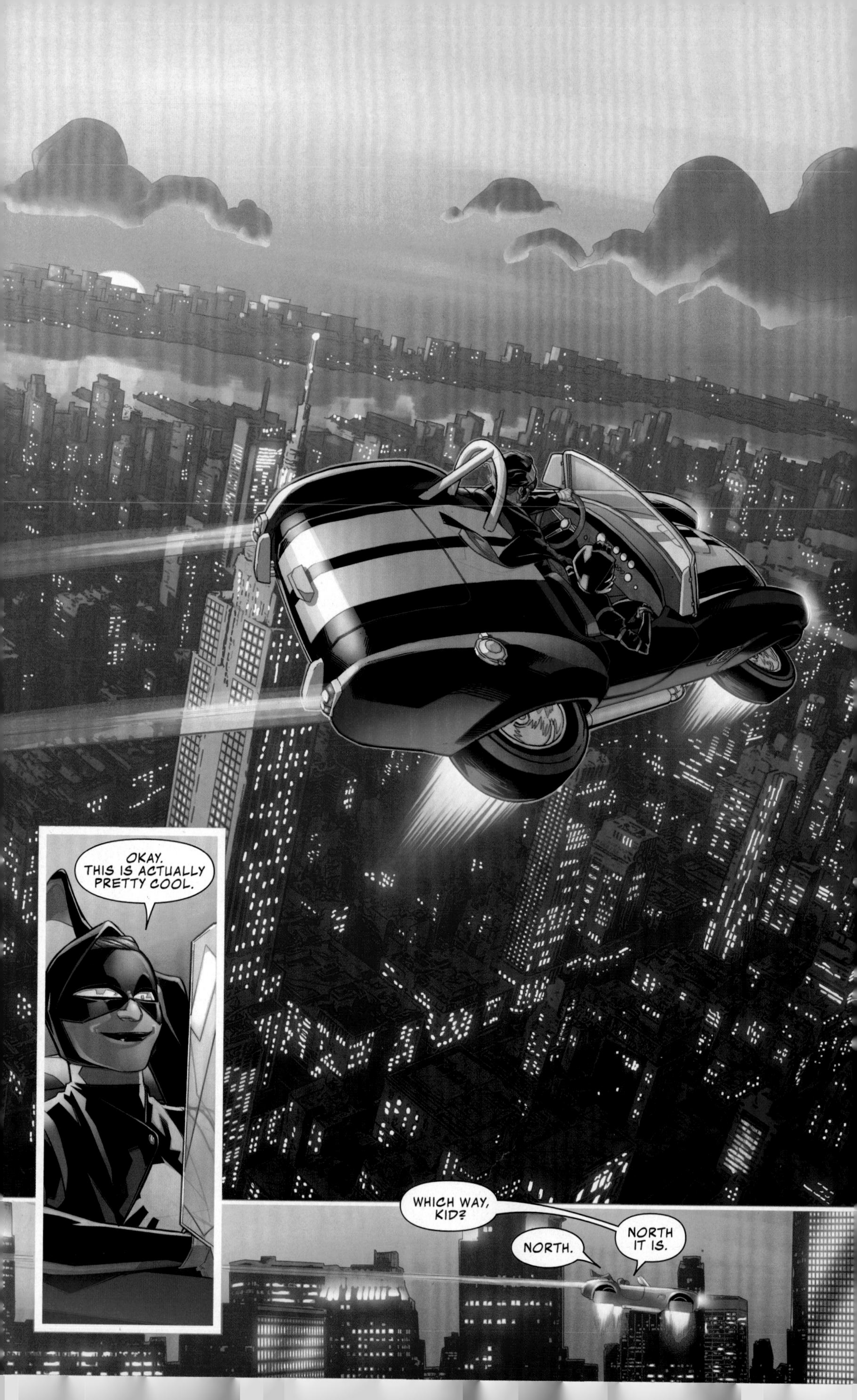
OKAY. THIS IS ACTUALLY PRETTY COOL.
WHICH WAY, KID?
NORTH.
NORTH IT IS.

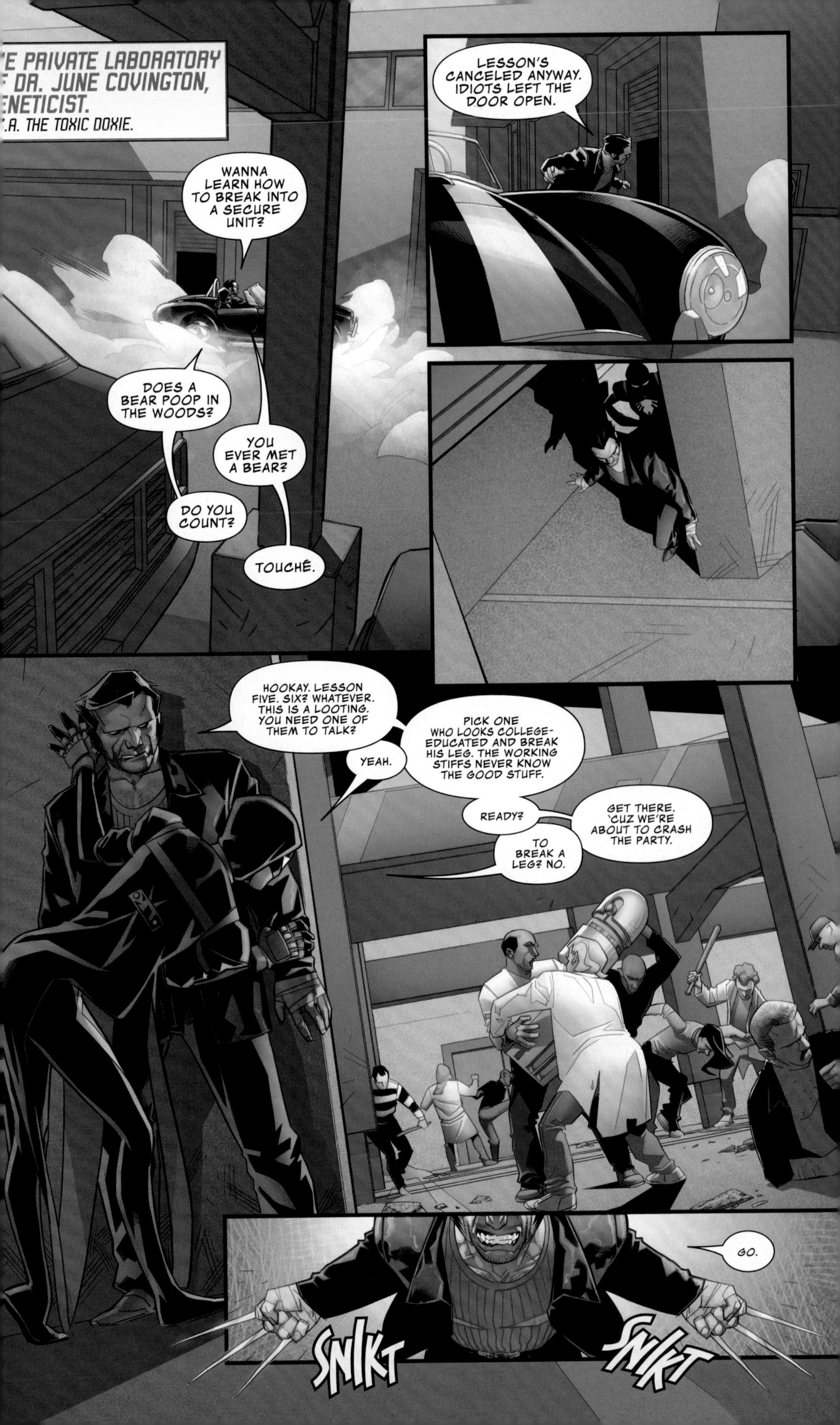

E PRIVATE LABORATORY
F DR. JUNE COVINGTON,
ENETICIST.
.A. THE TOXIC DOXIE.
WANNA LEARN HOW TO BREAK INTO A SECURE UNIT?
DOES A BEAR POOP IN THE WOODS?
YOU EVER MET A BEAR?
DO YOU COUNT?
TOUCHÉ.
LESSON'S CANCELED ANYWAY. IDIOTS LEFT THE DOOR OPEN.
HOOKAY. LESSON FIVE. SIX? WHATEVER. THIS IS A LOOTING. YOU NEED ONE OF THEM TO TALK?
YEAH.
PICK ONE WHO LOOKS COLLEGE-EDUCATED AND BREAK HIS LEG. THE WORKING STIFFS NEVER KNOW THE GOOD STUFF.
READY?
TO BREAK A LEG? NO.
GET THERE. 'CUZ WE'RE ABOUT TO CRASH THE PARTY.
GO.
SNIKT
SNIKT

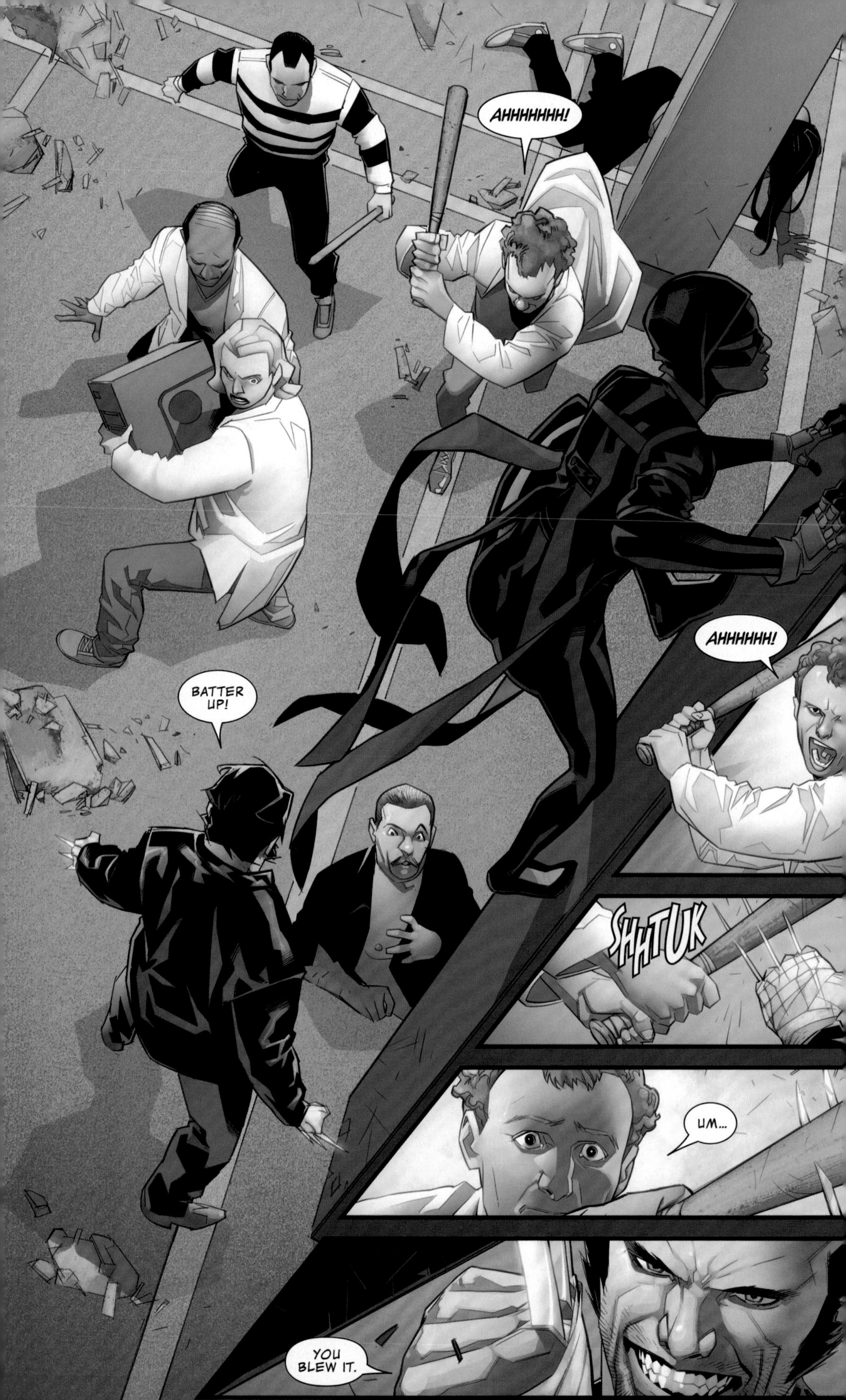
AHHHHHHH!
AHHHHHH!
BATTER UP!
SHHTUK
UM...
YOU BLEW IT.

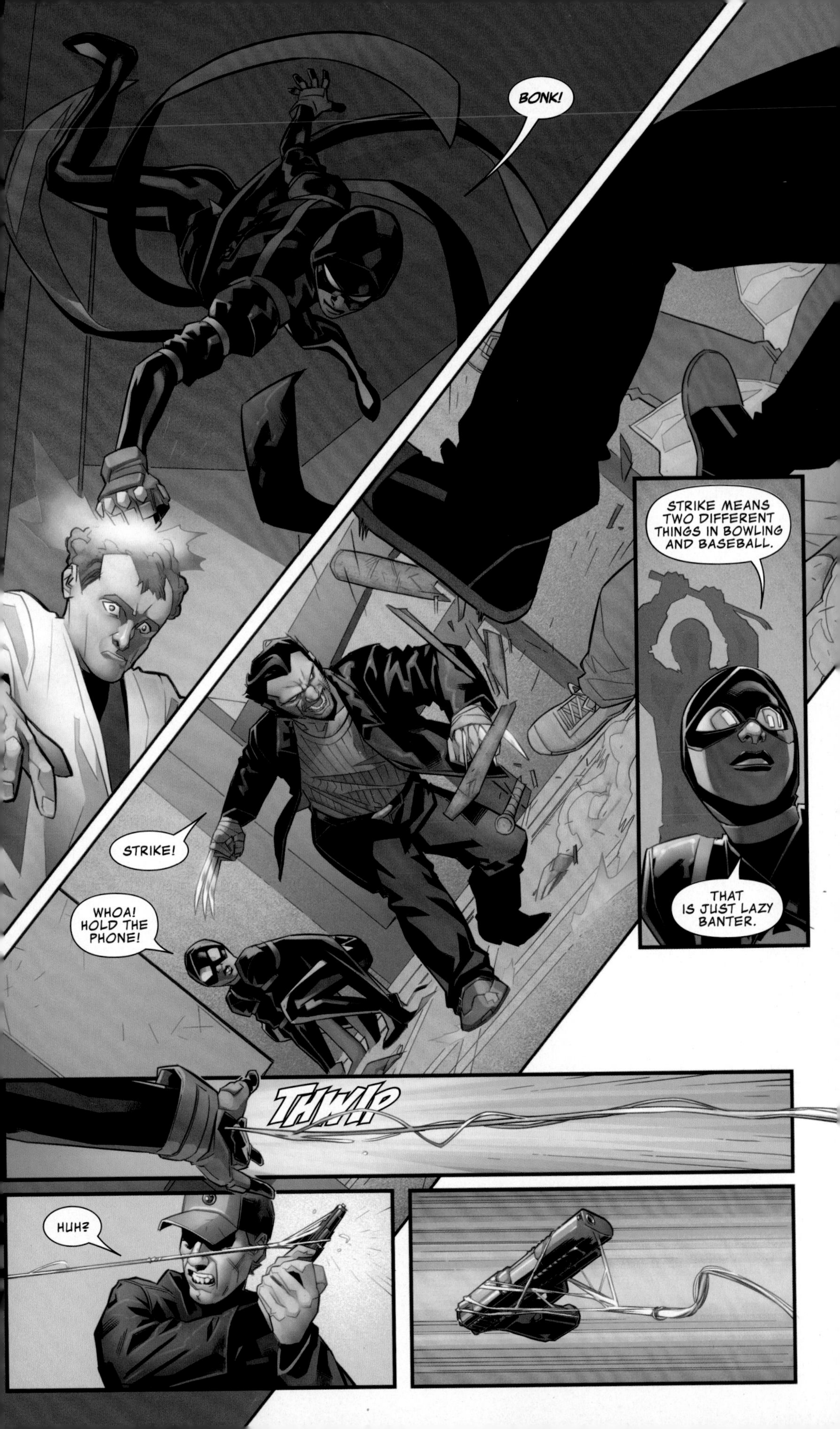
BONK!
STRIKE MEANS TWO DIFFERENT THINGS IN BOWLING AND BASEBALL.
STRIKE!
WHOA! HOLD THE PHONE!
THAT IS JUST LAZY BANTER.
THWIP
HUH?

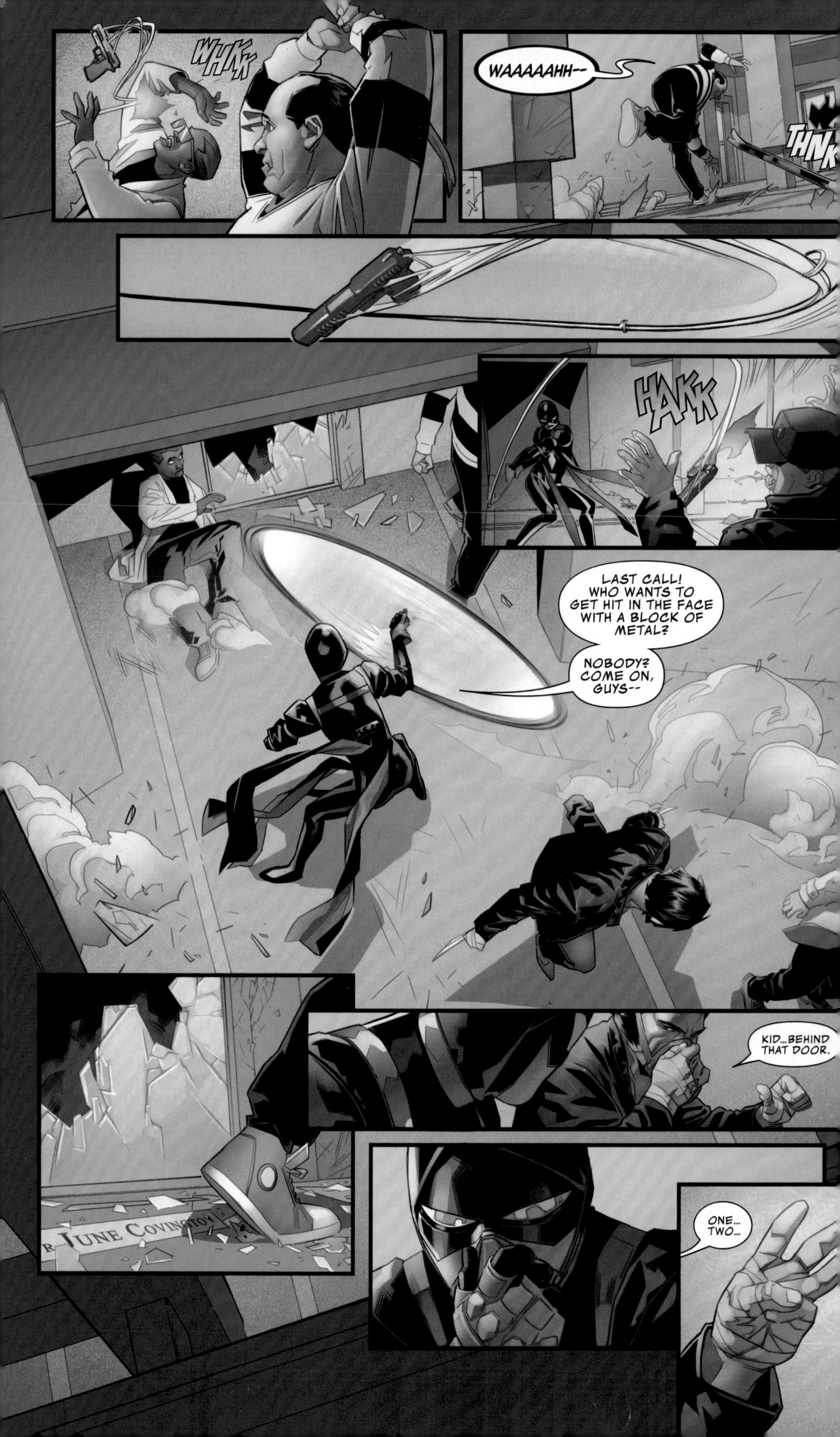
WHKK
WAAAAAHH--
THNK
HAKK
LAST CALL! WHO WANTS TO GET HIT IN THE FACE WITH A BLOCK OF METAL?
NOBODY? COME ON, GUYS--
KID...BEHIND THAT DOOR.
ONE... TWO...

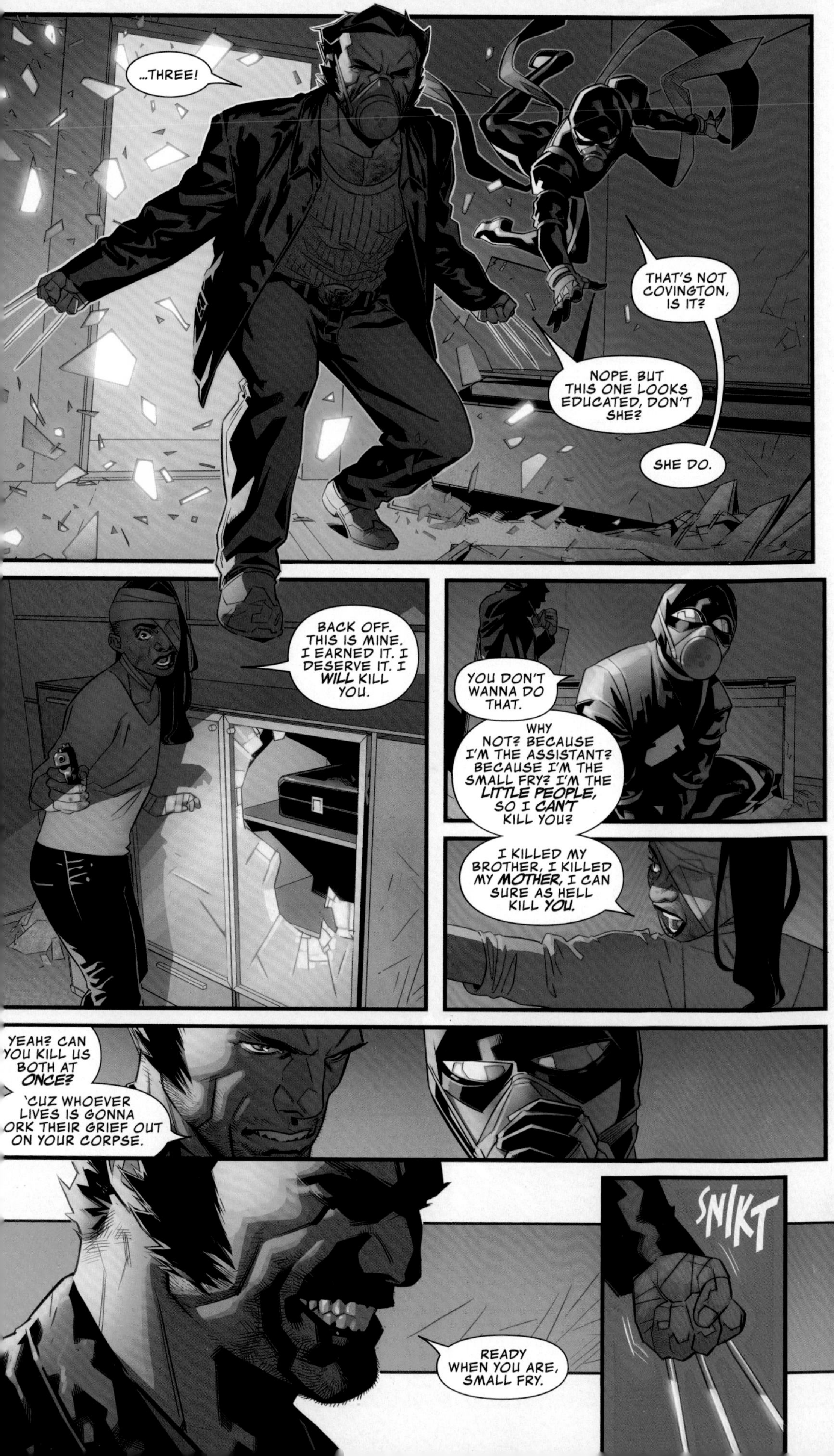
...THREE!
THAT'S NOT COVINGTON, IS IT?
NOPE. BUT THIS ONE LOOKS EDUCATED, DON'T SHE?
SHE DO.
BACK OFF. THIS IS MINE. I EARNED IT. I DESERVE IT. I WILL KILL YOU.
YOU DON'T WANNA DO THAT.
WHY NOT? BECAUSE I'M THE ASSISTANT? BECAUSE I'M THE SMALL FRY? I'M THE LITTLE PEOPLE, SO I CAN'T KILL YOU?
I KILLED MY BROTHER, I KILLED MY MOTHER, I CAN SURE AS HELL KILL YOU.
YEAH? CAN YOU KILL US BOTH AT ONCE?
'CUZ WHOEVER LIVES IS GONNA ORK THEIR GRIEF OUT ON YOUR CORPSE.
READY WHEN YOU ARE, SMALL FRY.
SNIKT

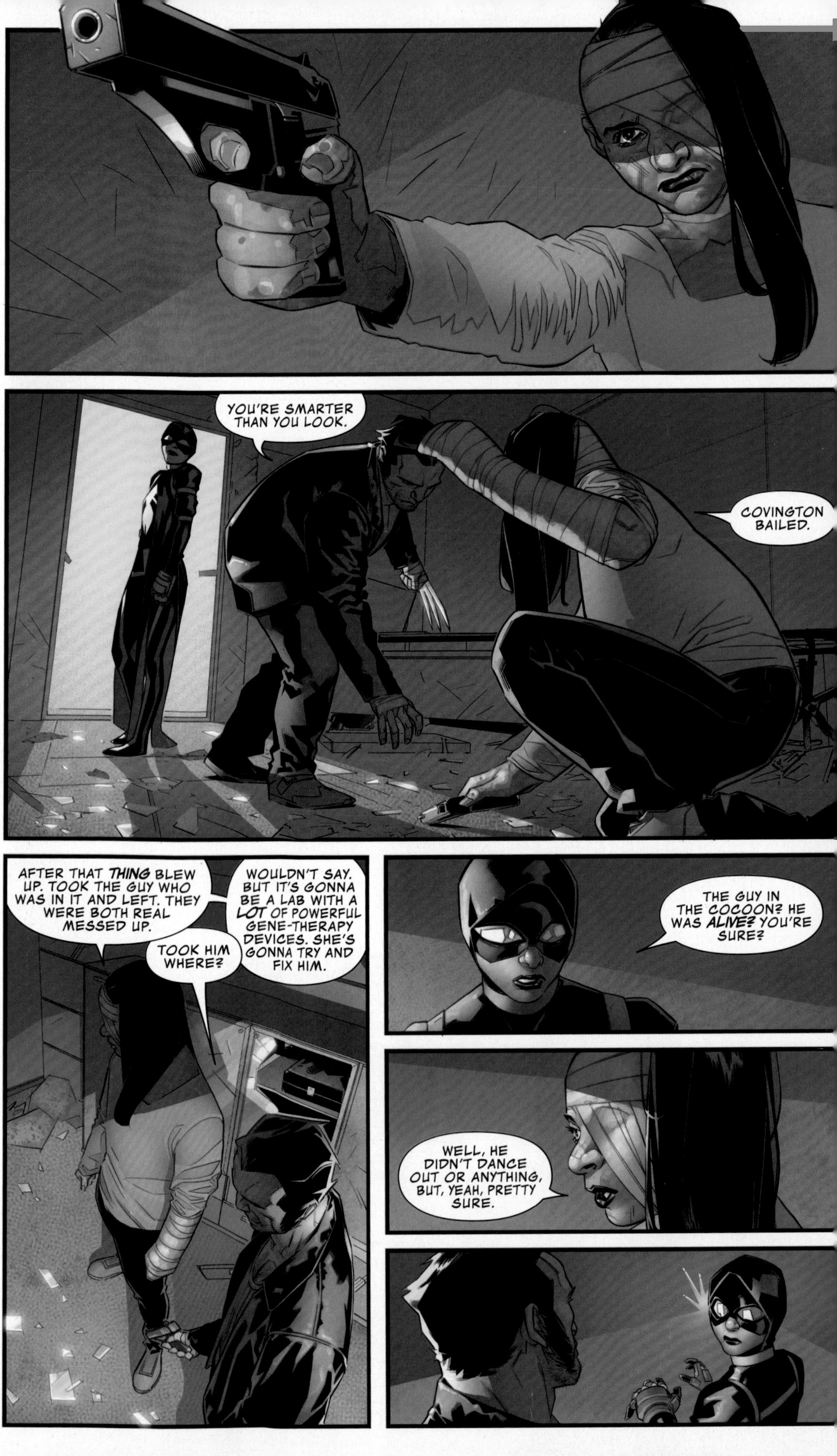

YOU'RE SMARTER THAN YOU LOOK.
COVINGTON BAILED.
AFTER THAT THING BLEW UP. TOOK THE GUY WHO WAS IN IT AND LEFT. THEY WERE BOTH REAL MESSED UP.
TOOK HIM WHERE?
WOULDN'T SAY. BUT IT'S GONNA BE A LAB WITH A LOT OF POWERFUL GENE-THERAPY DEVICES. SHE'S GONNA TRY AND FIX HIM.
THE GUY IN THE COCOON? HE WAS ALIVE? YOU'RE SURE?
WELL, HE DIDN'T DANCE OUT OR ANYTHING, BUT, YEAH, PRETTY SURE.

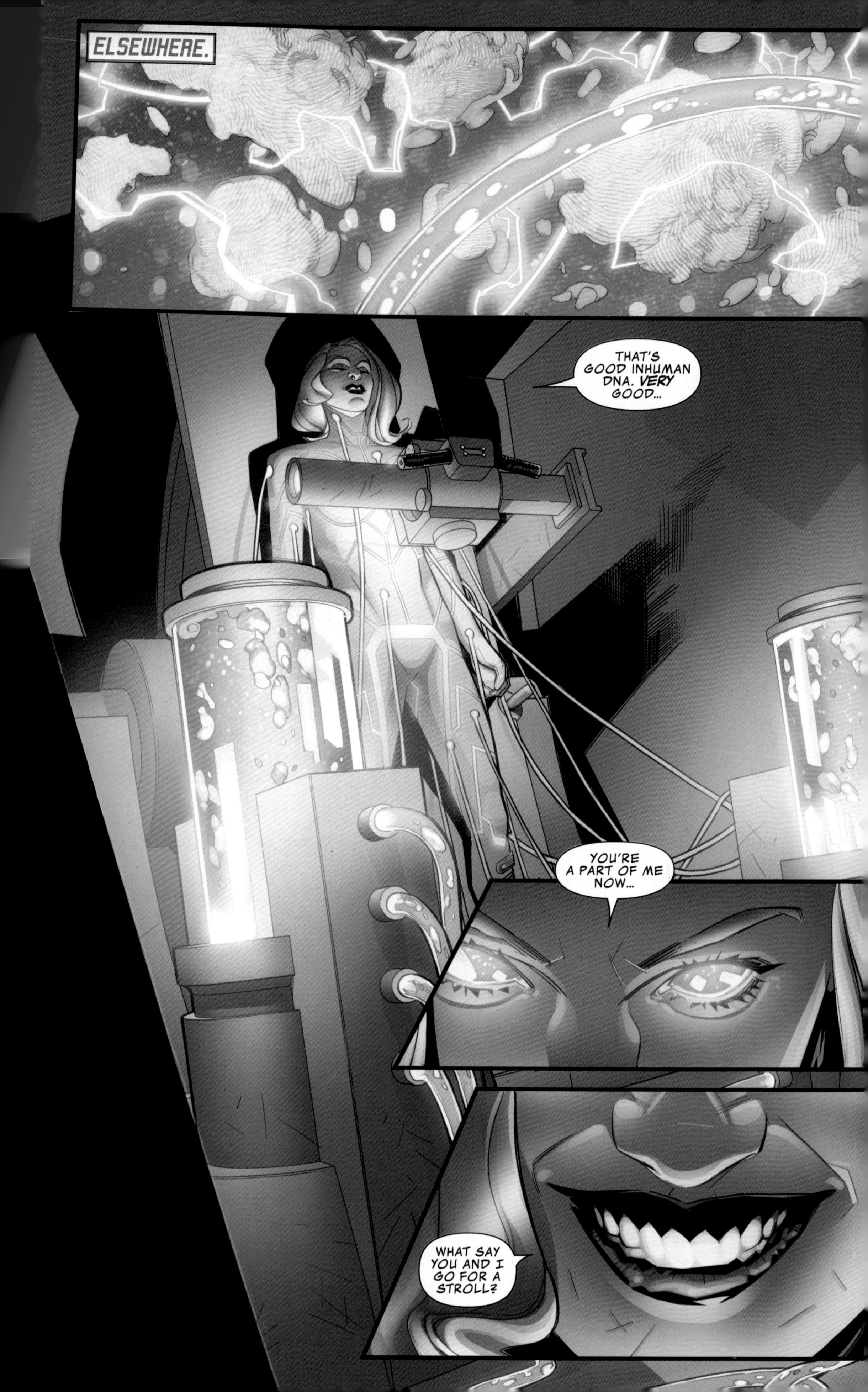
ELSEWHERE.
THAT'S GOOD INHUMAN DNA. VERY GOOD...
YOU'RE A PART OF ME NOW...
WHAT SAY YOU AND I GO FOR A STROLL?

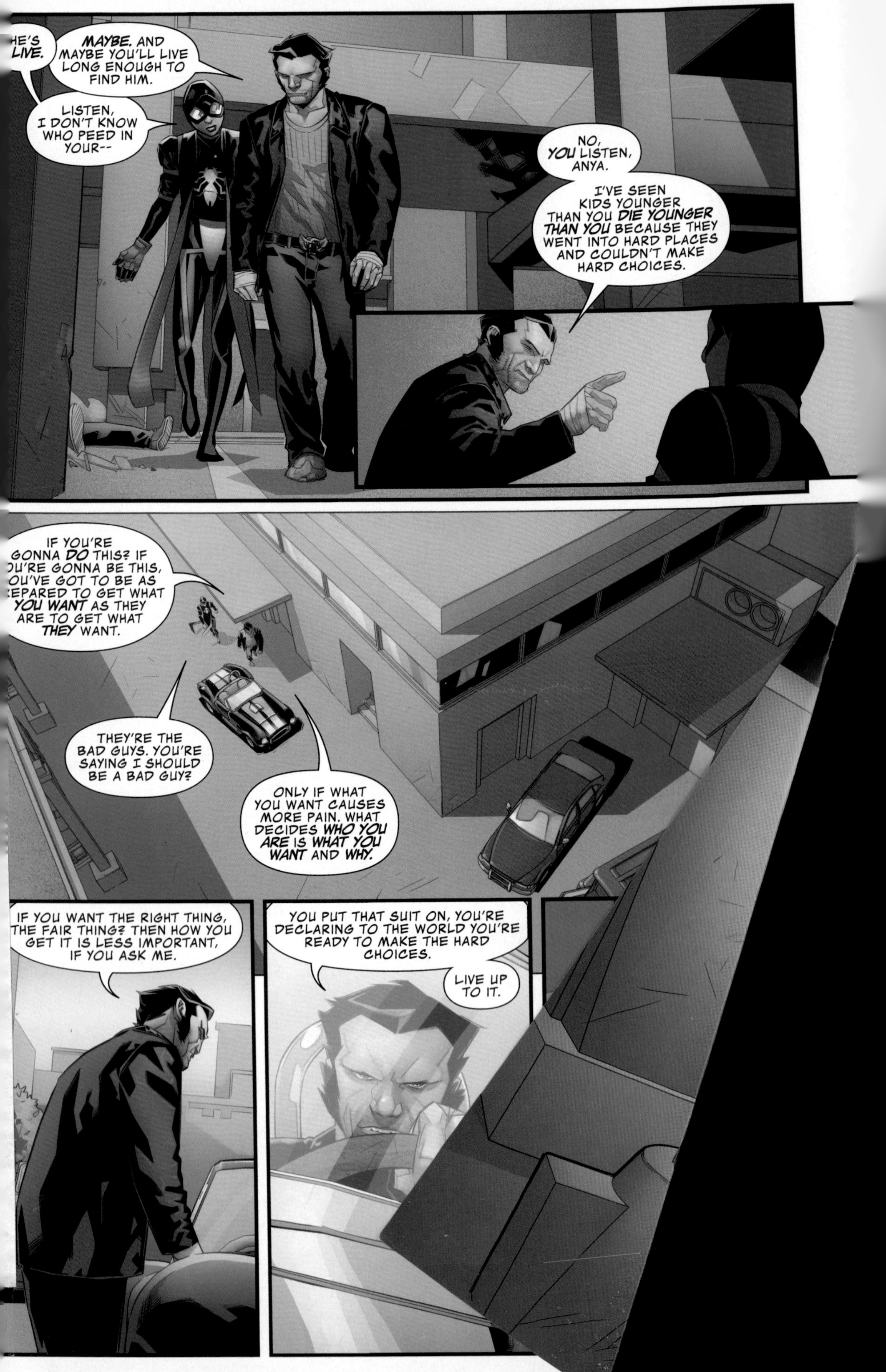
HE'S LIVE.
MAYBE. AND MAYBE YOU'LL LIVE LONG ENOUGH TO FIND HIM.
LISTEN, I DON'T KNOW WHO PEED IN YOUR--
NO, YOU LISTEN, ANYA.
I'VE SEEN KIDS YOUNGER THAN YOU DIE YOUNGER THAN YOU BECAUSE THEY WENT INTO HARD PLACES AND COULDN'T MAKE HARD CHOICES.
IF YOU'RE GONNA DO THIS? IF OU'RE GONNA BE THIS, OU'VE GOT TO BE AS EPARED TO GET WHAT YOU WANT AS THEY ARE TO GET WHAT THEY WANT.
THEY'RE THE BAD GUYS. YOU'RE SAYING I SHOULD BE A BAD GUY?
ONLY IF WHAT YOU WANT CAUSES MORE PAIN. WHAT DECIDES WHO YOU ARE IS WHAT YOU WANT AND WHY.
IF YOU WANT THE RIGHT THING, THE FAIR THING? THEN HOW YOU GET IT IS LESS IMPORTANT, IF YOU ASK ME.
YOU PUT THAT SUIT ON, YOU'RE DECLARING TO THE WORLD YOU'RE READY TO MAKE THE HARD CHOICES.
LIVE UP TO IT.

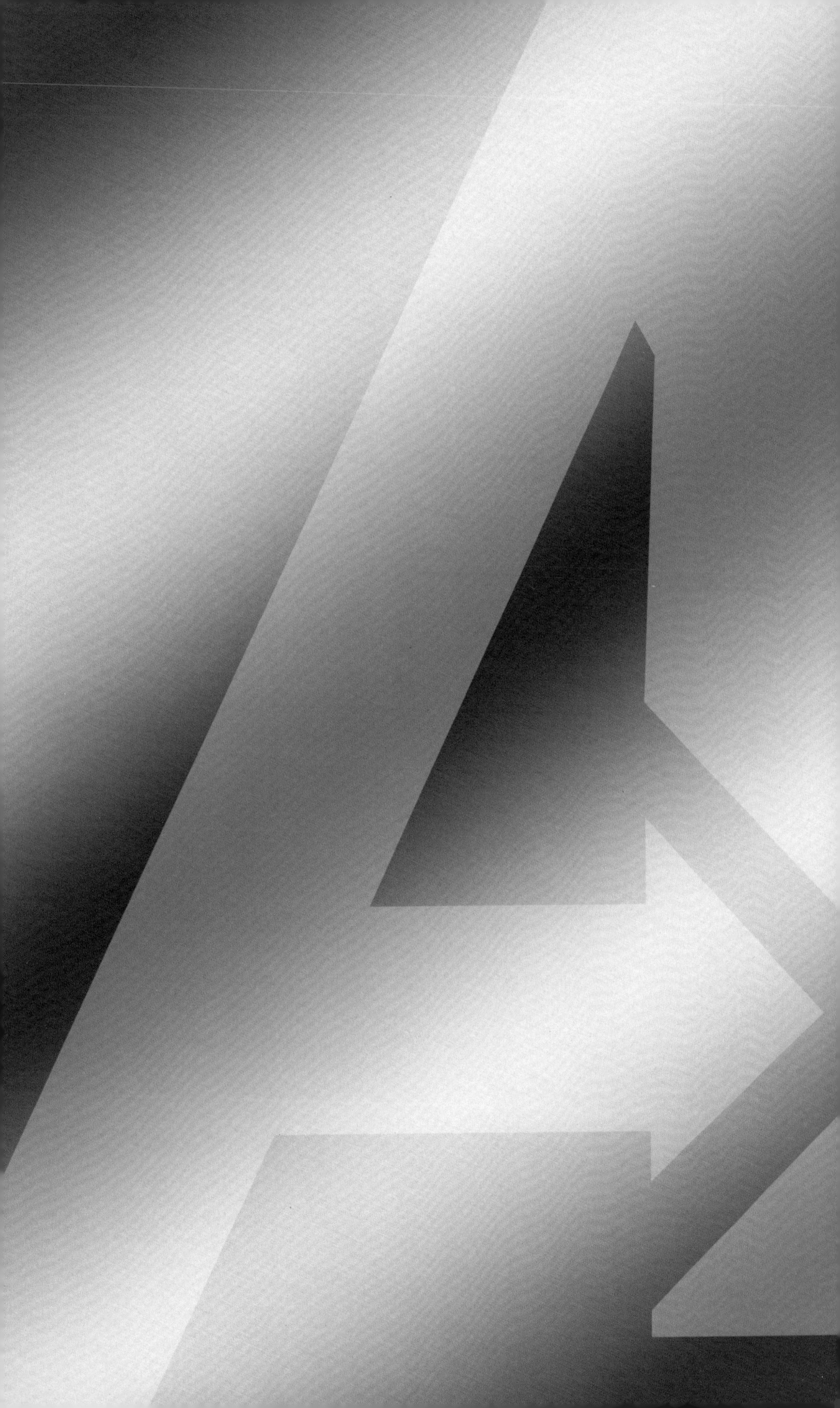

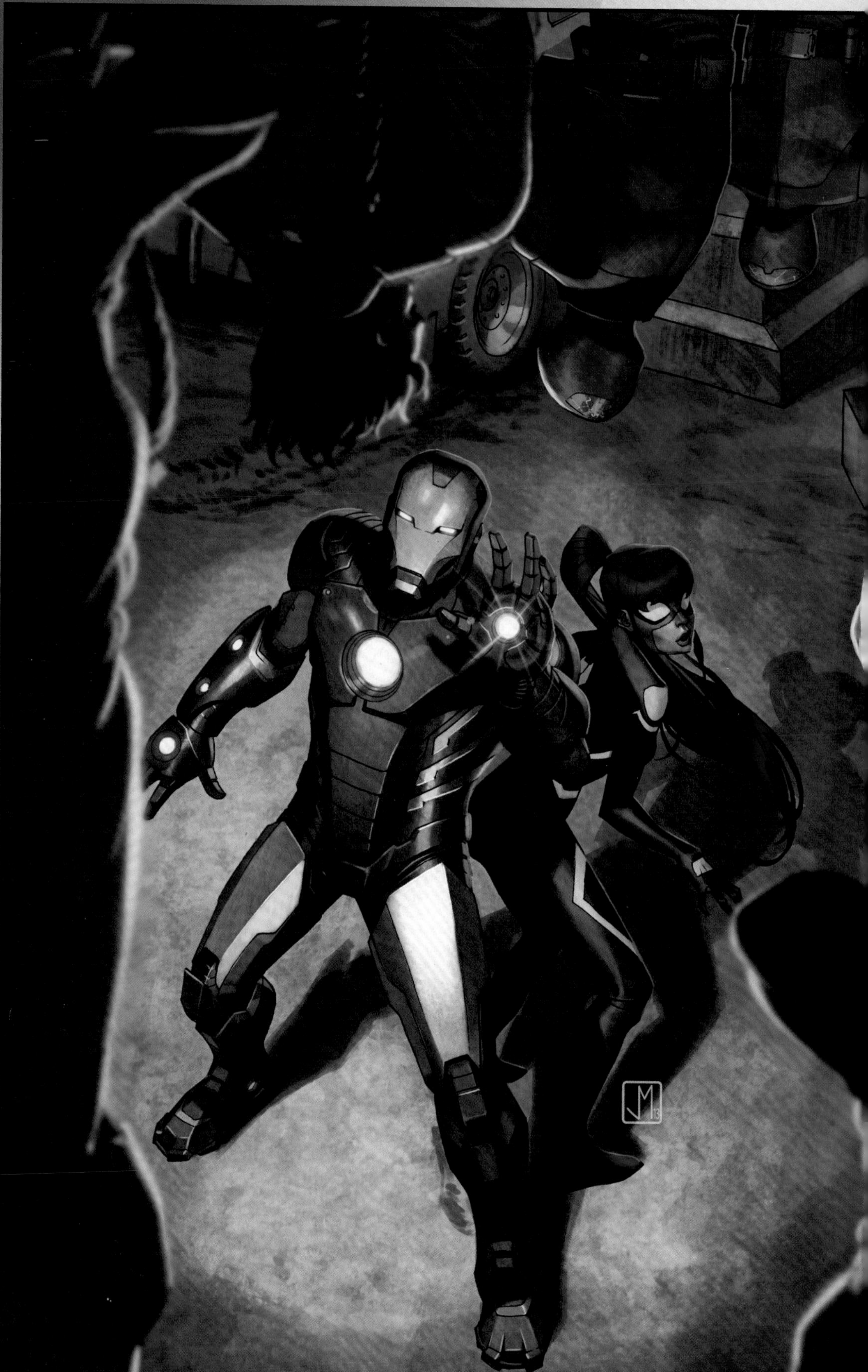

TWENTY-FOUR

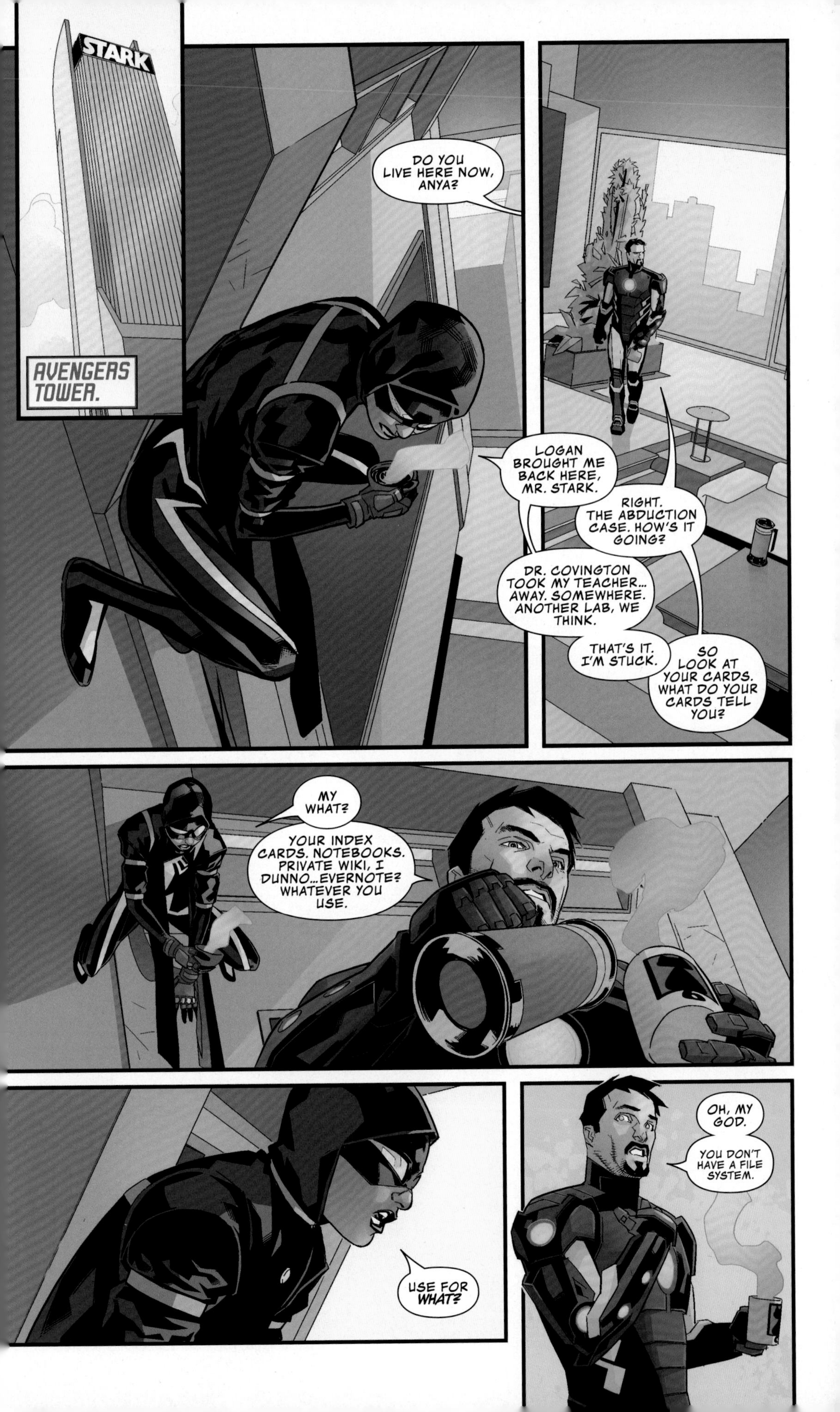
STARK
AVENGERS TOWER.
DO YOU LIVE HERE NOW, ANYA?
LOGAN BROUGHT ME BACK HERE, MR. STARK.
RIGHT. THE ABDUCTION CASE. HOW'S IT GOING?
DR. COVINGTON TOOK MY TEACHER... AWAY. SOMEWHERE. ANOTHER LAB, WE THINK.
THAT'S IT. I'M STUCK.
SO LOOK AT YOUR CARDS. WHAT DO YOUR CARDS TELL YOU?
MY WHAT?
YOUR INDEX CARDS. NOTEBOOKS. PRIVATE WIKI, I DUNNO...EVERNOTE? WHATEVER YOU USE.
USE FOR *WHAT?*
OH, MY GOD.
YOU DON'T HAVE A FILE SYSTEM.

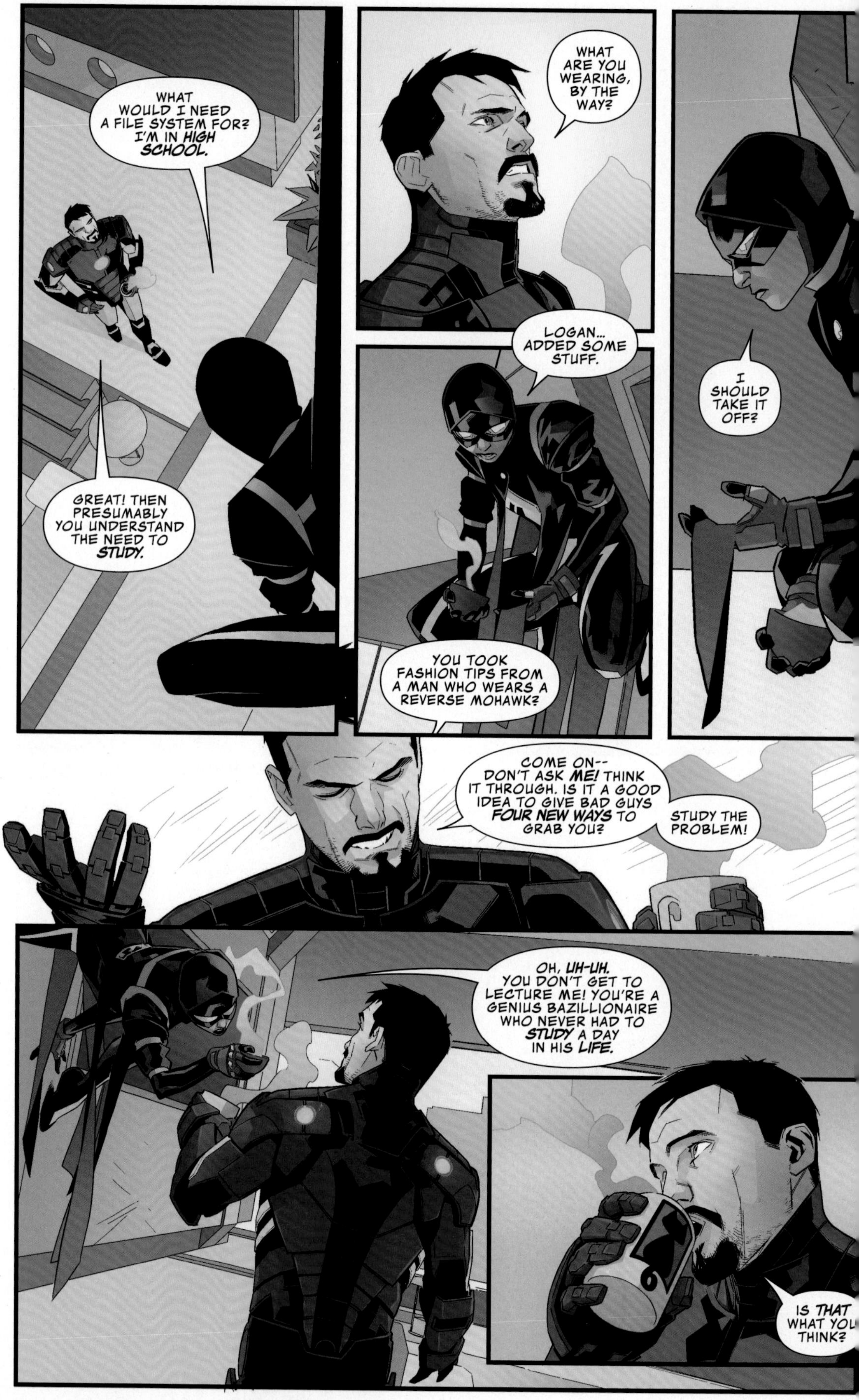
WHAT WOULD I NEED A FILE SYSTEM FOR? I'M IN HIGH SCHOOL.
GREAT! THEN PRESUMABLY YOU UNDERSTAND THE NEED TO STUDY.
WHAT ARE YOU WEARING, BY THE WAY?
LOGAN... ADDED SOME STUFF.
YOU TOOK FASHION TIPS FROM A MAN WHO WEARS A REVERSE MOHAWK?
I SHOULD TAKE IT OFF?
COME ON-- DON'T ASK ME! THINK IT THROUGH. IS IT A GOOD IDEA TO GIVE BAD GUYS FOUR NEW WAYS TO GRAB YOU?
STUDY THE PROBLEM!
OH, UH-UH. YOU DON'T GET TO LECTURE ME! YOU'RE A GENIUS BAZILLIONAIRE WHO NEVER HAD TO STUDY A DAY IN HIS LIFE.
IS THAT WHAT YOU THINK?

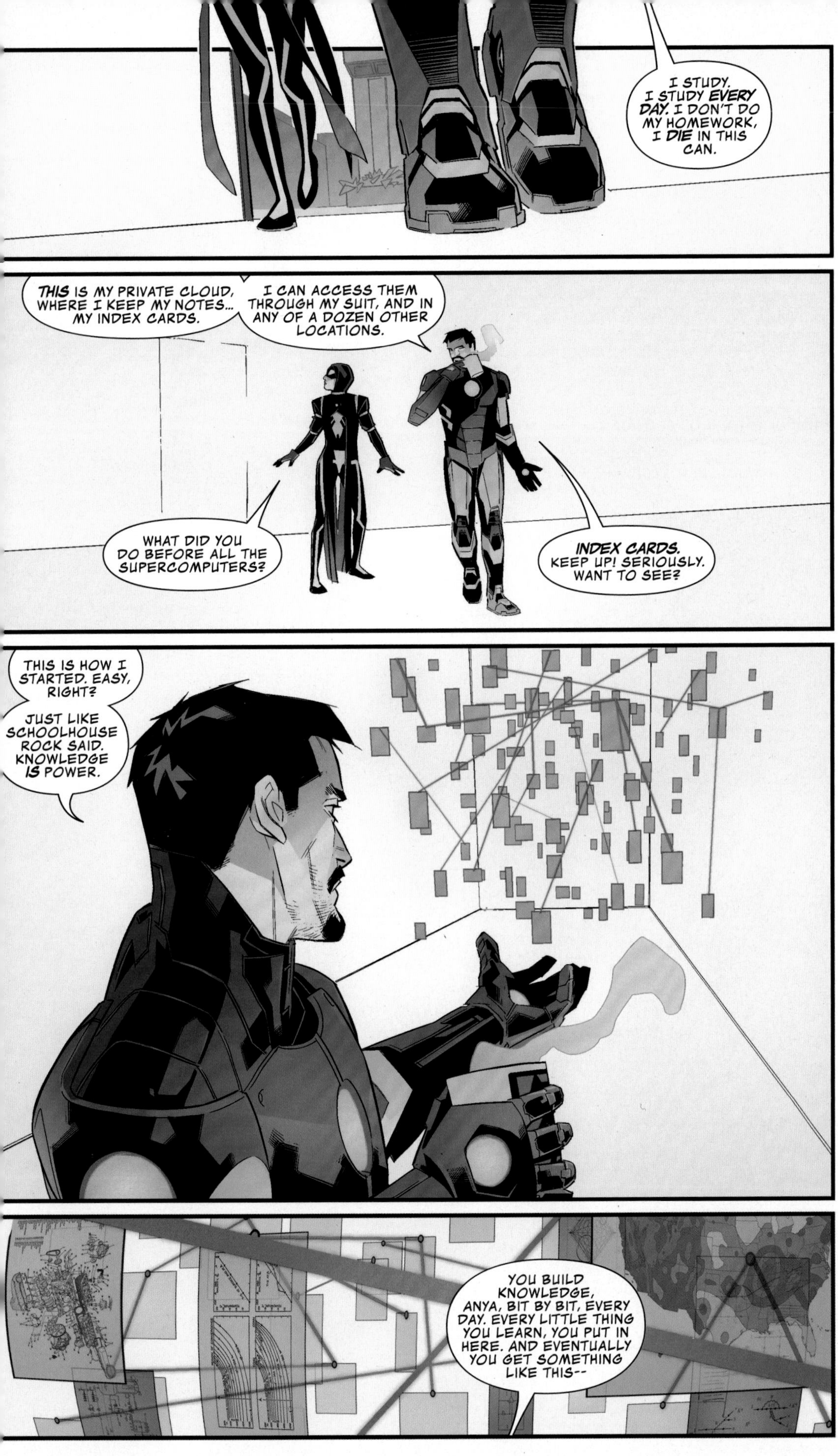
I STUDY. I STUDY EVERY DAY. I DON'T DO MY HOMEWORK, I DIE IN THIS CAN.
THIS IS MY PRIVATE CLOUD, WHERE I KEEP MY NOTES... MY INDEX CARDS.
I CAN ACCESS THEM THROUGH MY SUIT, AND IN ANY OF A DOZEN OTHER LOCATIONS.
WHAT DID YOU DO BEFORE ALL THE SUPERCOMPUTERS?
INDEX CARDS. KEEP UP! SERIOUSLY. WANT TO SEE?
THIS IS HOW I STARTED. EASY, RIGHT?
JUST LIKE SCHOOLHOUSE ROCK SAID. KNOWLEDGE IS POWER.
YOU BUILD KNOWLEDGE, ANYA, BIT BY BIT, EVERY DAY. EVERY LITTLE THING YOU LEARN, YOU PUT IN HERE. AND EVENTUALLY YOU GET SOMETHING LIKE THIS--

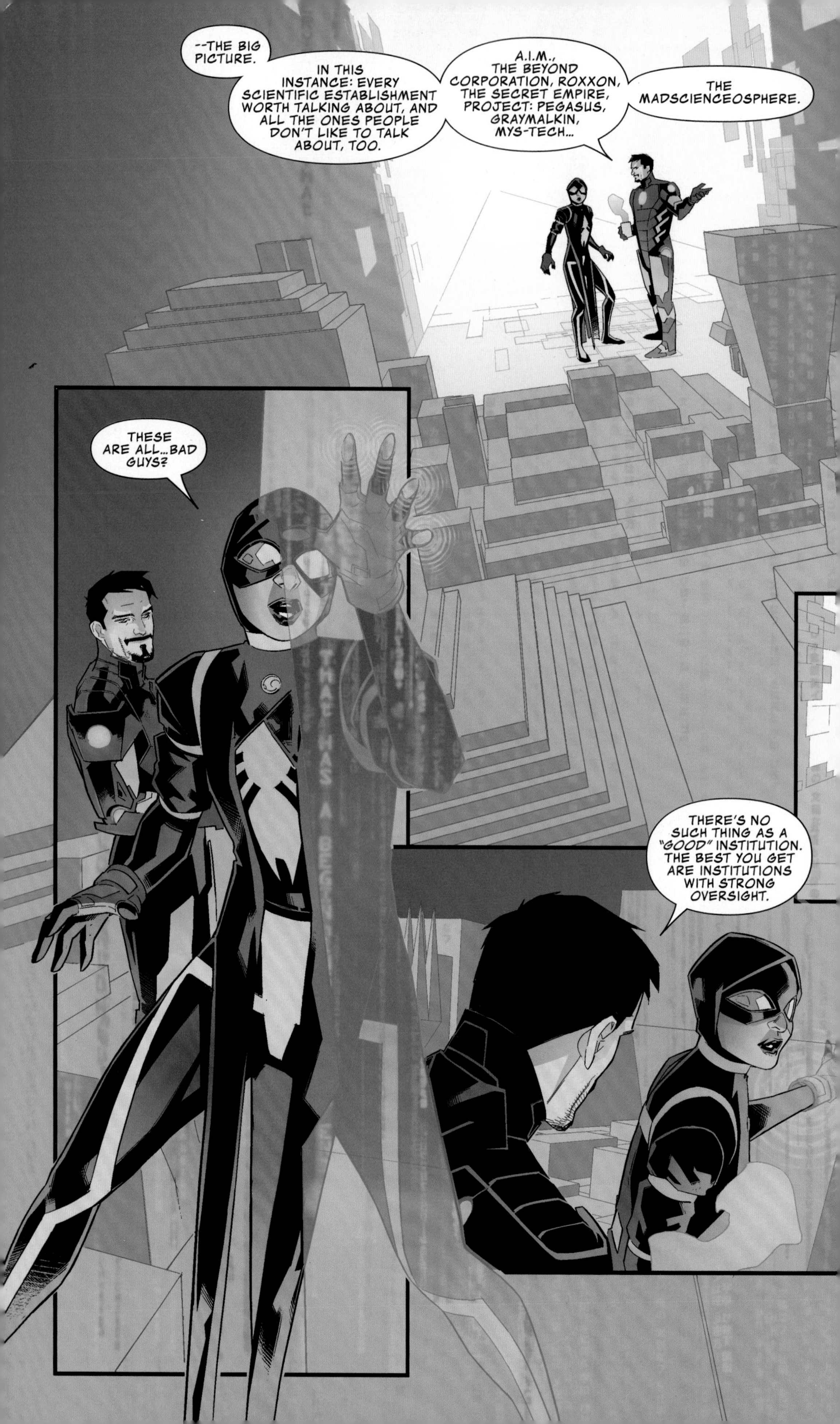
--THE BIG PICTURE.
IN THIS INSTANCE: EVERY SCIENTIFIC ESTABLISHMENT WORTH TALKING ABOUT, AND ALL THE ONES PEOPLE DON'T LIKE TO TALK ABOUT, TOO.
A.I.M., THE BEYOND CORPORATION, ROXXON, THE SECRET EMPIRE, PROJECT: PEGASUS, GRAYMALKIN, MYS-TECH...
THE MADSCIENCEOSPHERE.
THESE ARE ALL...BAD GUYS?
THERE'S NO SUCH THING AS A "GOOD" INSTITUTION. THE BEST YOU GET ARE INSTITUTIONS WITH STRONG OVERSIGHT.

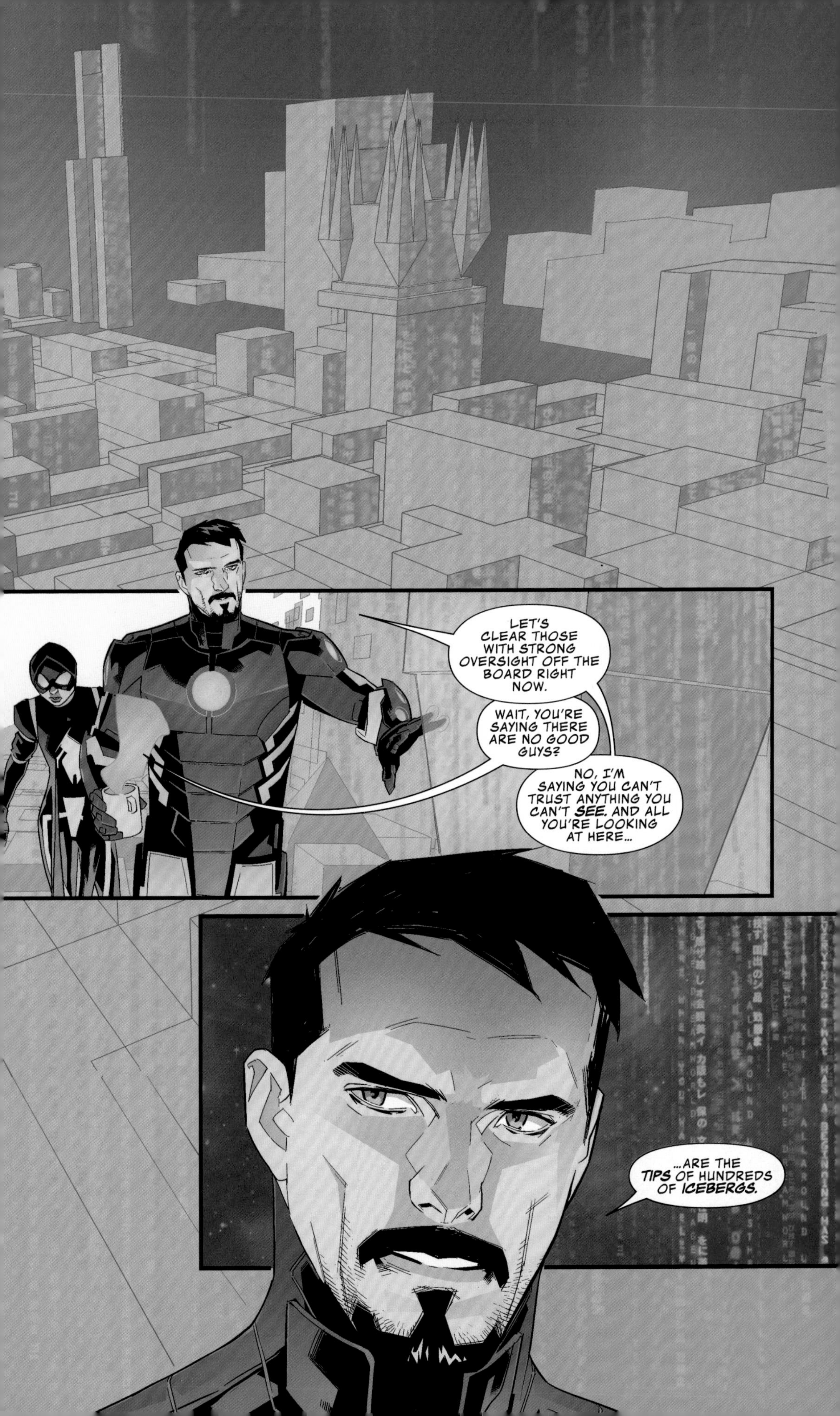
LET'S CLEAR THOSE WITH STRONG OVERSIGHT OFF THE BOARD RIGHT NOW.
WAIT, YOU'RE SAYING THERE ARE NO GOOD GUYS?
NO, I'M SAYING YOU CAN'T TRUST ANYTHING YOU CAN'T SEE. AND ALL YOU'RE LOOKING AT HERE...
...ARE THE TIPS OF HUNDREDS OF ICEBERGS.

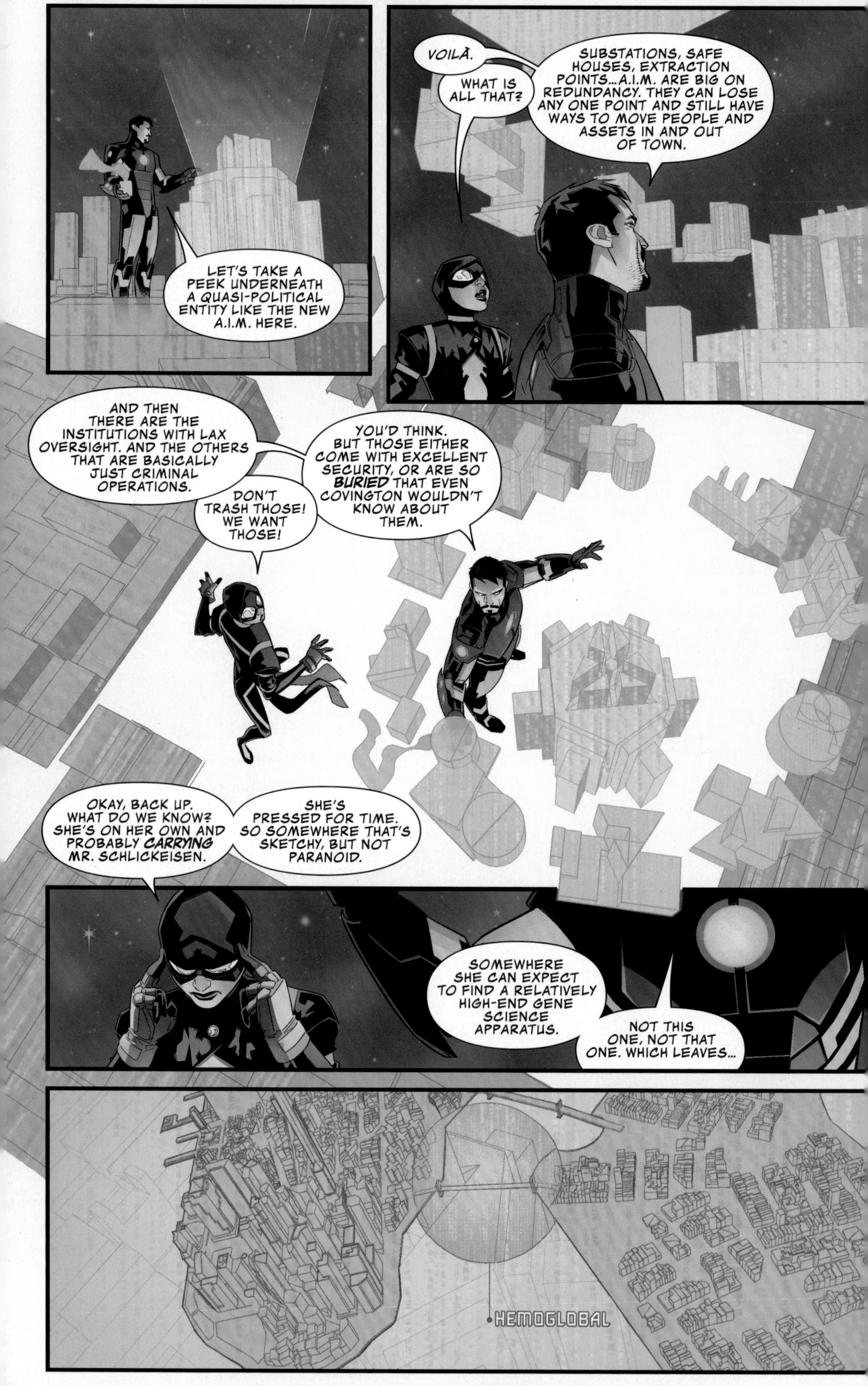
LET'S TAKE A PEEK UNDERNEATH A QUASI-POLITICAL ENTITY LIKE THE NEW A.I.M. HERE.
VOILÀ.
WHAT IS ALL THAT?
SUBSTATIONS, SAFE HOUSES, EXTRACTION POINTS...A.I.M. ARE BIG ON REDUNDANCY. THEY CAN LOSE ANY ONE POINT AND STILL HAVE WAYS TO MOVE PEOPLE AND ASSETS IN AND OUT OF TOWN.
AND THEN THERE ARE THE INSTITUTIONS WITH LAX OVERSIGHT. AND THE OTHERS THAT ARE BASICALLY JUST CRIMINAL OPERATIONS.
DON'T TRASH THOSE! WE WANT THOSE!
YOU'D THINK. BUT THOSE EITHER COME WITH EXCELLENT SECURITY, OR ARE SO *BURIED* THAT EVEN COVINGTON WOULDN'T KNOW ABOUT THEM.
OKAY, BACK UP. WHAT DO WE KNOW? SHE'S ON HER OWN AND PROBABLY *CARRYING* MR. SCHLICKEISEN.
SHE'S PRESSED FOR TIME. SO SOMEWHERE THAT'S SKETCHY, BUT NOT PARANOID.
SOMEWHERE SHE CAN EXPECT TO FIND A RELATIVELY HIGH-END GENE SCIENCE APPARATUS.
NOT THIS ONE, NOT THAT ONE. WHICH LEAVES...
HEMOGLOBAL

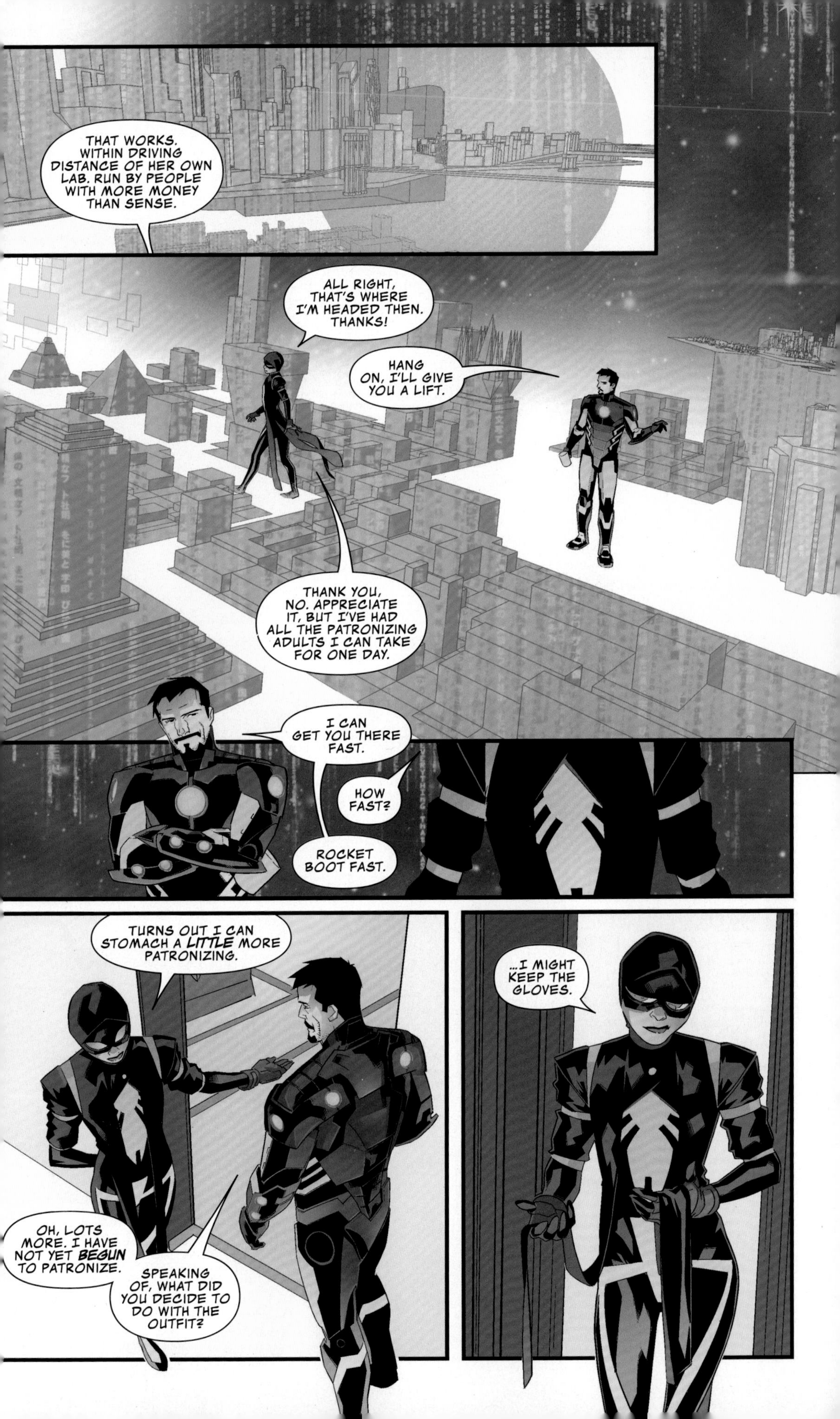

THAT WORKS. WITHIN DRIVING DISTANCE OF HER OWN LAB. RUN BY PEOPLE WITH MORE MONEY THAN SENSE.
ALL RIGHT, THAT'S WHERE I'M HEADED THEN. THANKS!
HANG ON, I'LL GIVE YOU A LIFT.
THANK YOU, NO. APPRECIATE IT, BUT I'VE HAD ALL THE PATRONIZING ADULTS I CAN TAKE FOR ONE DAY.
I CAN GET YOU THERE FAST.
HOW FAST?
ROCKET BOOT FAST.
TURNS OUT I CAN STOMACH A LITTLE MORE PATRONIZING.
OH, LOTS MORE. I HAVE NOT YET BEGUN TO PATRONIZE.
SPEAKING OF, WHAT DID YOU DECIDE TO DO WITH THE OUTFIT?
...I MIGHT KEEP THE GLOVES.

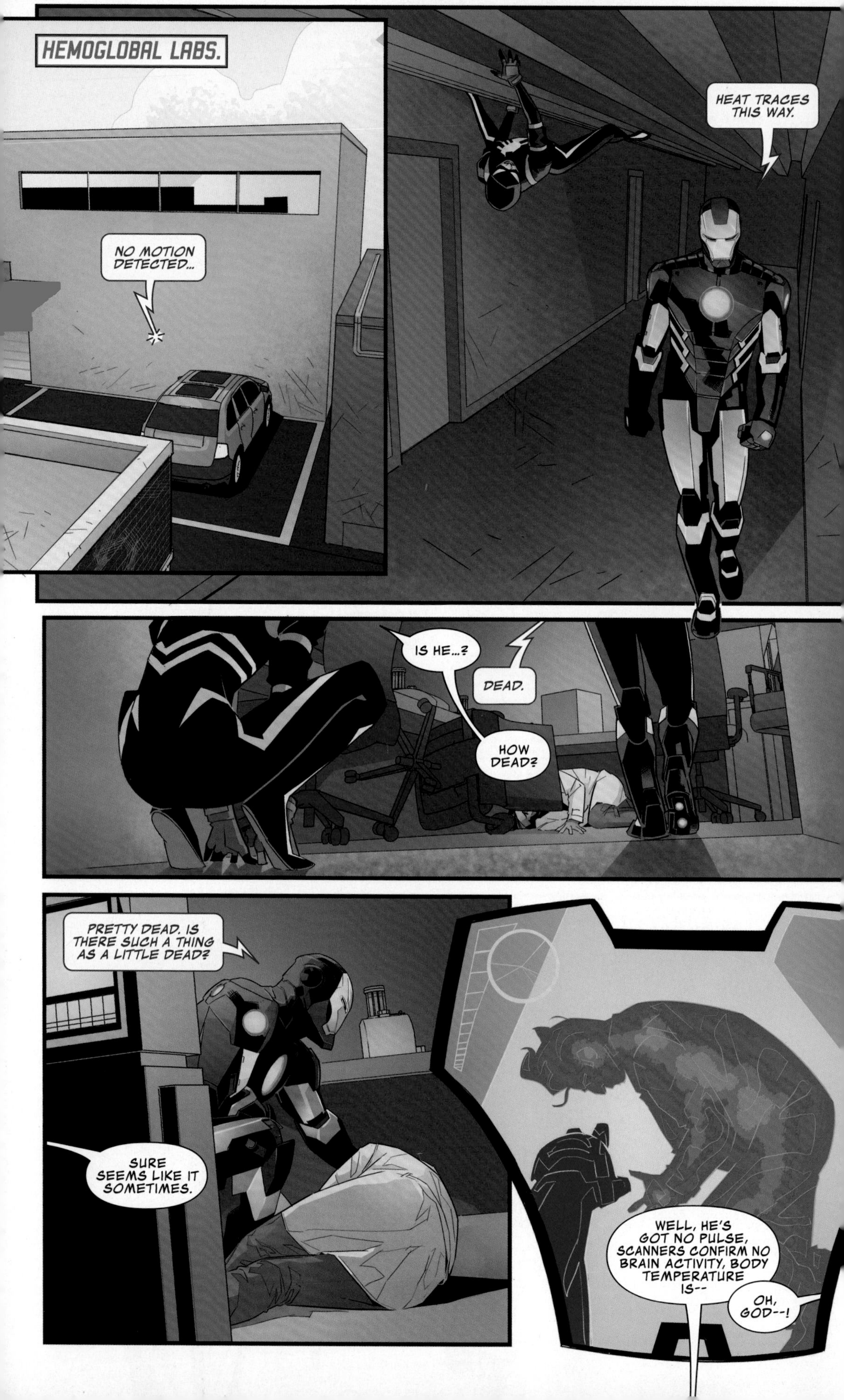
HEMOGLOBAL LABS.
NO MOTION DETECTED...
HEAT TRACES THIS WAY.
IS HE...?
DEAD.
HOW DEAD?
PRETTY DEAD. IS THERE SUCH A THING AS A LITTLE DEAD?
SURE SEEMS LIKE IT SOMETIMES.
WELL, HE'S GOT NO PULSE, SCANNERS CONFIRM NO BRAIN ACTIVITY, BODY TEMPERATURE IS--
OH, GOD--!

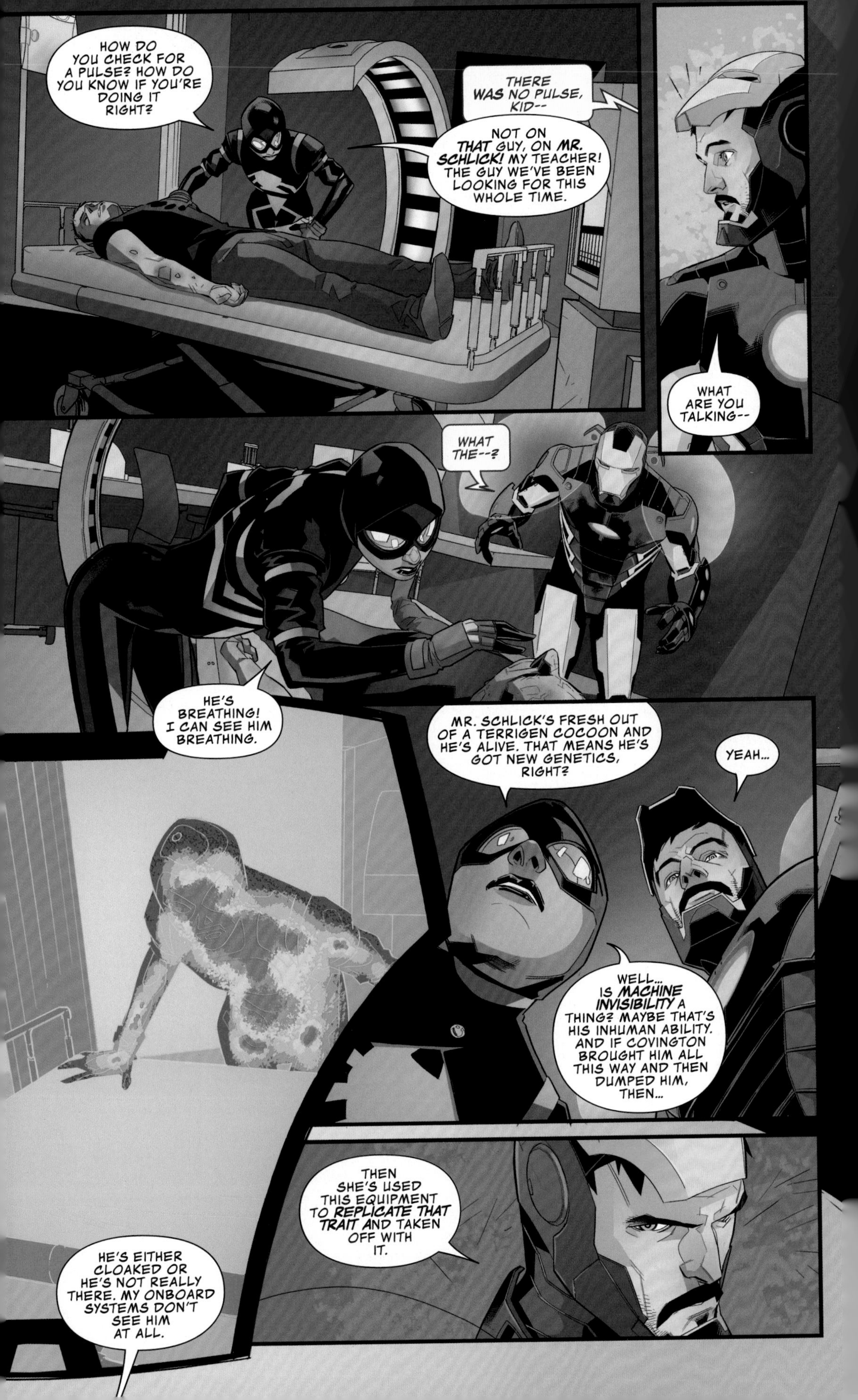
HOW DO YOU CHECK FOR A PULSE? HOW DO YOU KNOW IF YOU'RE DOING IT RIGHT?
THERE WAS NO PULSE, KID--
NOT ON THAT GUY, ON MR. SCHLICK! MY TEACHER! THE GUY WE'VE BEEN LOOKING FOR THIS WHOLE TIME.
WHAT ARE YOU TALKING--
WHAT THE--?
HE'S BREATHING! I CAN SEE HIM BREATHING.
HE'S EITHER CLOAKED OR HE'S NOT REALLY THERE. MY ONBOARD SYSTEMS DON'T SEE HIM AT ALL.
MR. SCHLICK'S FRESH OUT OF A TERRIGEN COCOON AND HE'S ALIVE. THAT MEANS HE'S GOT NEW GENETICS, RIGHT?
YEAH...
WELL... IS MACHINE INVISIBILITY A THING? MAYBE THAT'S HIS INHUMAN ABILITY. AND IF COVINGTON BROUGHT HIM ALL THIS WAY AND THEN DUMPED HIM, THEN...
THEN SHE'S USED THIS EQUIPMENT TO REPLICATE THAT TRAIT AND TAKEN OFF WITH IT.

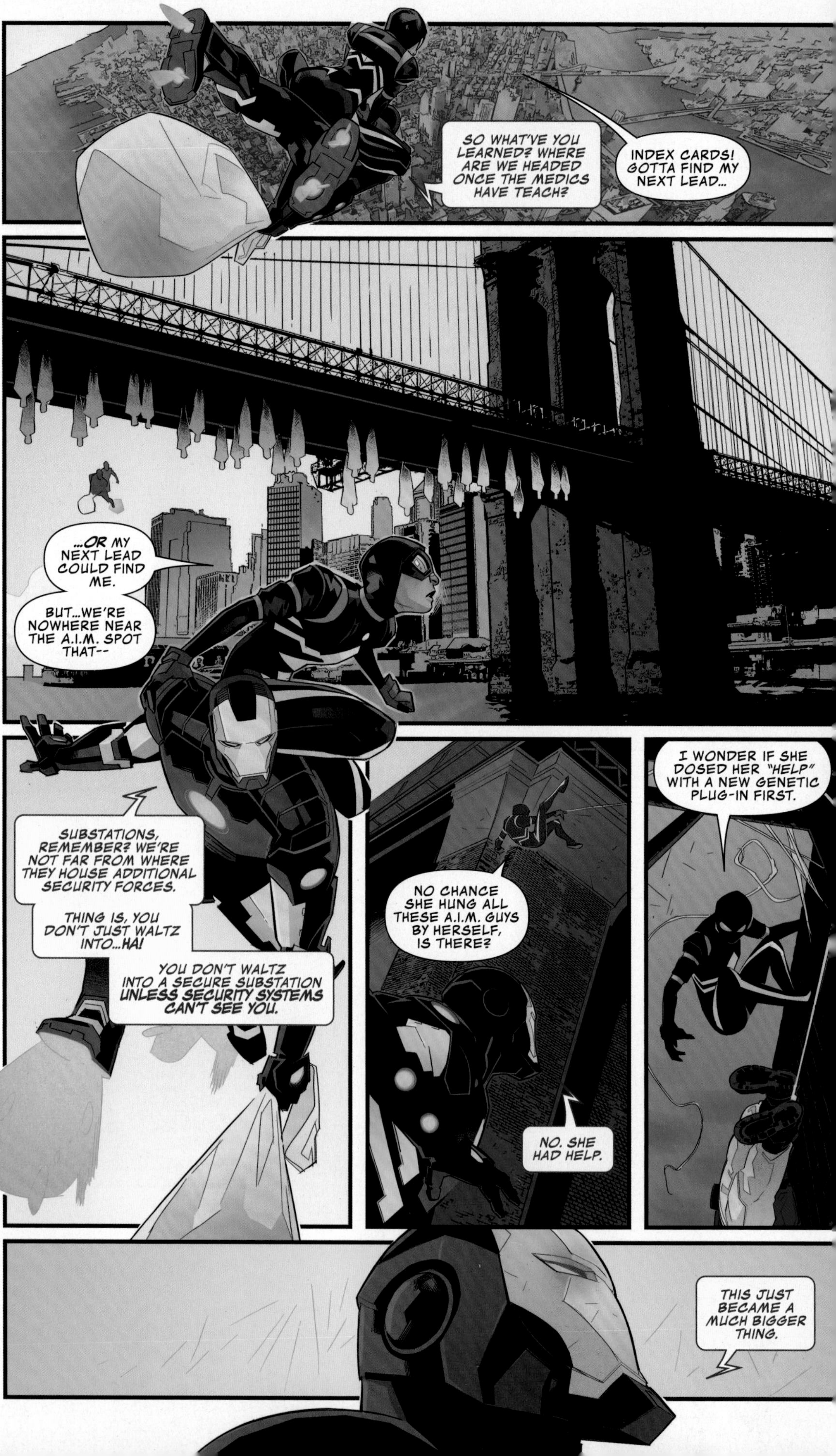
SO WHAT'VE YOU LEARNED? WHERE ARE WE HEADED ONCE THE MEDICS HAVE TEACH?
INDEX CARDS! GOTTA FIND MY NEXT LEAD...
...OR MY NEXT LEAD COULD FIND ME.
BUT...WE'RE NOWHERE NEAR THE A.I.M. SPOT THAT--
SUBSTATIONS, REMEMBER? WE'RE NOT FAR FROM WHERE THEY HOUSE ADDITIONAL SECURITY FORCES.
THING IS, YOU DON'T JUST WALTZ INTO...HA!
YOU DON'T WALTZ INTO A SECURE SUBSTATION UNLESS SECURITY SYSTEMS CAN'T SEE YOU.
NO CHANCE SHE HUNG ALL THESE A.I.M. GUYS BY HERSELF, IS THERE?
NO. SHE HAD HELP.
I WONDER IF SHE DOSED HER "HELP" WITH A NEW GENETIC PLUG-IN FIRST.
THIS JUST BECAME A MUCH BIGGER THING.

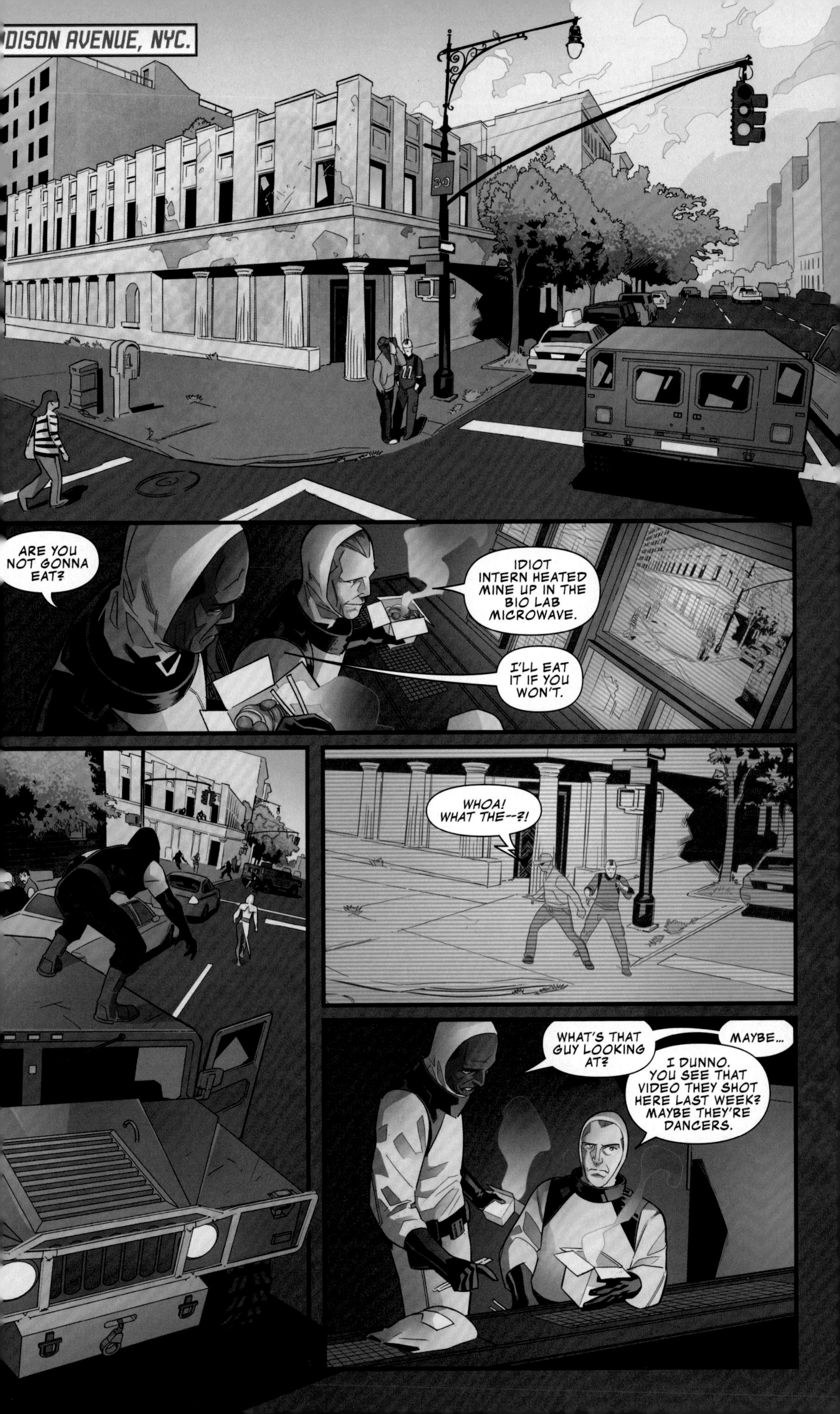
DISON AVENUE, NYC.
30
22
ARE YOU NOT GONNA EAT?
IDIOT INTERN HEATED MINE UP IN THE BIO LAB MICROWAVE.
I'LL EAT IT IF YOU WON'T.
WHOA! WHAT THE--?!
WHAT'S THAT GUY LOOKING AT?
MAYBE...
I DUNNO. YOU SEE THAT VIDEO THEY SHOT HERE LAST WEEK? MAYBE THEY'RE DANCERS.

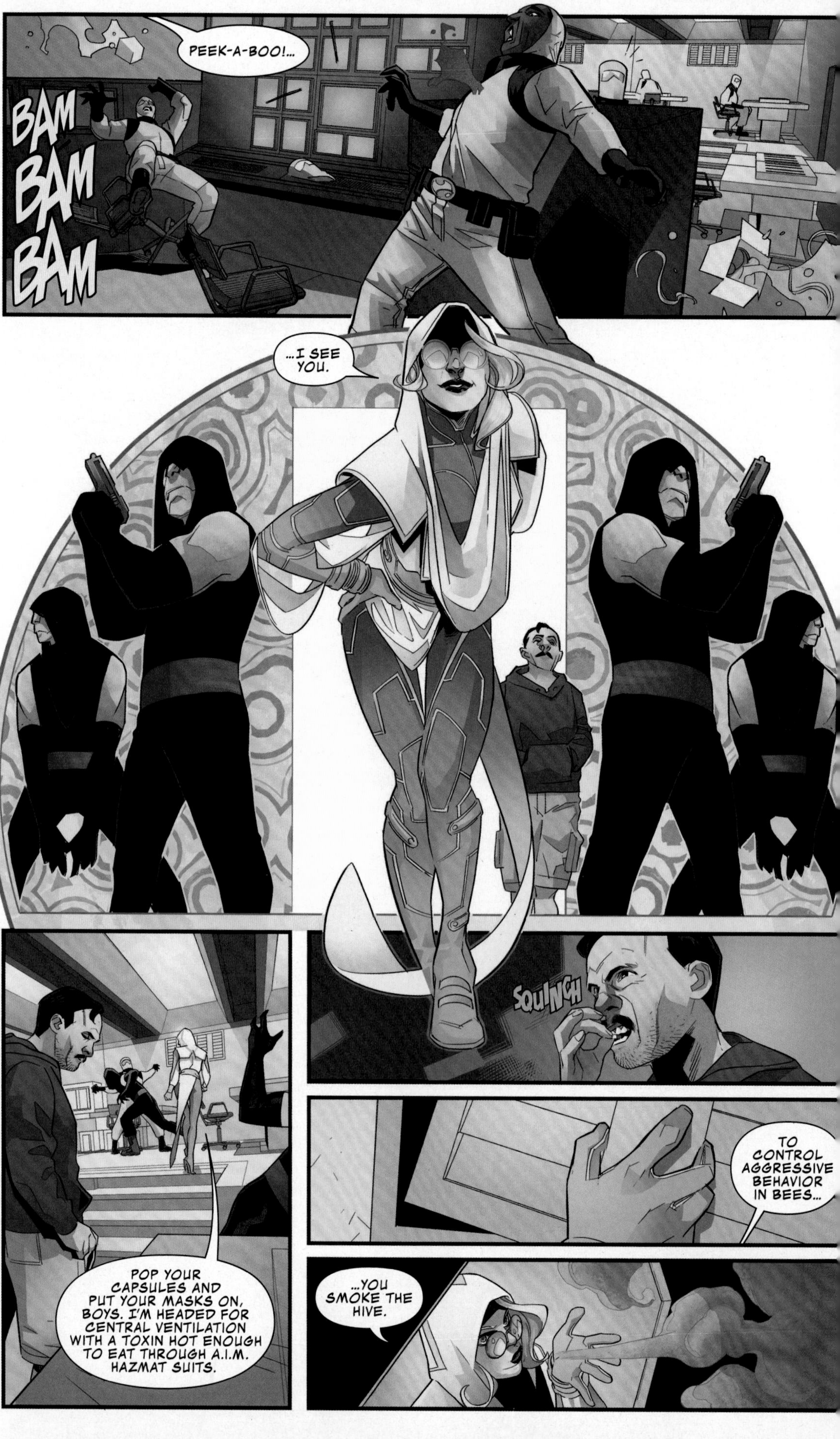
PEEK-A-BOO!...
BAM BAM BAM
...I SEE YOU.
POP YOUR CAPSULES AND PUT YOUR MASKS ON, BOYS. I'M HEADED FOR CENTRAL VENTILATION WITH A TOXIN HOT ENOUGH TO EAT THROUGH A.I.M. HAZMAT SUITS.
SQUINCH
TO CONTROL AGGRESSIVE BEHAVIOR IN BEES...
...YOU SMOKE THE HIVE.

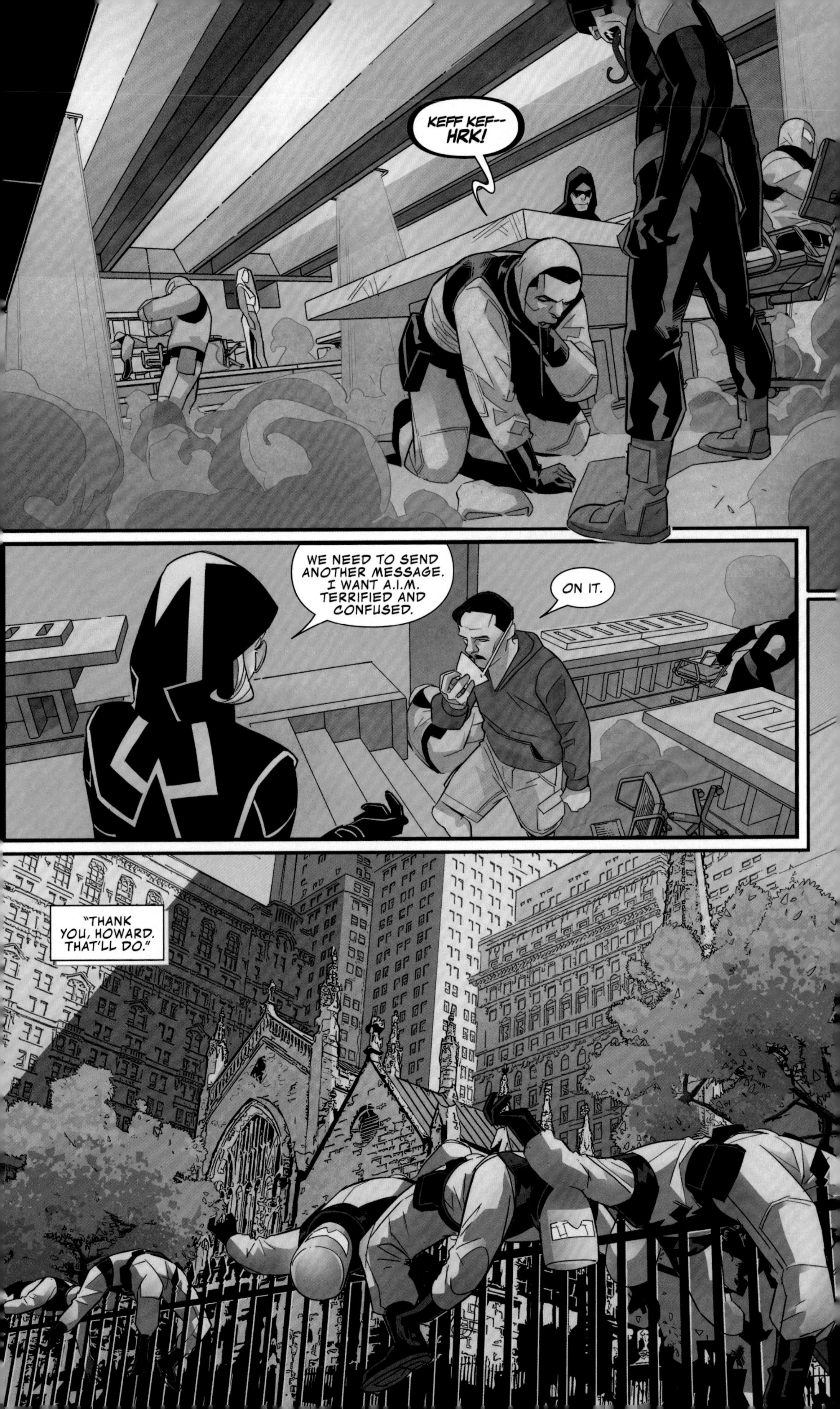
KEFF KEF-- HRK!
WE NEED TO SEND ANOTHER MESSAGE. I WANT A.I.M. TERRIFIED AND CONFUSED.
ON IT.
"THANK YOU, HOWARD. THAT'LL DO."

BELLEVUE
HOSPITAL.

IT'S NOT A COMA.
IT'S A MINIMALLY
CONSCIOUS
STATE.

BUT AS
WE CAN'T SCAN HIS
BRAIN OR GET ANY KIND
OF READING OFF HIM,
OUR OPTIONS ARE
REALLY LIMITED.

I'D LIKE HIM TO BE ABLE TO TELL
ME SOMETHING. WE'RE AT THE SHARP
END OF A SUDDEN GLOBAL MEDICAL
CRISIS AND I COULD USE SOME
INFORMATION.

LOOK, WE'RE
NOT EXPECTING
HIM TO BE ABLE TO
TELL US ANYTHING.
WE JUST--

JUST FIVE
MINUTES WITH
SOME KIND OF
COMMUNICATION
COULD--

I NEED
ZOLPIDEM
TARTRATE.
RIGHT
NOW.

ZOLPIDEM IS
AMBIEN. THAT'S A
SLEEPING PILL, DOC.

NOT FOR
PEOPLE IN MCS.
IN A PERCENTAGE
OF THOSE CASE
IT WAKES THEM
UP. *FAST.*

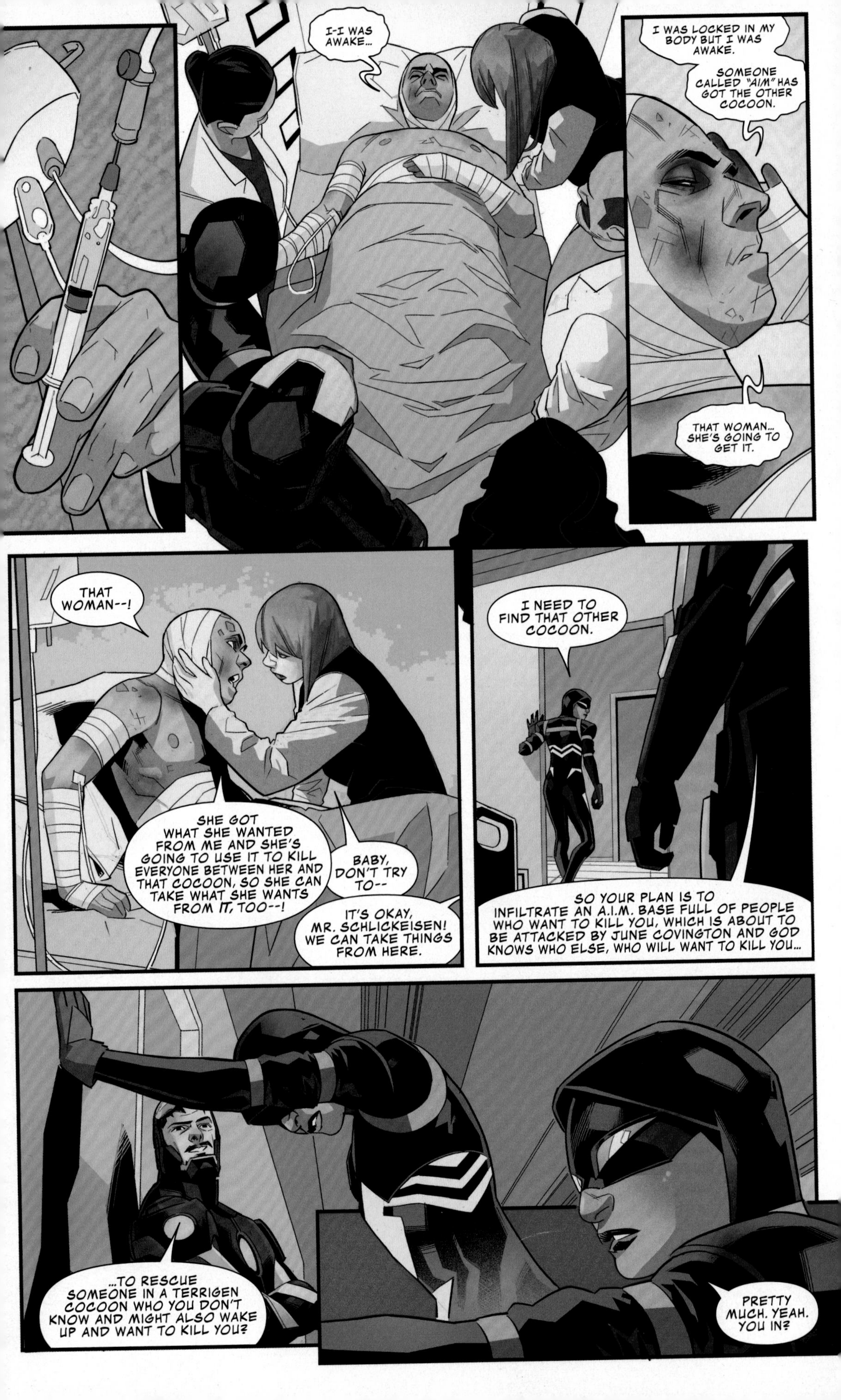

I-I WAS AWAKE...
I WAS LOCKED IN MY BODY BUT I WAS AWAKE.
SOMEONE CALLED "AIM" HAS GOT THE OTHER COCOON.
THAT WOMAN... SHE'S GOING TO GET IT.
THAT WOMAN--!
SHE GOT WHAT SHE WANTED FROM ME AND SHE'S GOING TO USE IT TO KILL EVERYONE BETWEEN HER AND THAT COCOON, SO SHE CAN TAKE WHAT SHE WANTS FROM IT, TOO--!
BABY, DON'T TRY TO--
IT'S OKAY, MR. SCHLICKEISEN! WE CAN TAKE THINGS FROM HERE.
I NEED TO FIND THAT OTHER COCOON.
SO YOUR PLAN IS TO INFILTRATE AN A.I.M. BASE FULL OF PEOPLE WHO WANT TO KILL YOU, WHICH IS ABOUT TO BE ATTACKED BY JUNE COVINGTON AND GOD KNOWS WHO ELSE, WHO WILL WANT TO KILL YOU...
...TO RESCUE SOMEONE IN A TERRIGEN COCOON WHO YOU DON'T KNOW AND MIGHT ALSO WAKE UP AND WANT TO KILL YOU?
PRETTY MUCH. YEAH. YOU IN?

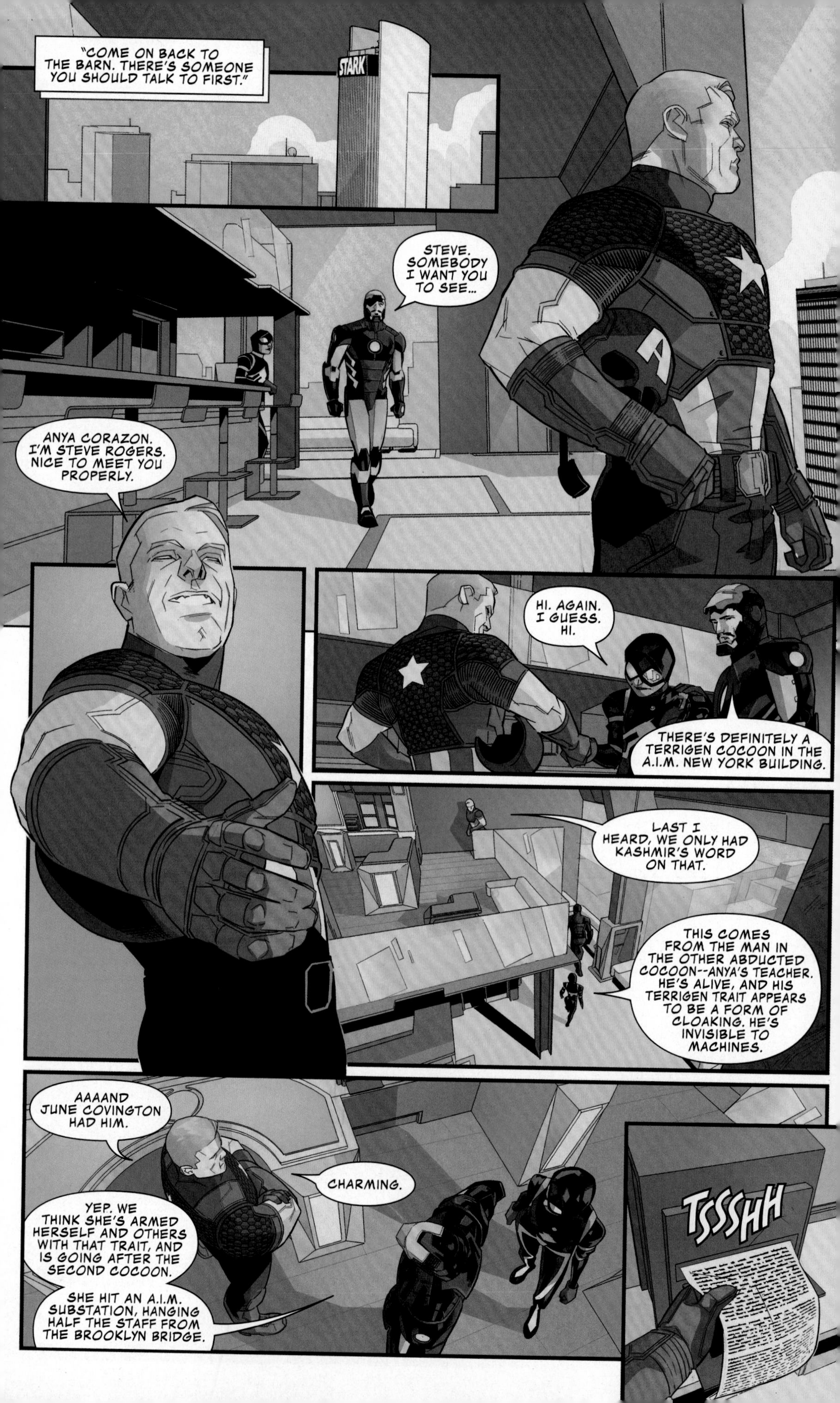
"COME ON BACK TO THE BARN. THERE'S SOMEONE YOU SHOULD TALK TO FIRST."
STARK
STEVE. SOMEBODY I WANT YOU TO SEE...
ANYA CORAZON. I'M STEVE ROGERS. NICE TO MEET YOU PROPERLY.
HI. AGAIN. I GUESS. HI.
THERE'S DEFINITELY A TERRIGEN COCOON IN THE A.I.M. NEW YORK BUILDING.
LAST I HEARD, WE ONLY HAD KASHMIR'S WORD ON THAT.
THIS COMES FROM THE MAN IN THE OTHER ABDUCTED COCOON--ANYA'S TEACHER. HE'S ALIVE, AND HIS TERRIGEN TRAIT APPEARS TO BE A FORM OF CLOAKING. HE'S INVISIBLE TO MACHINES.
AAAAND JUNE COVINGTON HAD HIM.
CHARMING.
YEP. WE THINK SHE'S ARMED HERSELF AND OTHERS WITH THAT TRAIT, AND IS GOING AFTER THE SECOND COCOON.
SHE HIT AN A.I.M. SUBSTATION, HANGING HALF THE STAFF FROM THE BROOKLYN BRIDGE.
TSSSHH

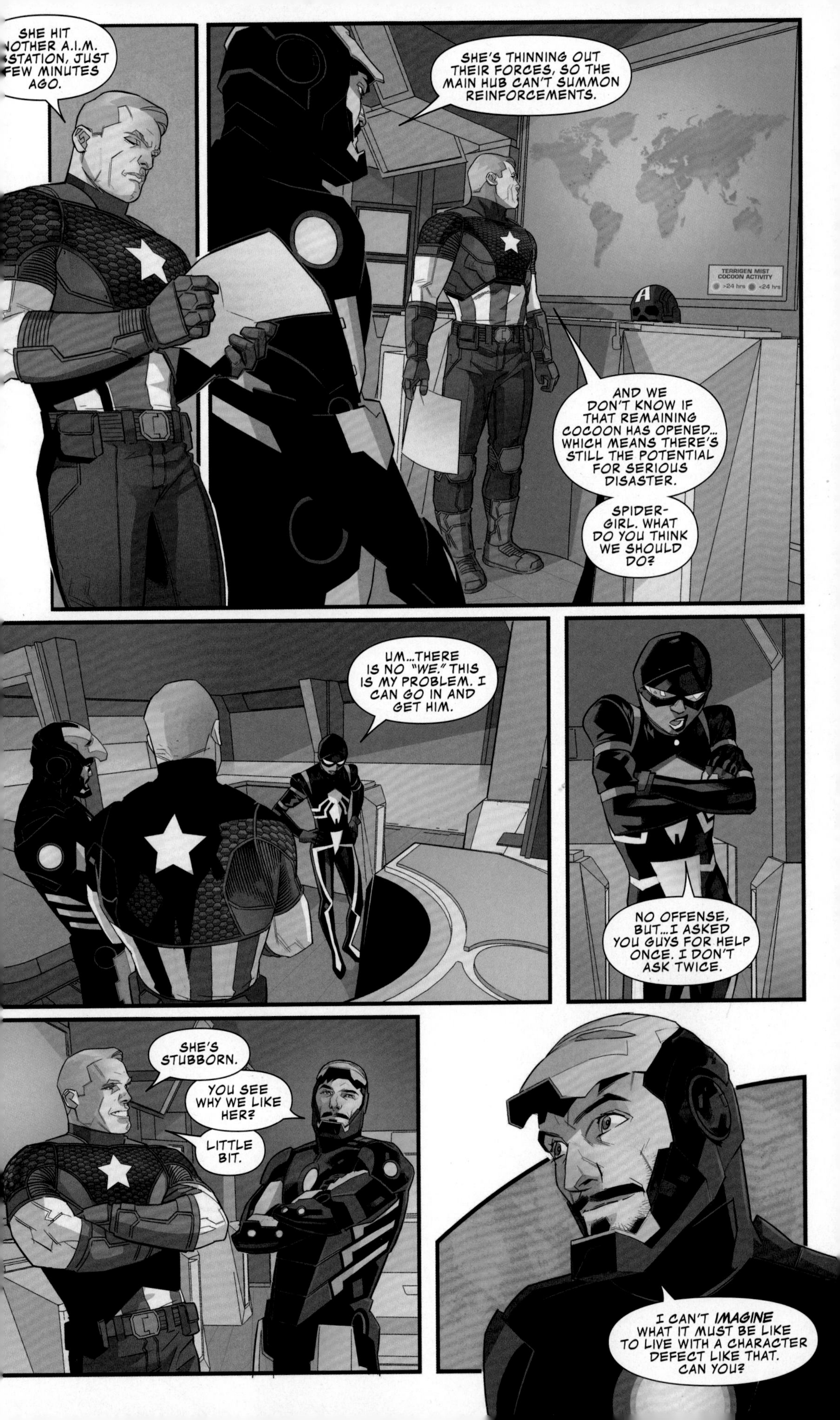
SHE HIT NOTHER A.I.M. STATION, JUST FEW MINUTES AGO.
SHE'S THINNING OUT THEIR FORCES, SO THE MAIN HUB CAN'T SUMMON REINFORCEMENTS.
TERRIGEN MIST COCOON ACTIVITY
>24 hrs
<24 hrs
AND WE DON'T KNOW IF THAT REMAINING COCOON HAS OPENED... WHICH MEANS THERE'S STILL THE POTENTIAL FOR SERIOUS DISASTER.
SPIDER-GIRL. WHAT DO YOU THINK WE SHOULD DO?
UM...THERE IS NO "WE." THIS IS MY PROBLEM. I CAN GO IN AND GET HIM.
NO OFFENSE, BUT...I ASKED YOU GUYS FOR HELP ONCE. I DON'T ASK TWICE.
SHE'S STUBBORN.
YOU SEE WHY WE LIKE HER?
LITTLE BIT.
I CAN'T *IMAGINE* WHAT IT MUST BE LIKE TO LIVE WITH A CHARACTER DEFECT LIKE THAT. CAN YOU?

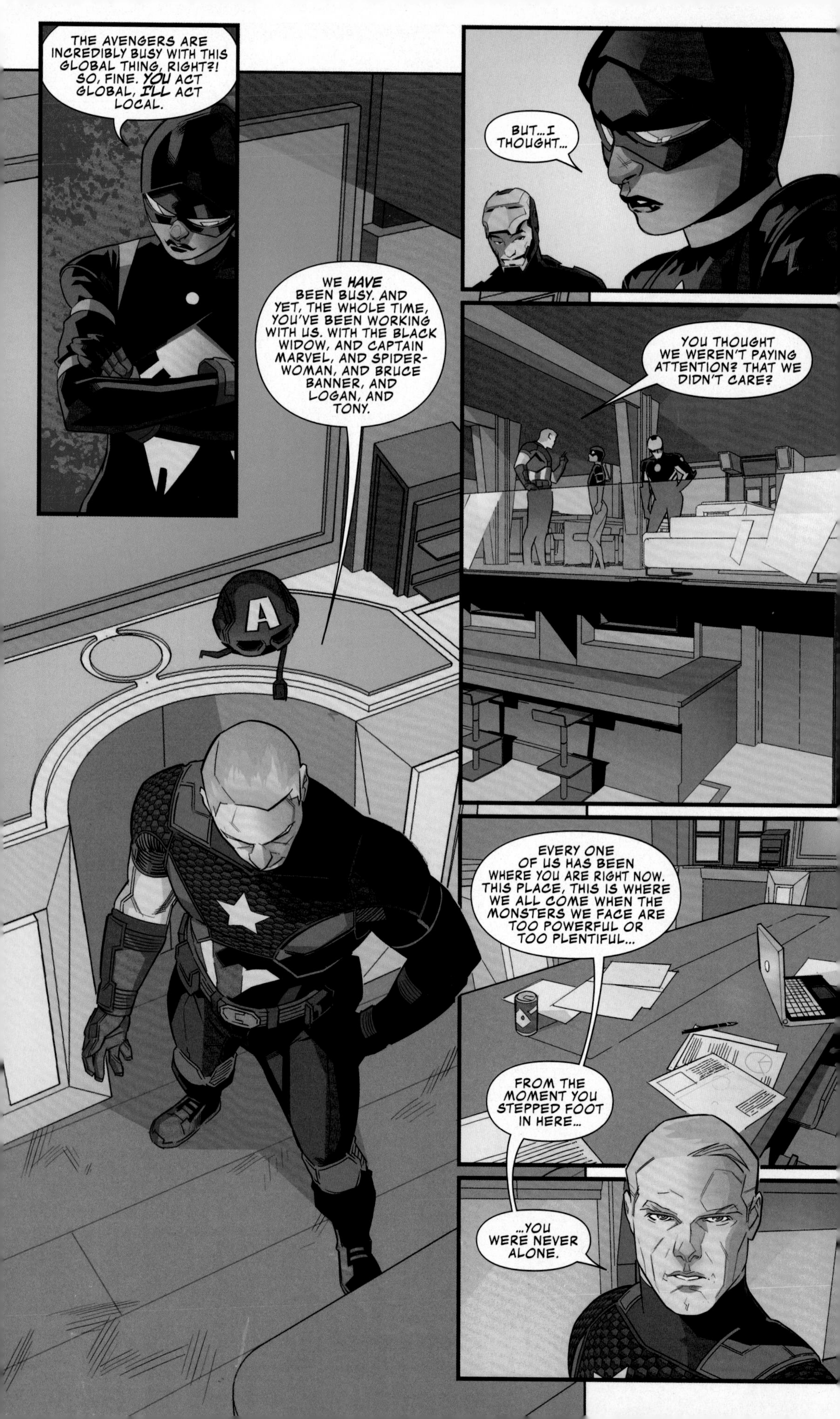
THE AVENGERS ARE INCREDIBLY BUSY WITH THIS GLOBAL THING, RIGHT?! SO, FINE. *YOU* ACT GLOBAL, *I'LL* ACT LOCAL.
BUT... I THOUGHT...
WE *HAVE* BEEN BUSY. AND YET, THE WHOLE TIME, YOU'VE BEEN WORKING WITH US. WITH THE BLACK WIDOW, AND CAPTAIN MARVEL, AND SPIDER-WOMAN, AND BRUCE BANNER, AND LOGAN, AND TONY.
YOU THOUGHT WE WEREN'T PAYING ATTENTION? THAT WE DIDN'T CARE?
EVERY ONE OF US HAS BEEN WHERE YOU ARE RIGHT NOW. THIS PLACE, THIS IS WHERE WE ALL COME WHEN THE MONSTERS WE FACE ARE TOO POWERFUL OR TOO PLENTIFUL...
FROM THE MOMENT YOU STEPPED FOOT IN HERE...
...YOU WERE NEVER ALONE.

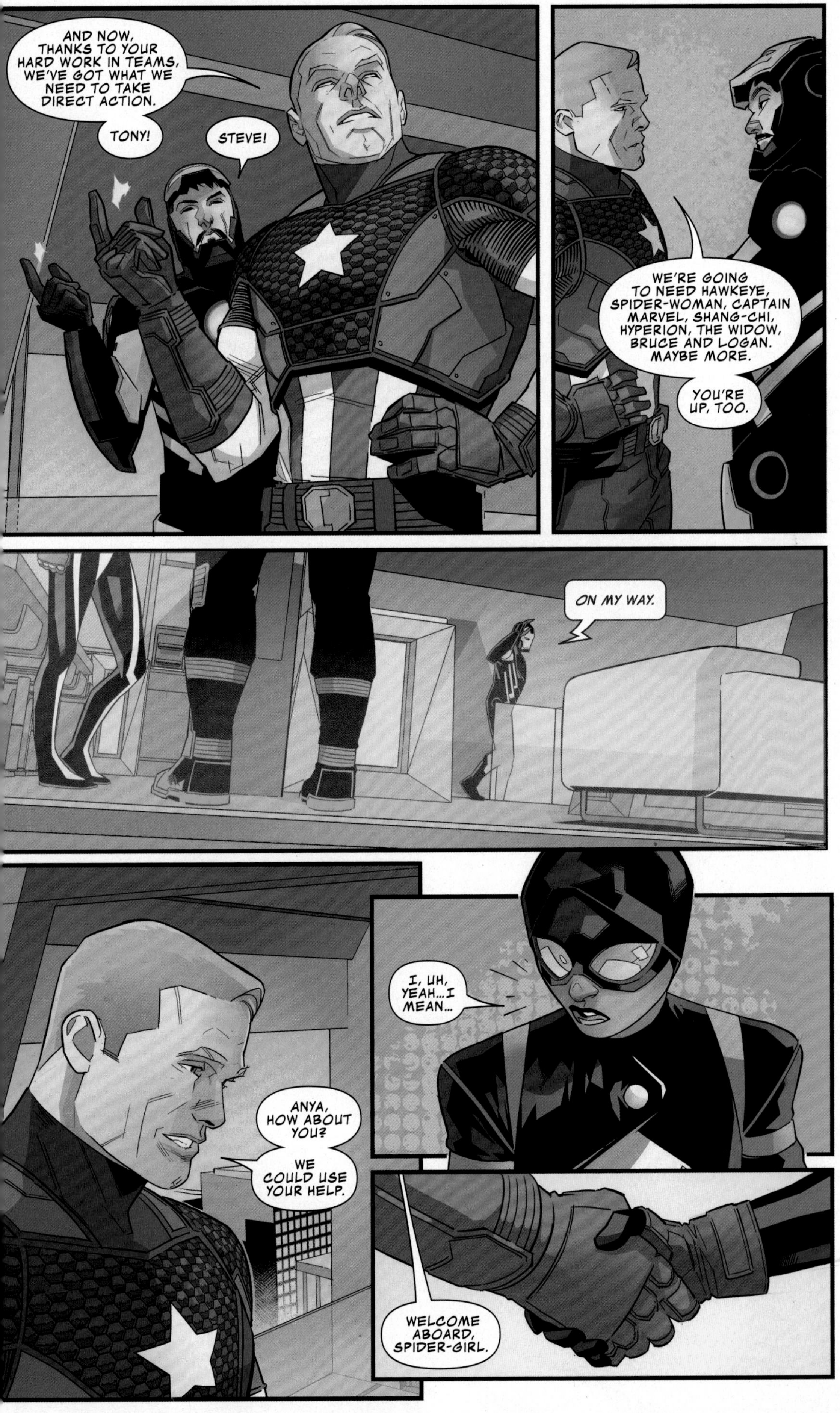
AND NOW, THANKS TO YOUR HARD WORK IN TEAMS, WE'VE GOT WHAT WE NEED TO TAKE DIRECT ACTION.
TONY!
STEVE!
WE'RE GOING TO NEED HAWKEYE, SPIDER-WOMAN, CAPTAIN MARVEL, SHANG-CHI, HYPERION, THE WIDOW, BRUCE AND LOGAN. MAYBE MORE.
YOU'RE UP, TOO.
ON MY WAY.
ANYA, HOW ABOUT YOU?
WE COULD USE YOUR HELP.
I, UH, YEAH...I MEAN...
WELCOME ABOARD, SPIDER-GIRL.

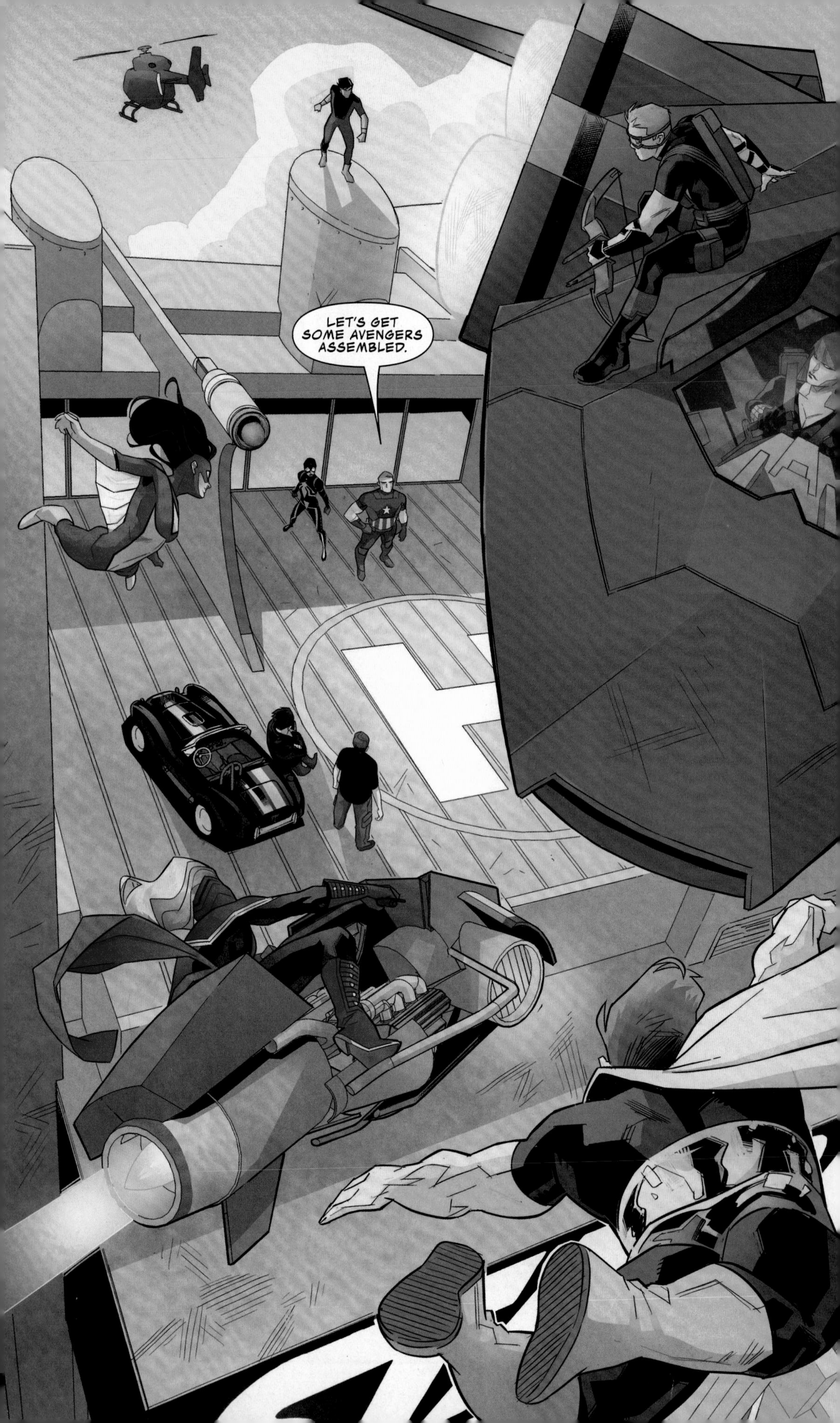
LET'S GET SOME AVENGERS ASSEMBLED.

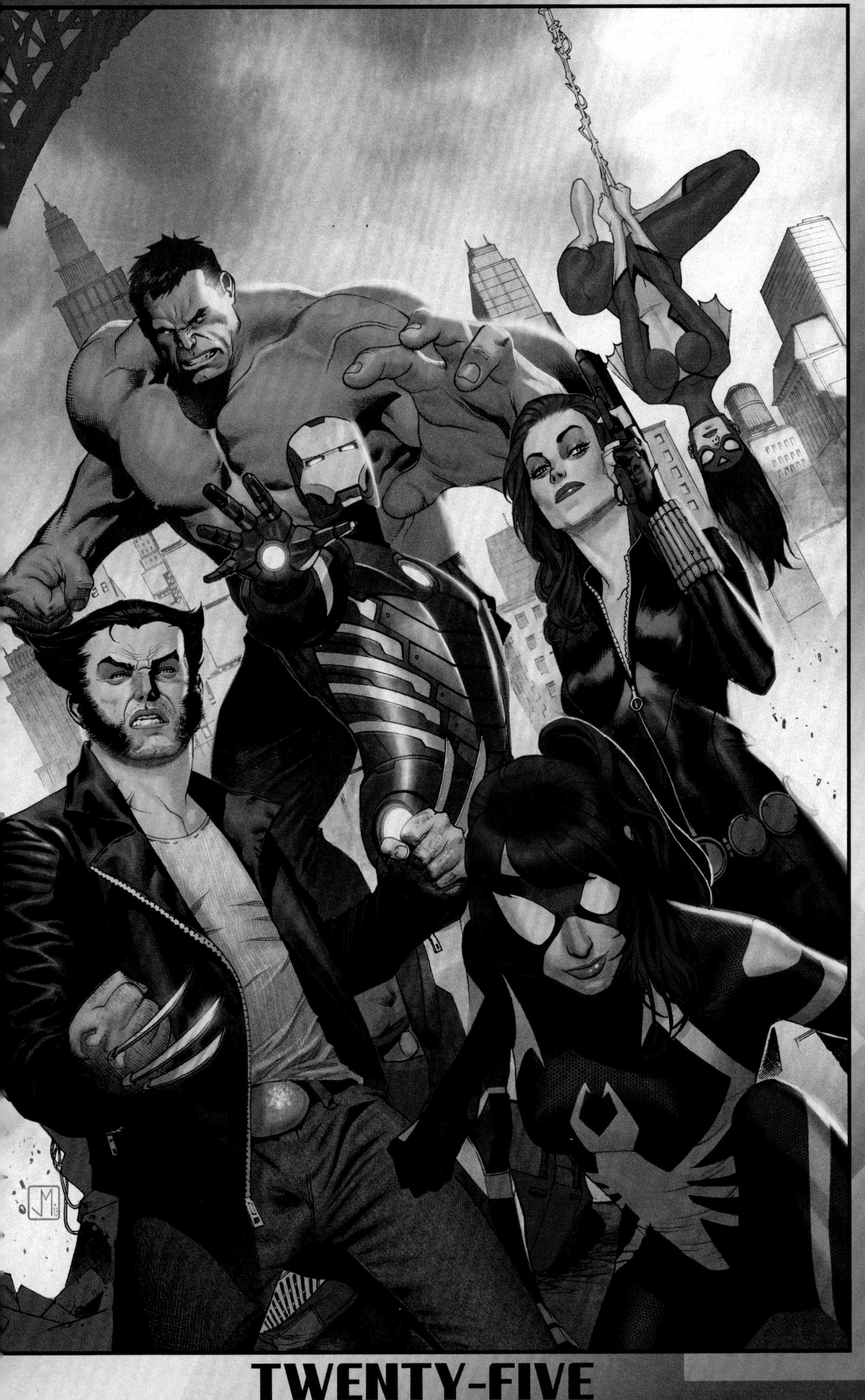

TWENTY-FIVE

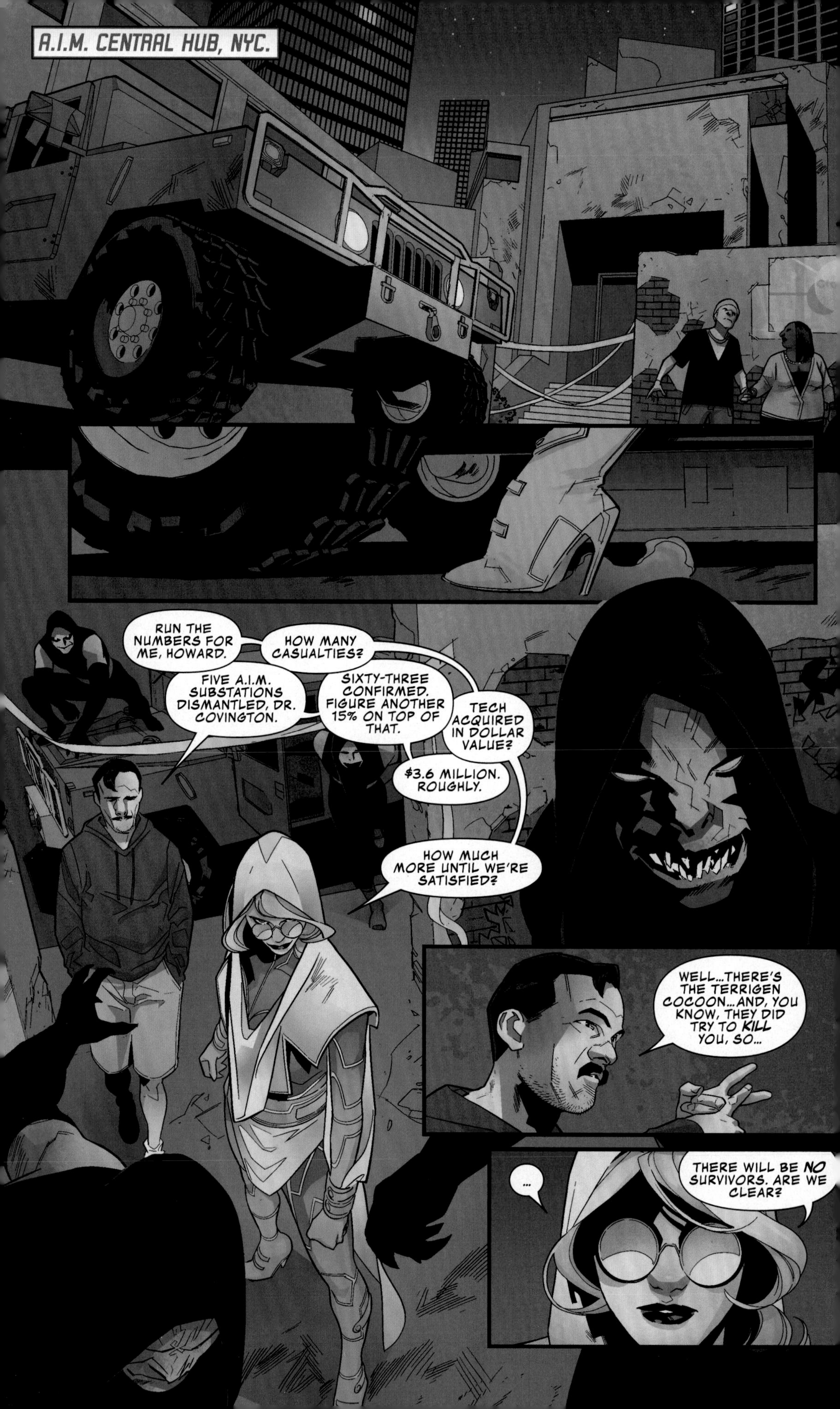
A.I.M. CENTRAL HUB, NYC.
RUN THE NUMBERS FOR ME, HOWARD.
FIVE A.I.M. SUBSTATIONS DISMANTLED, DR. COVINGTON.
HOW MANY CASUALTIES?
SIXTY-THREE CONFIRMED. FIGURE ANOTHER 15% ON TOP OF THAT.
TECH ACQUIRED IN DOLLAR VALUE?
$3.6 MILLION. ROUGHLY.
HOW MUCH MORE UNTIL WE'RE SATISFIED?
WELL...THERE'S THE TERRIGEN COCOON...AND, YOU KNOW, THEY DID TRY TO KILL YOU, SO...
...
THERE WILL BE NO SURVIVORS. ARE WE CLEAR?

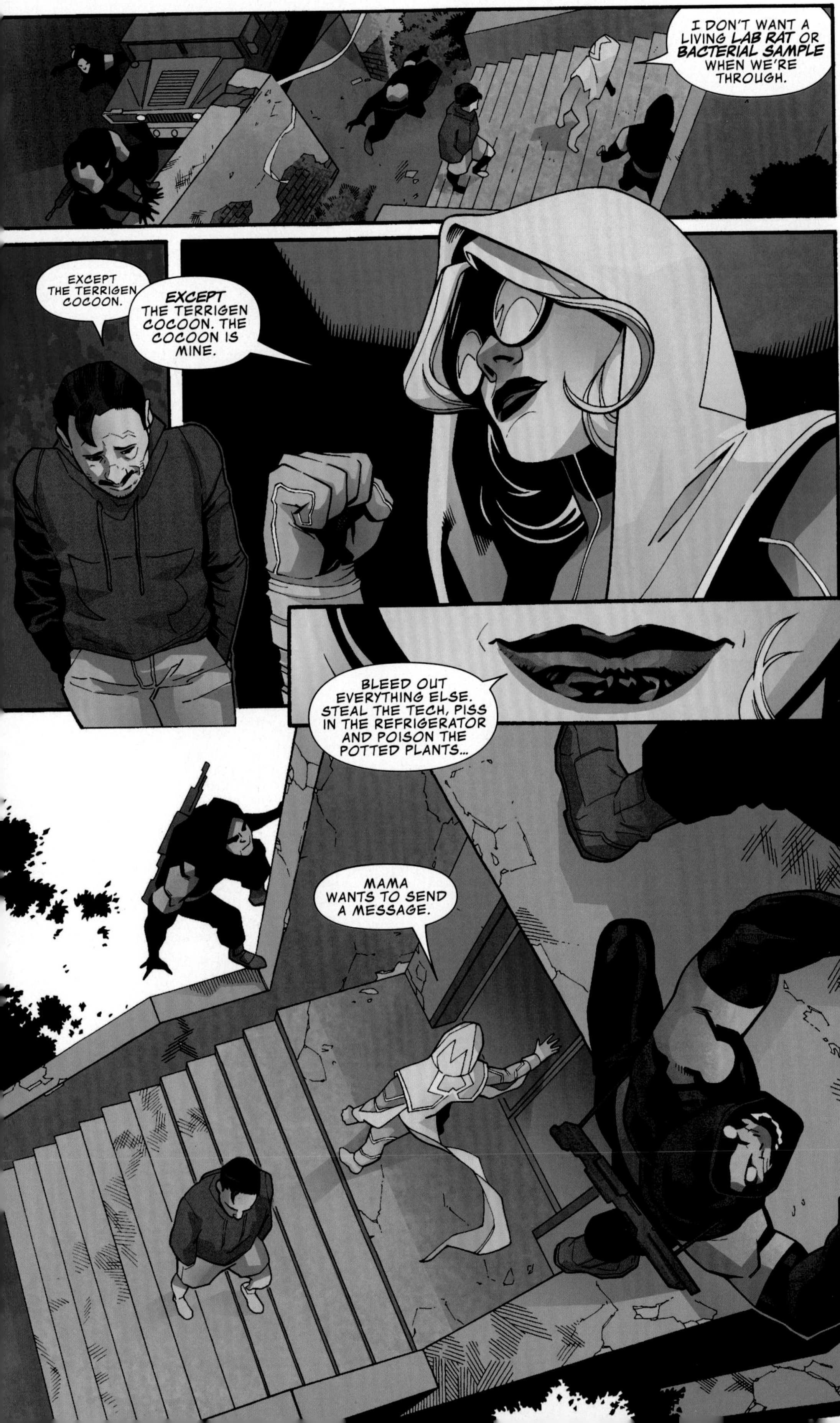
I DON'T WANT A LIVING LAB RAT OR BACTERIAL SAMPLE WHEN WE'RE THROUGH.
EXCEPT THE TERRIGEN COCOON.
EXCEPT THE TERRIGEN COCOON. THE COCOON IS MINE.
BLEED OUT EVERYTHING ELSE. STEAL THE TECH, PISS IN THE REFRIGERATOR AND POISON THE POTTED PLANTS...
MAMA WANTS TO SEND A MESSAGE.

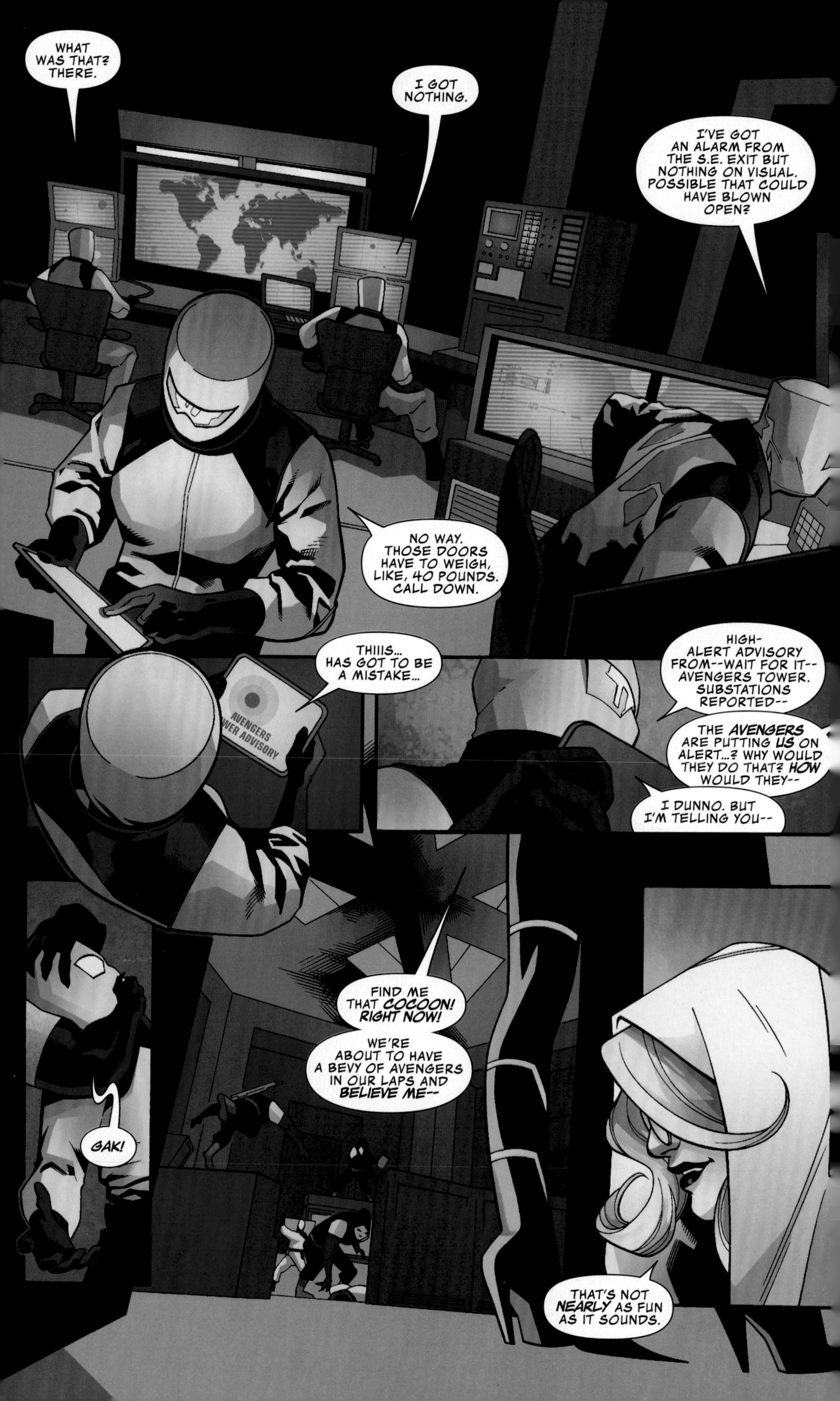

WHAT WAS THAT? THERE.
I GOT NOTHING.
I'VE GOT AN ALARM FROM THE S.E. EXIT BUT NOTHING ON VISUAL. POSSIBLE THAT COULD HAVE BLOWN OPEN?
NO WAY. THOSE DOORS HAVE TO WEIGH, LIKE, 40 POUNDS. CALL DOWN.
THIIIS... HAS GOT TO BE A MISTAKE...
AVENGERS
ALERT ADVISORY
HIGH-ALERT ADVISORY FROM--WAIT FOR IT--AVENGERS TOWER. SUBSTATIONS REPORTED--
THE AVENGERS ARE PUTTING US ON ALERT...? WHY WOULD THEY DO THAT? HOW WOULD THEY--
I DUNNO. BUT I'M TELLING YOU--
FIND ME THAT COCOON! RIGHT NOW!
WE'RE ABOUT TO HAVE A BEVY OF AVENGERS IN OUR LAPS AND BELIEVE ME--
GAK!
THAT'S NOT NEARLY AS FUN AS IT SOUNDS.

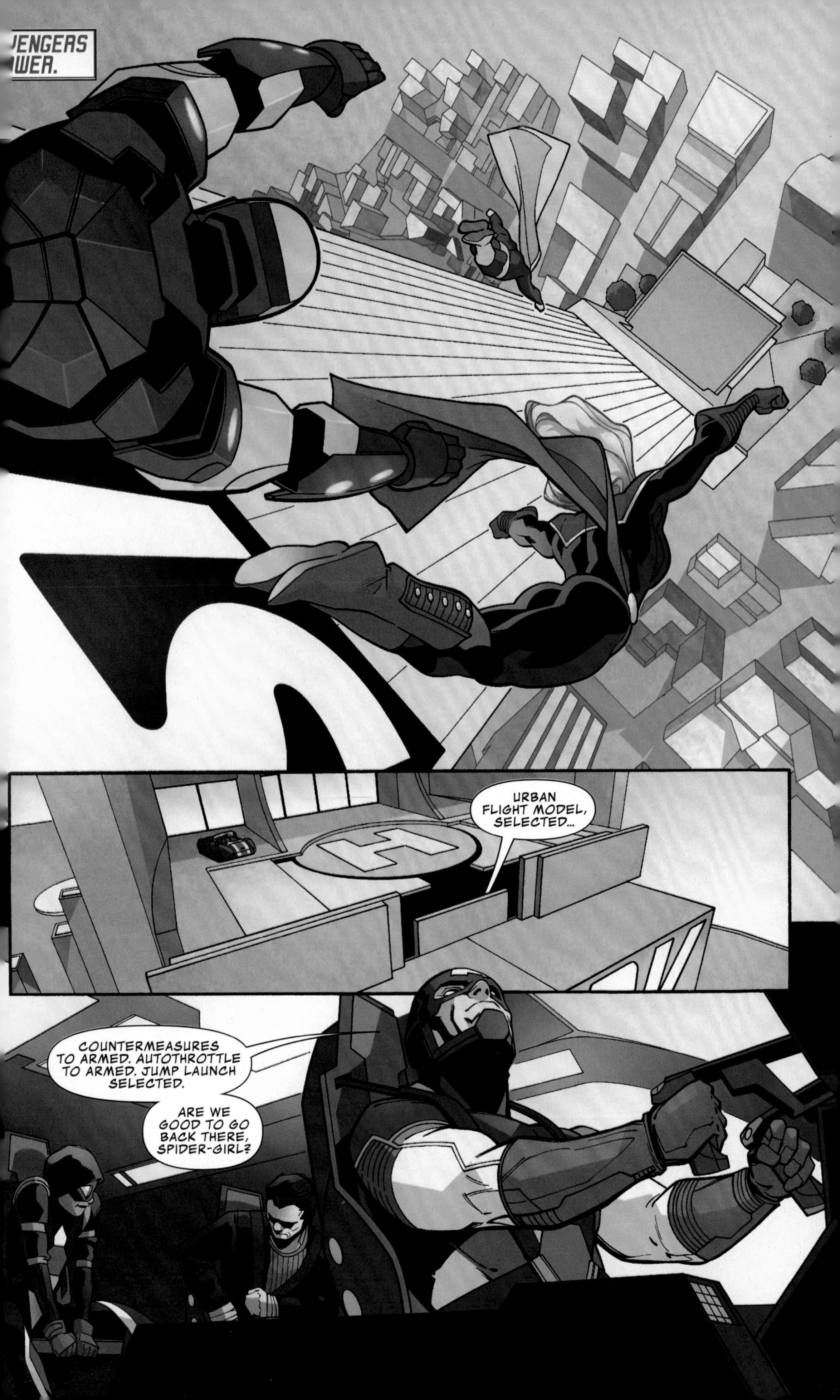

VENGERS
WER.
URBAN FLIGHT MODEL, SELECTED...
COUNTERMEASURES TO ARMED. AUTOTHROTTLE TO ARMED. JUMP LAUNCH SELECTED.
ARE WE GOOD TO GO BACK THERE, SPIDER-GIRL?

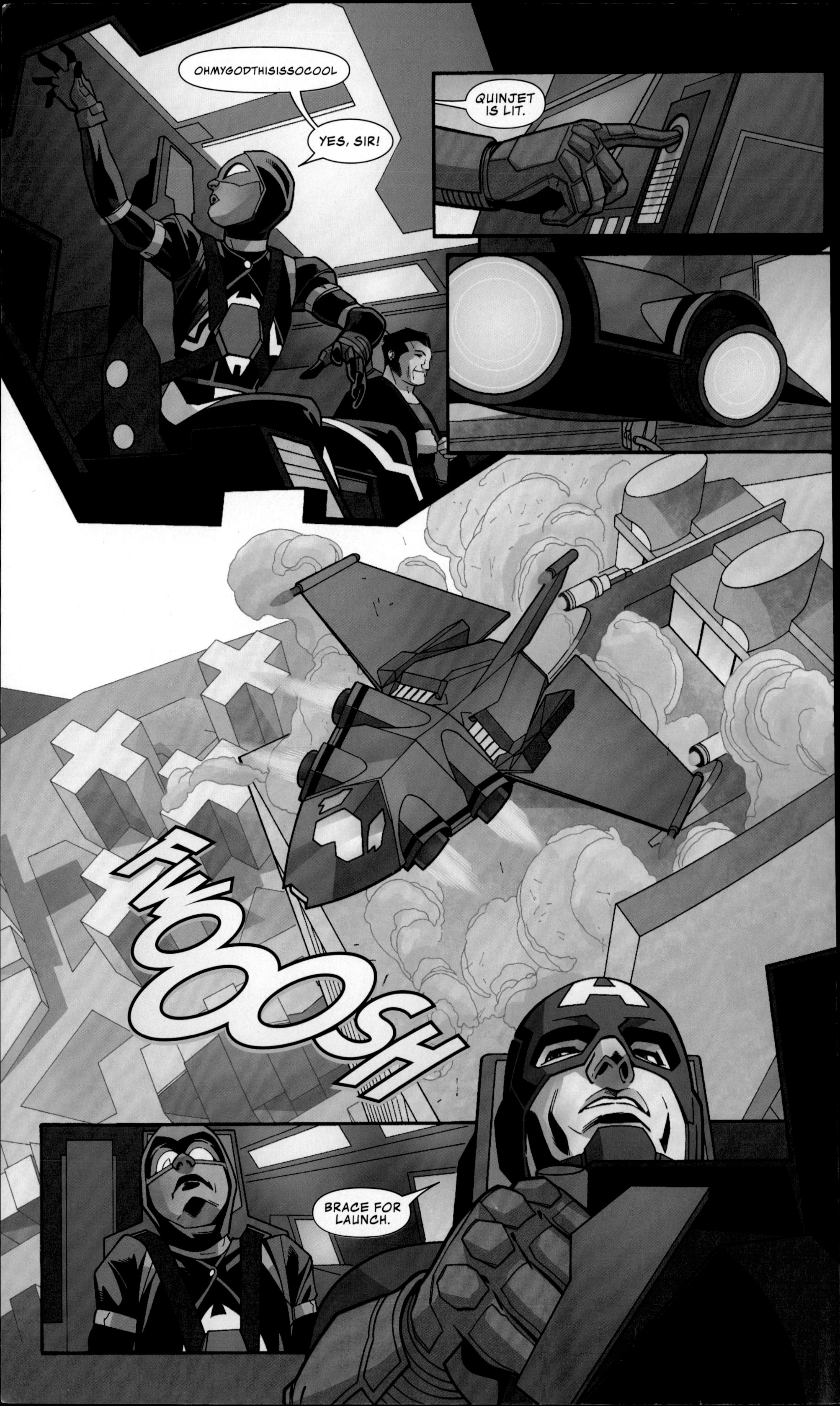
OHMYGODTHISISSOCOOL
YES, SIR!
QUINJET IS LIT.
FWOOOSH
BRACE FOR LAUNCH.

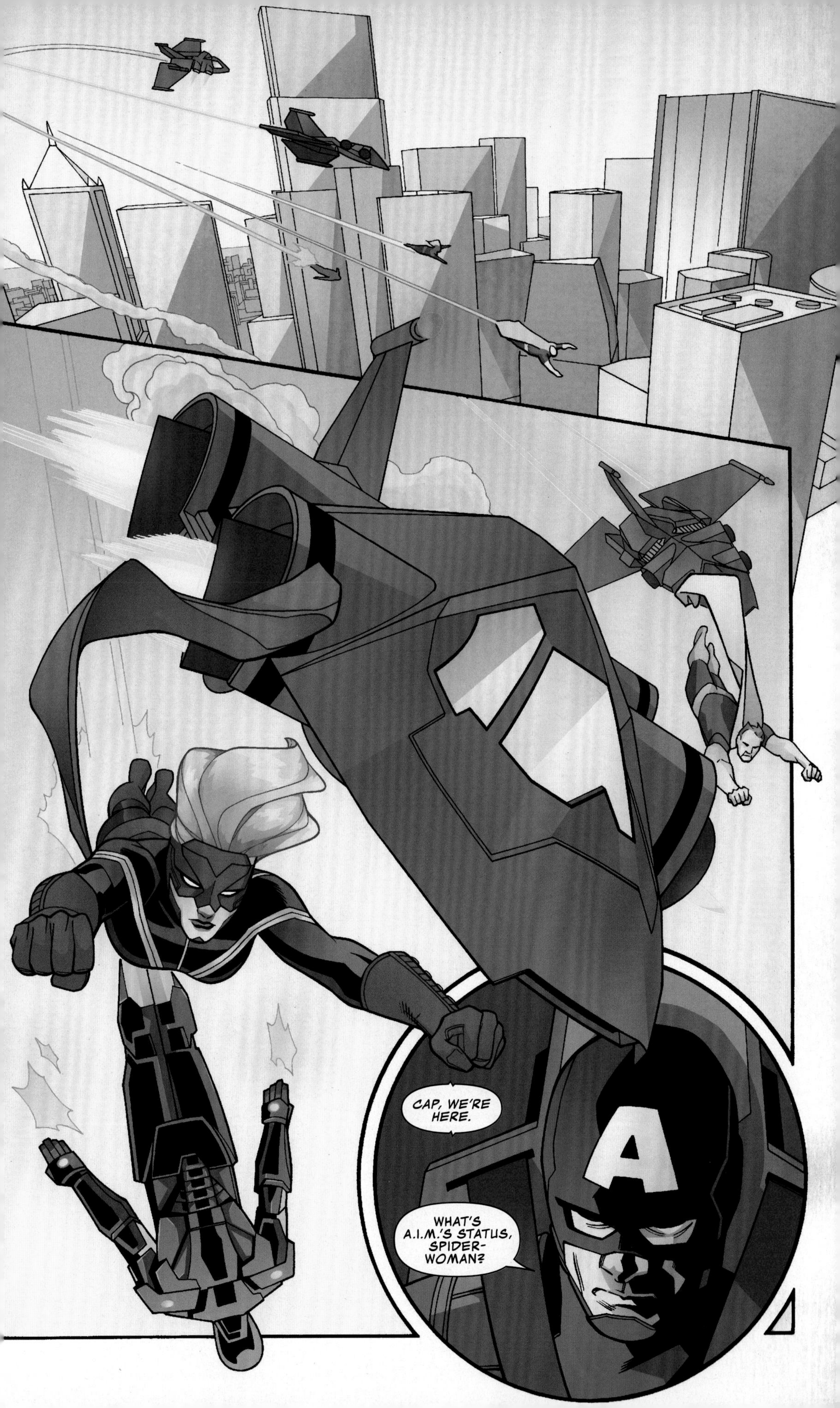
CAP, WE'RE HERE.
WHAT'S A.I.M.'S STATUS, SPIDER-WOMAN?

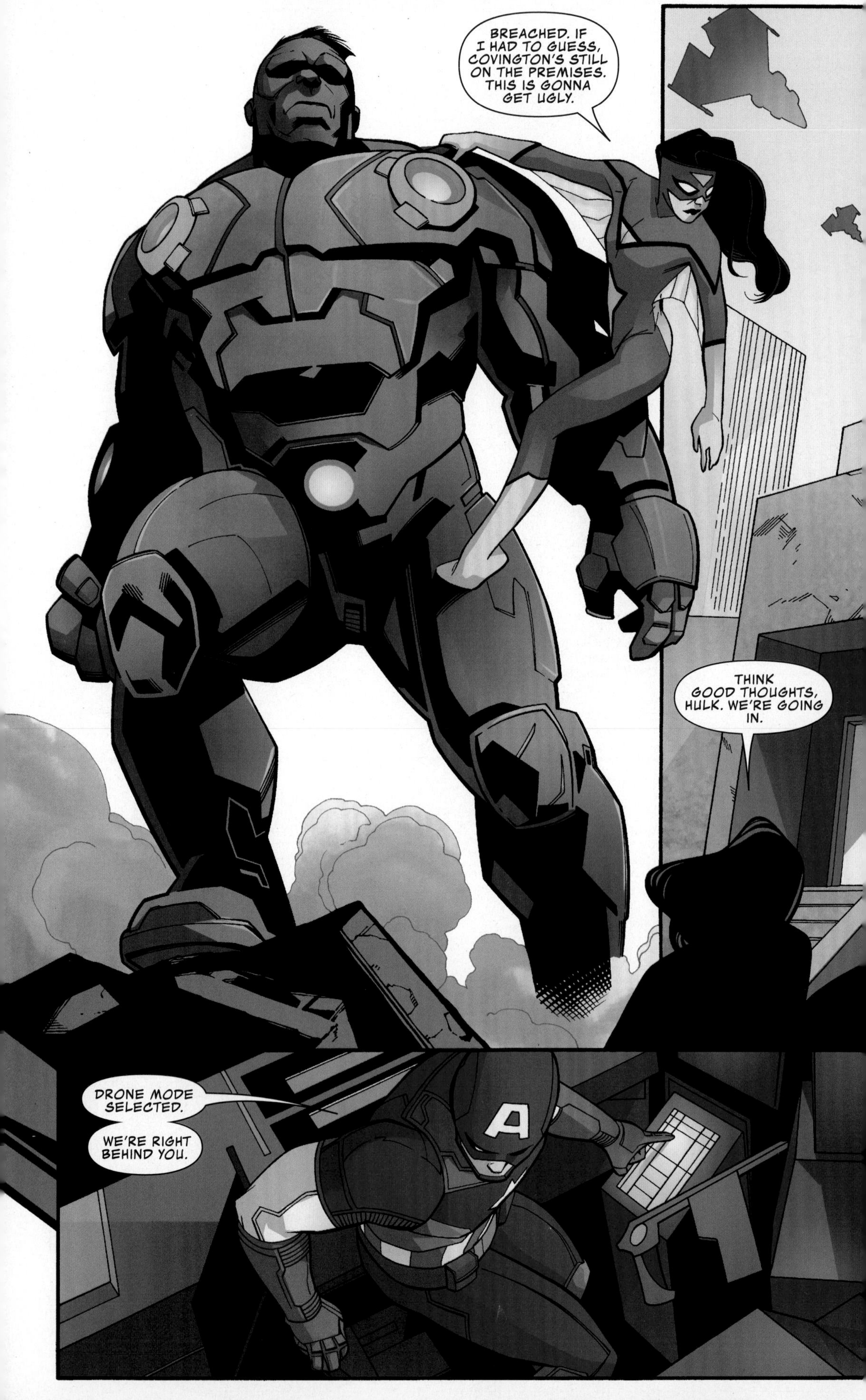
BREACHED. IF I HAD TO GUESS, COVINGTON'S STILL ON THE PREMISES. THIS IS GONNA GET UGLY.
THINK GOOD THOUGHTS, HULK. WE'RE GOING IN.
DRONE MODE SELECTED.
WE'RE RIGHT BEHIND YOU.

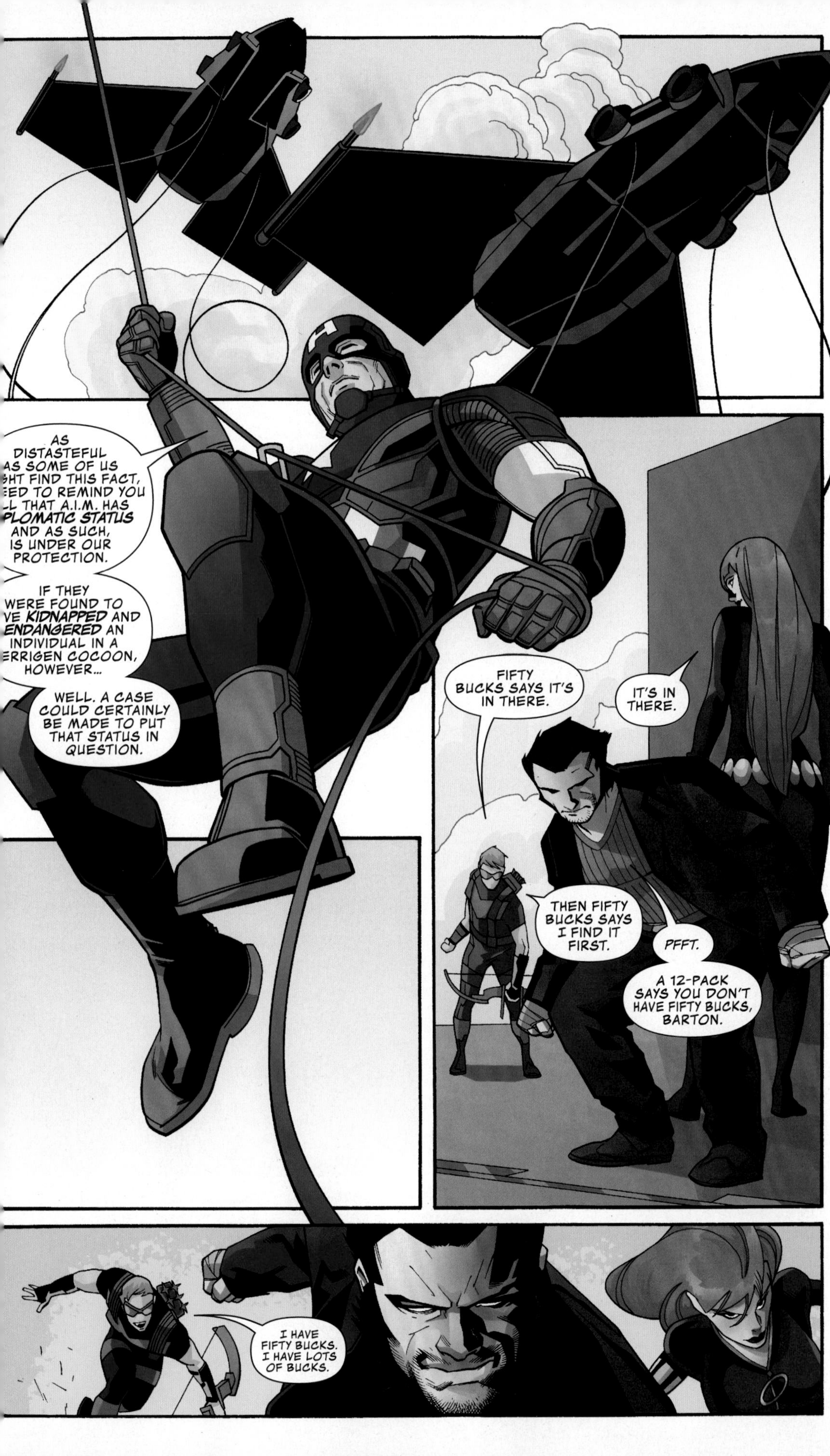
AS DISTASTEFUL AS SOME OF US GHT FIND THIS FACT, EED TO REMIND YOU L THAT A.I.M. HAS PLOMATIC STATUS AND AS SUCH, IS UNDER OUR PROTECTION.
IF THEY WERE FOUND TO VE KIDNAPPED AND ENDANGERED AN INDIVIDUAL IN A ERRIGEN COCOON, HOWEVER...
WELL. A CASE COULD CERTAINLY BE MADE TO PUT THAT STATUS IN QUESTION.
FIFTY BUCKS SAYS IT'S IN THERE.
IT'S IN THERE.
THEN FIFTY BUCKS SAYS I FIND IT FIRST.
PFFT.
A 12-PACK SAYS YOU DON'T HAVE FIFTY BUCKS, BARTON.
I HAVE FIFTY BUCKS. I HAVE LOTS OF BUCKS.

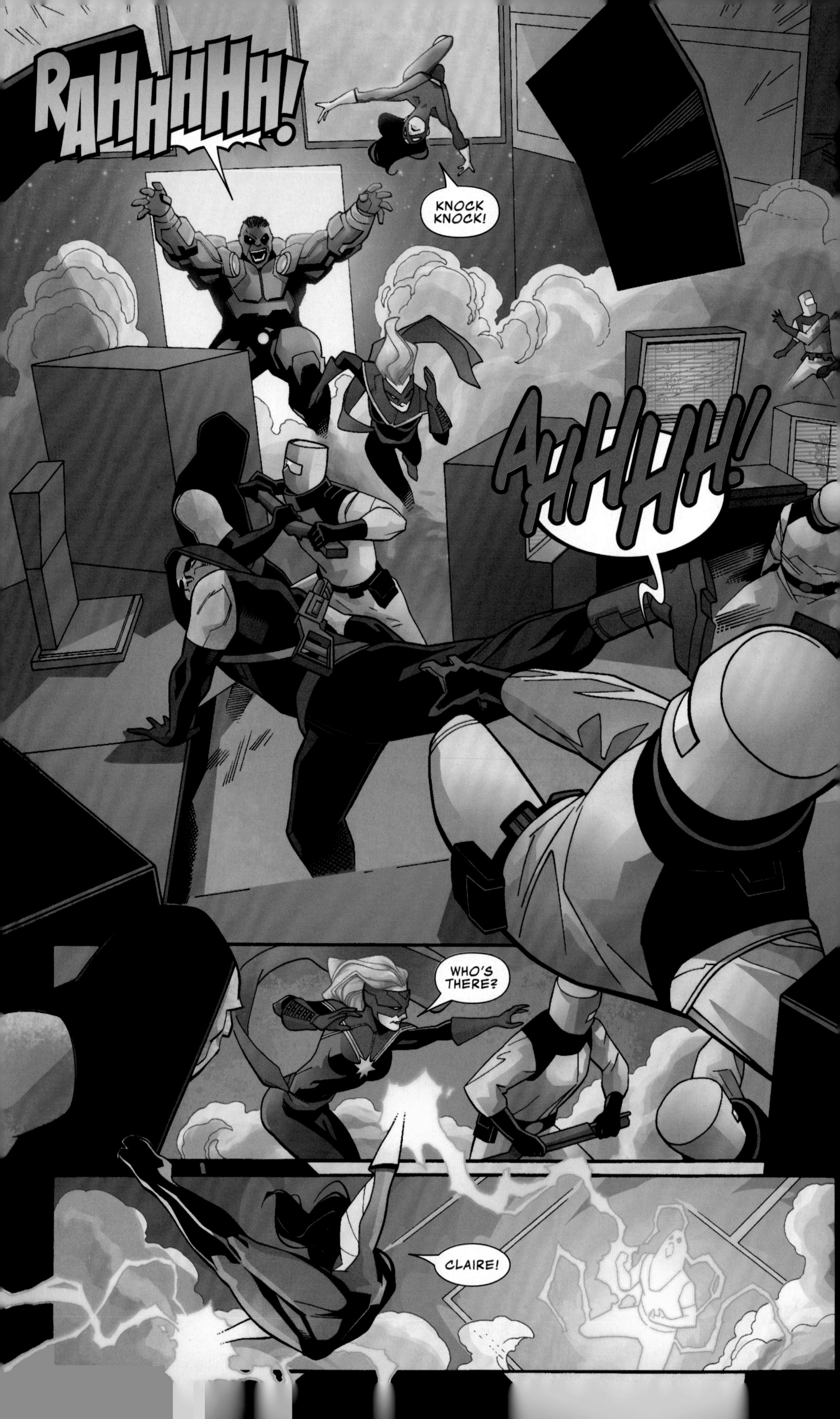
RAHHHHH!
KNOCK KNOCK!
AHHHHH!
WHO'S THERE?
CLAIRE!

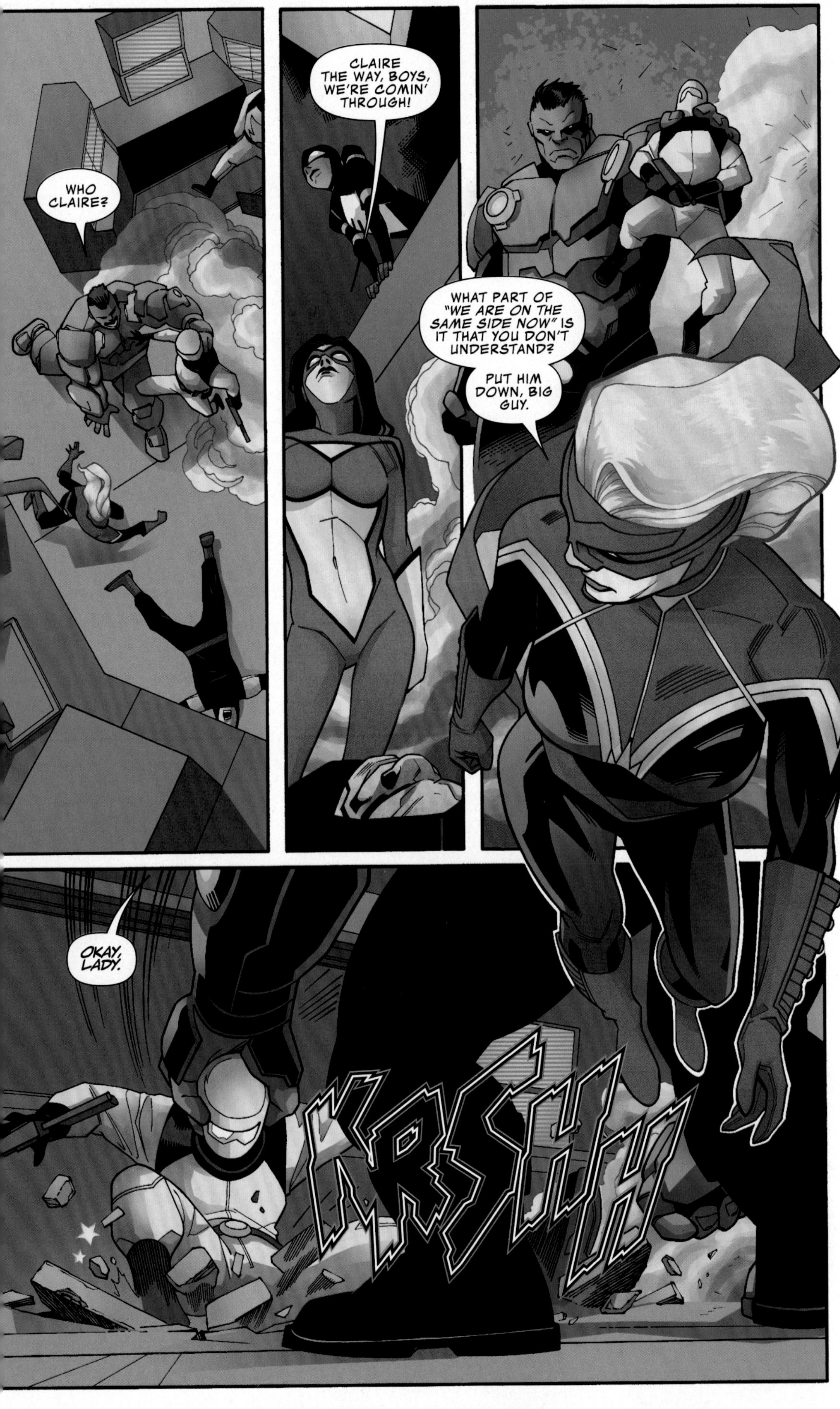
WHO CLAIRE?
CLAIRE THE WAY, BOYS, WE'RE COMIN' THROUGH!
WHAT PART OF "WE ARE ON THE SAME SIDE NOW" IS IT THAT YOU DON'T UNDERSTAND?
PUT HIM DOWN, BIG GUY.
OKAY, LADY.
KRSSHH

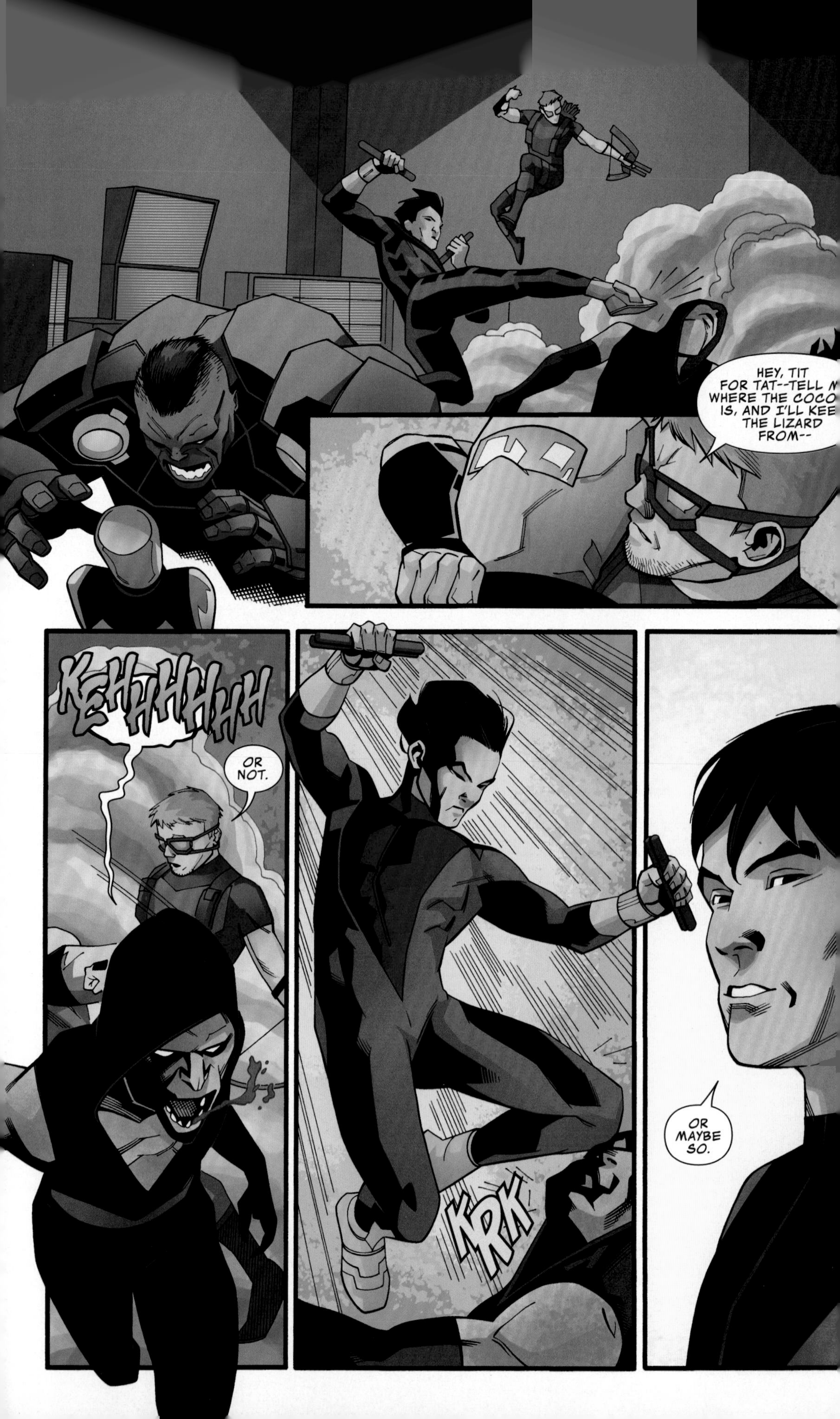

HEY, TIT FOR TAT--TELL M WHERE THE COCO IS, AND I'LL KEE THE LIZARD FROM--
KEHHHHHH
OR NOT.
KRK
OR MAYBE SO.

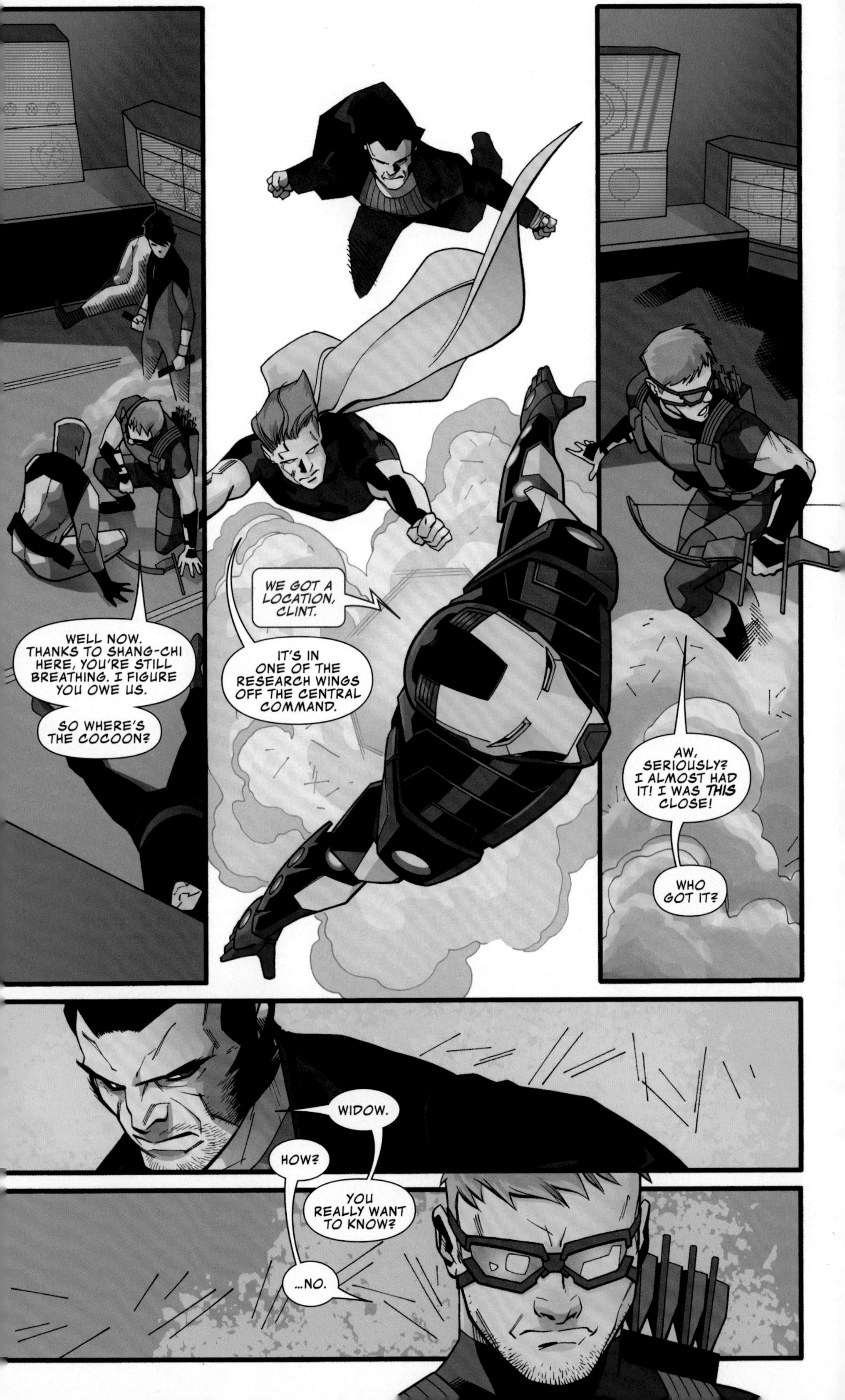
WELL NOW. THANKS TO SHANG-CHI HERE, YOU'RE STILL BREATHING. I FIGURE YOU OWE US.
SO WHERE'S THE COCOON?
WE GOT A LOCATION, CLINT.
IT'S IN ONE OF THE RESEARCH WINGS OFF THE CENTRAL COMMAND.
AW, SERIOUSLY? I ALMOST HAD IT! I WAS THIS CLOSE!
WHO GOT IT?
WIDOW.
HOW?
YOU REALLY WANT TO KNOW?
...NO.

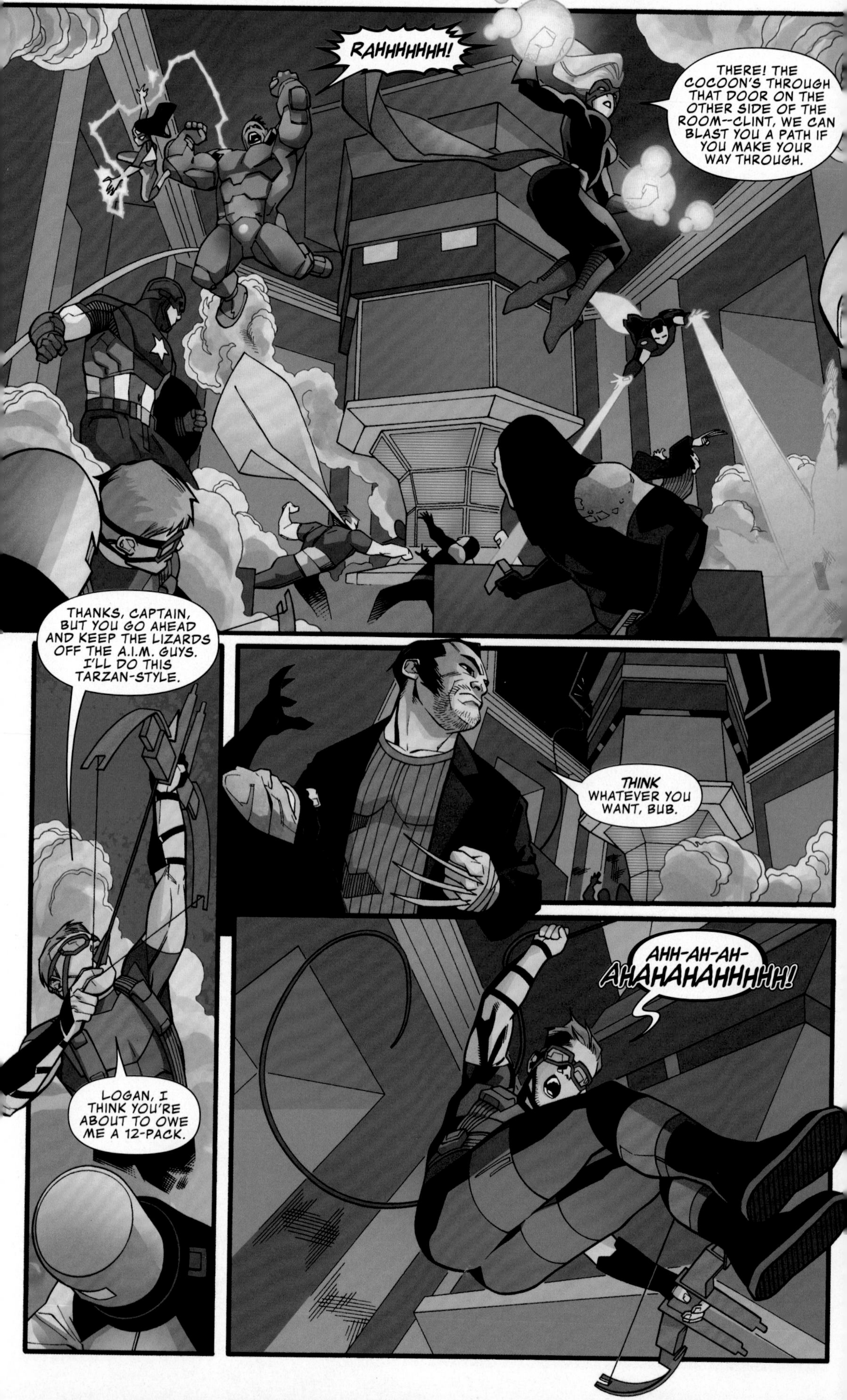
RAHHHHHHH!
THERE! THE COCOON'S THROUGH THAT DOOR ON THE OTHER SIDE OF THE ROOM--CLINT, WE CAN BLAST YOU A PATH IF YOU MAKE YOUR WAY THROUGH.
THANKS, CAPTAIN, BUT YOU GO AHEAD AND KEEP THE LIZARDS OFF THE A.I.M. GUYS. I'LL DO THIS TARZAN-STYLE.
LOGAN, I THINK YOU'RE ABOUT TO OWE ME A 12-PACK.
THINK WHATEVER YOU WANT, BUB.
AHH-AH-AH-AHAHAHAHHHHH!

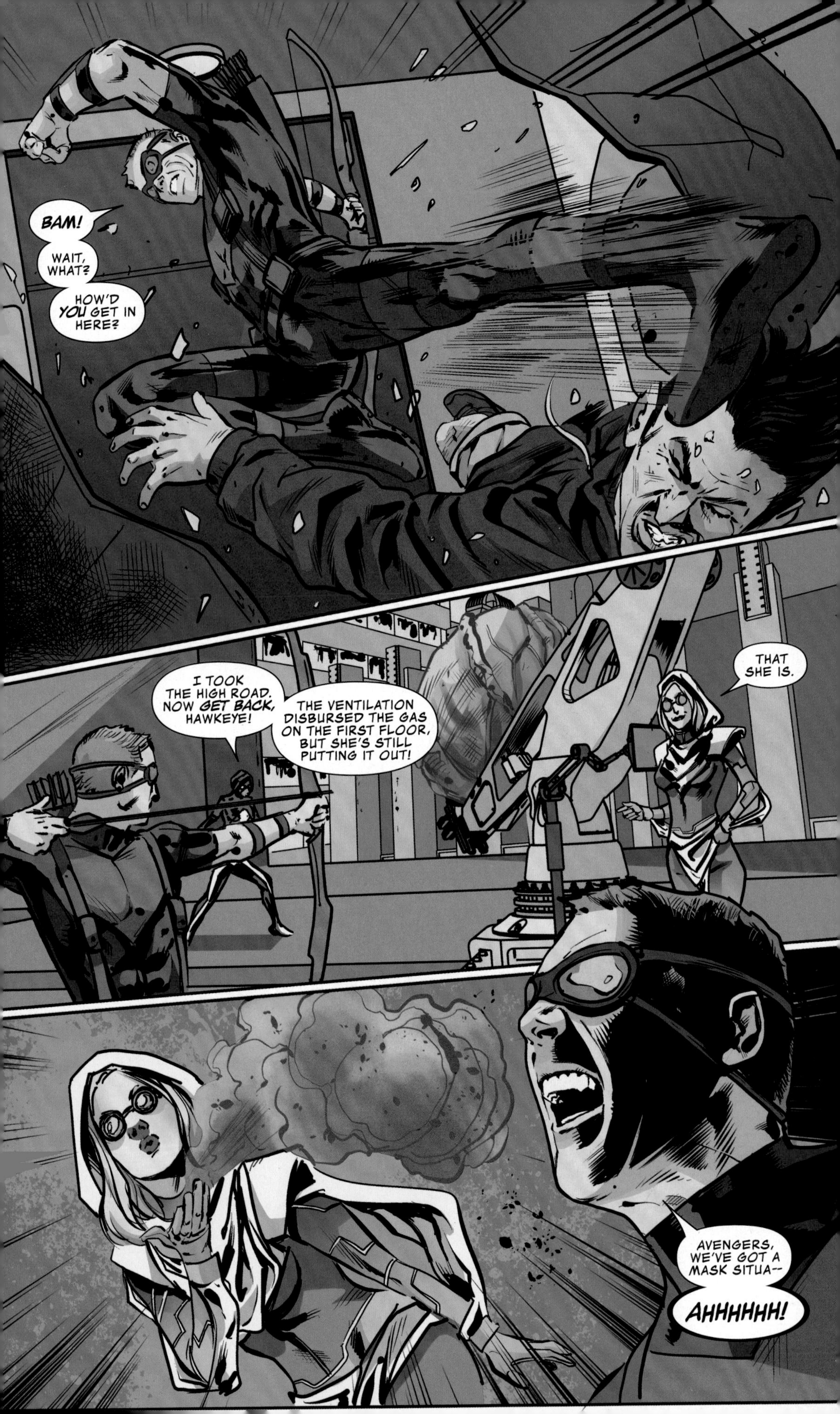
BAM!
WAIT, WHAT?
HOW'D YOU GET IN HERE?
I TOOK THE HIGH ROAD. NOW GET BACK, HAWKEYE!
THE VENTILATION DISBURSED THE GAS ON THE FIRST FLOOR, BUT SHE'S STILL PUTTING IT OUT!
THAT SHE IS.
AVENGERS, WE'VE GOT A MASK SITUA--
AHHHHHH!

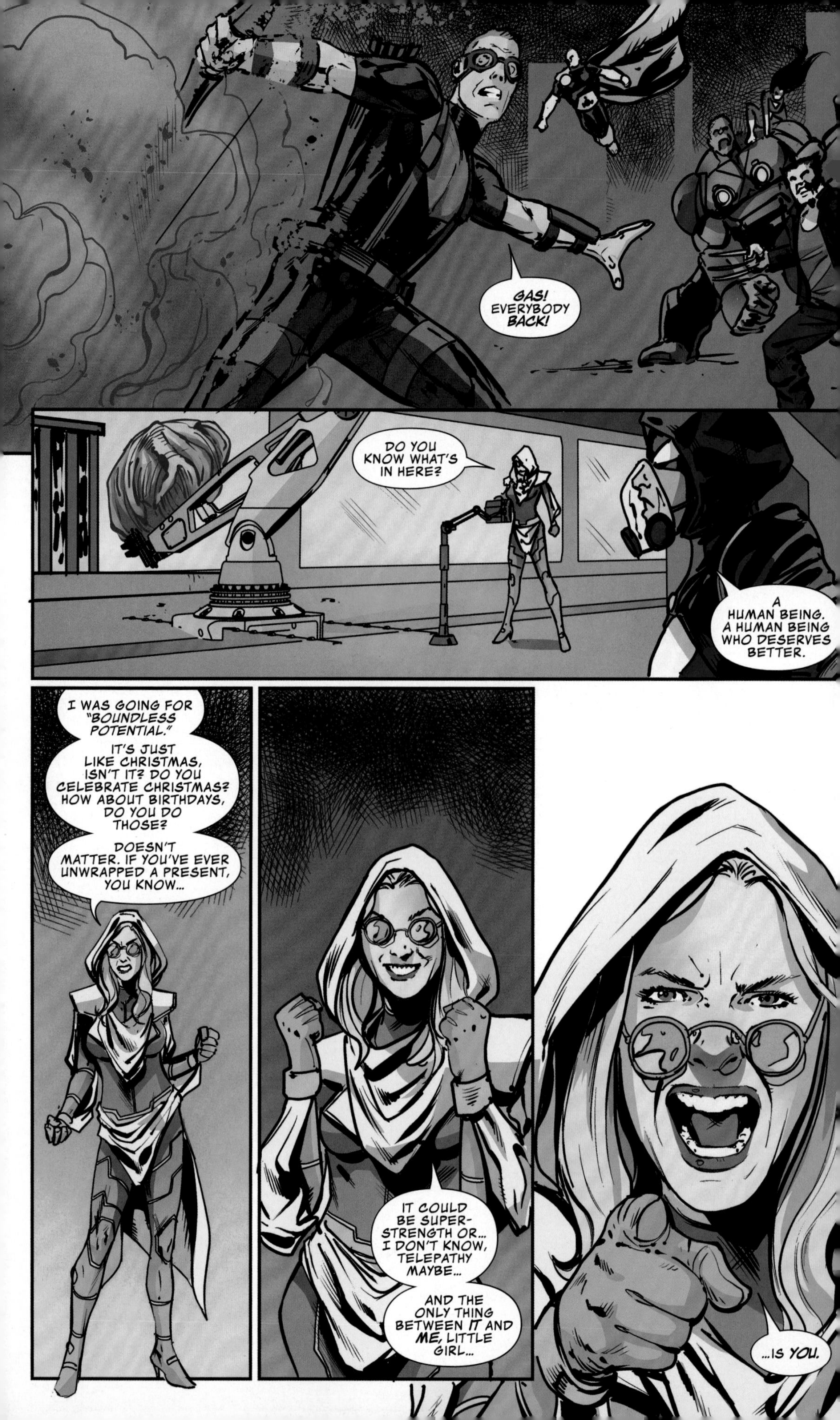
GAS! EVERYBODY BACK!
DO YOU KNOW WHAT'S IN HERE?
A HUMAN BEING. A HUMAN BEING WHO DESERVES BETTER.
I WAS GOING FOR "BOUNDLESS POTENTIAL."
IT'S JUST LIKE CHRISTMAS, ISN'T IT? DO YOU CELEBRATE CHRISTMAS? HOW ABOUT BIRTHDAYS, DO YOU DO THOSE?
DOESN'T MATTER. IF YOU'VE EVER UNWRAPPED A PRESENT, YOU KNOW...
IT COULD BE SUPER-STRENGTH OR... I DON'T KNOW, TELEPATHY MAYBE...
AND THE ONLY THING BETWEEN IT AND ME, LITTLE GIRL...
...IS YOU.

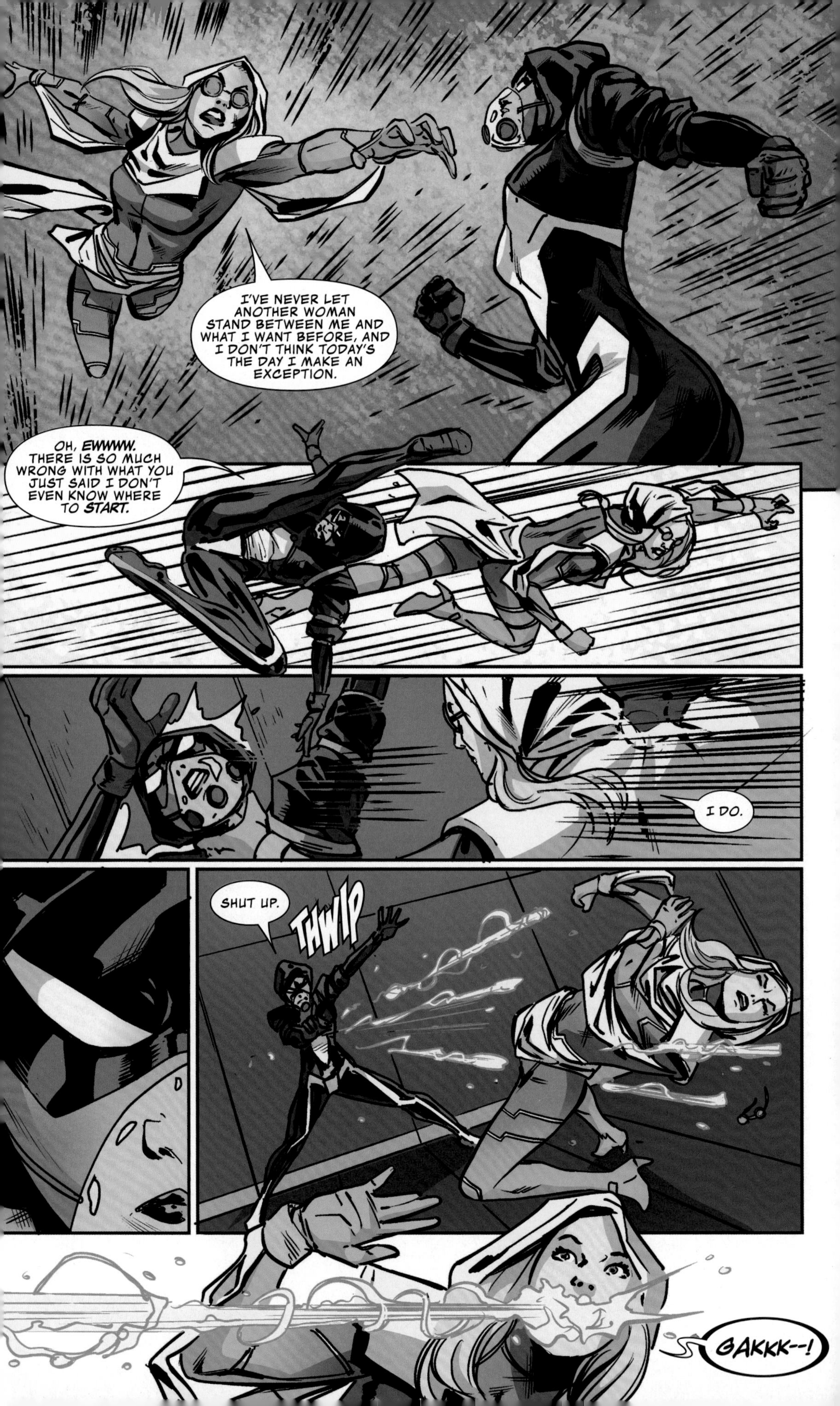
I'VE NEVER LET ANOTHER WOMAN STAND BETWEEN ME AND WHAT I WANT BEFORE, AND I DON'T THINK TODAY'S THE DAY I MAKE AN EXCEPTION.
OH, EWWWW. THERE IS SO MUCH WRONG WITH WHAT YOU JUST SAID I DON'T EVEN KNOW WHERE TO START.
I DO.
SHUT UP.
THWIP
GAKKK--!

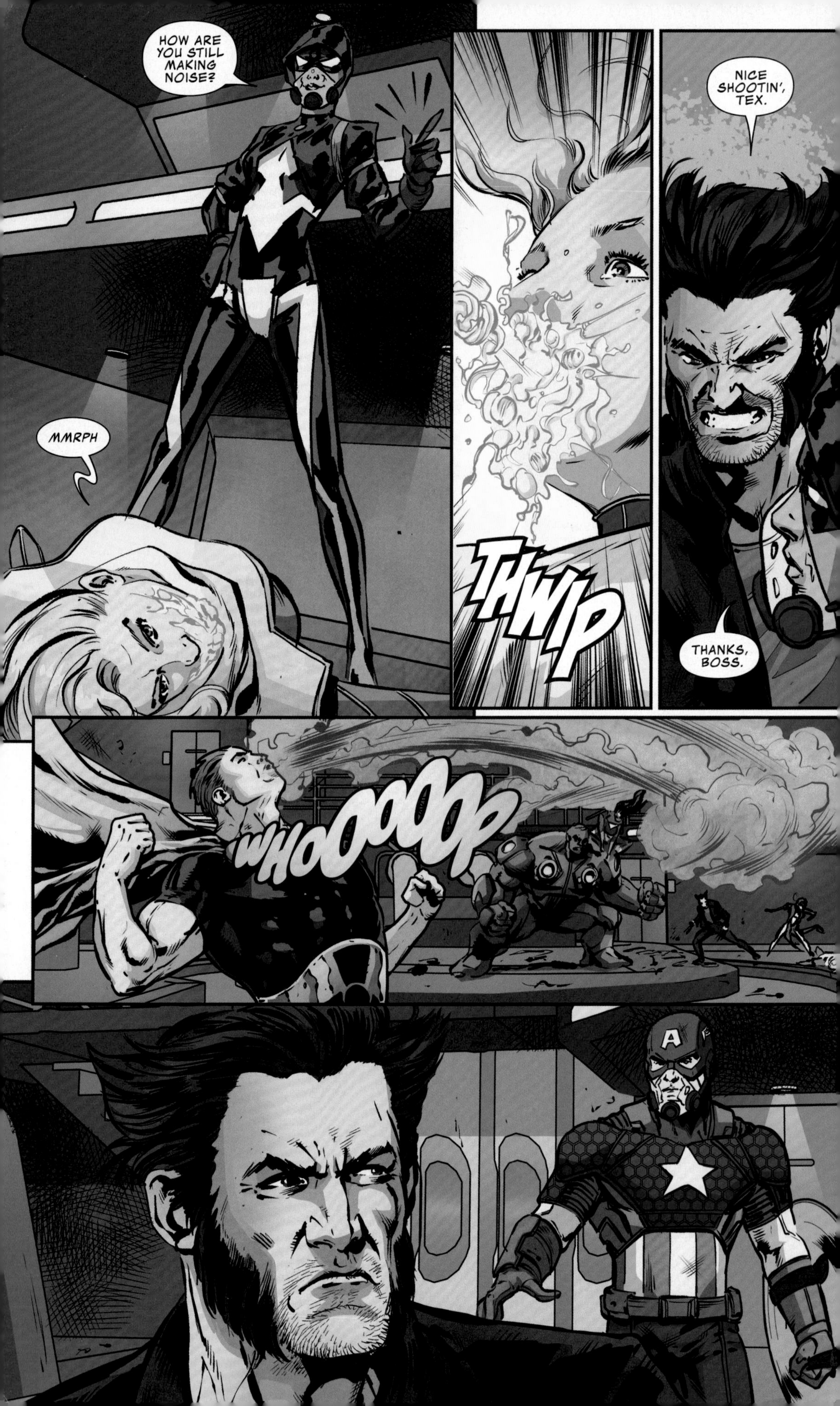
HOW ARE YOU STILL MAKING NOISE?
MMRPH
THWIP
NICE SHOOTIN', TEX.
THANKS, BOSS.
WHOOOOOOP

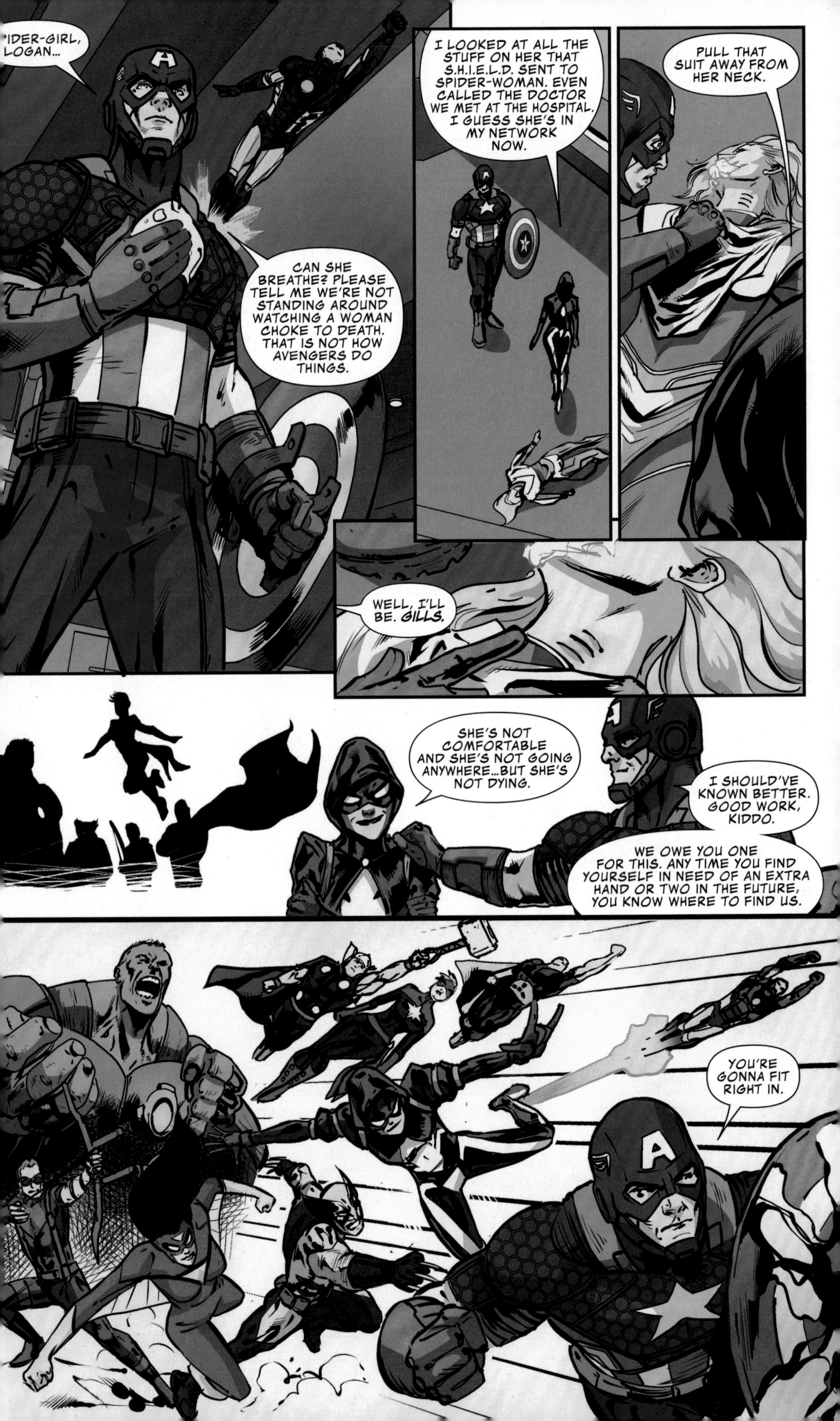

PIDER-GIRL, LOGAN...
CAN SHE BREATHE? PLEASE TELL ME WE'RE NOT STANDING AROUND WATCHING A WOMAN CHOKE TO DEATH. THAT IS NOT HOW AVENGERS DO THINGS.
I LOOKED AT ALL THE STUFF ON HER THAT S.H.I.E.L.D. SENT TO SPIDER-WOMAN. EVEN CALLED THE DOCTOR WE MET AT THE HOSPITAL. I GUESS SHE'S IN MY NETWORK NOW.
PULL THAT SUIT AWAY FROM HER NECK.
WELL, I'LL BE. GILLS.
SHE'S NOT COMFORTABLE AND SHE'S NOT GOING ANYWHERE...BUT SHE'S NOT DYING.
I SHOULD'VE KNOWN BETTER. GOOD WORK, KIDDO.
WE OWE YOU ONE FOR THIS. ANY TIME YOU FIND YOURSELF IN NEED OF AN EXTRA HAND OR TWO IN THE FUTURE, YOU KNOW WHERE TO FIND US.
YOU'RE GONNA FIT RIGHT IN.

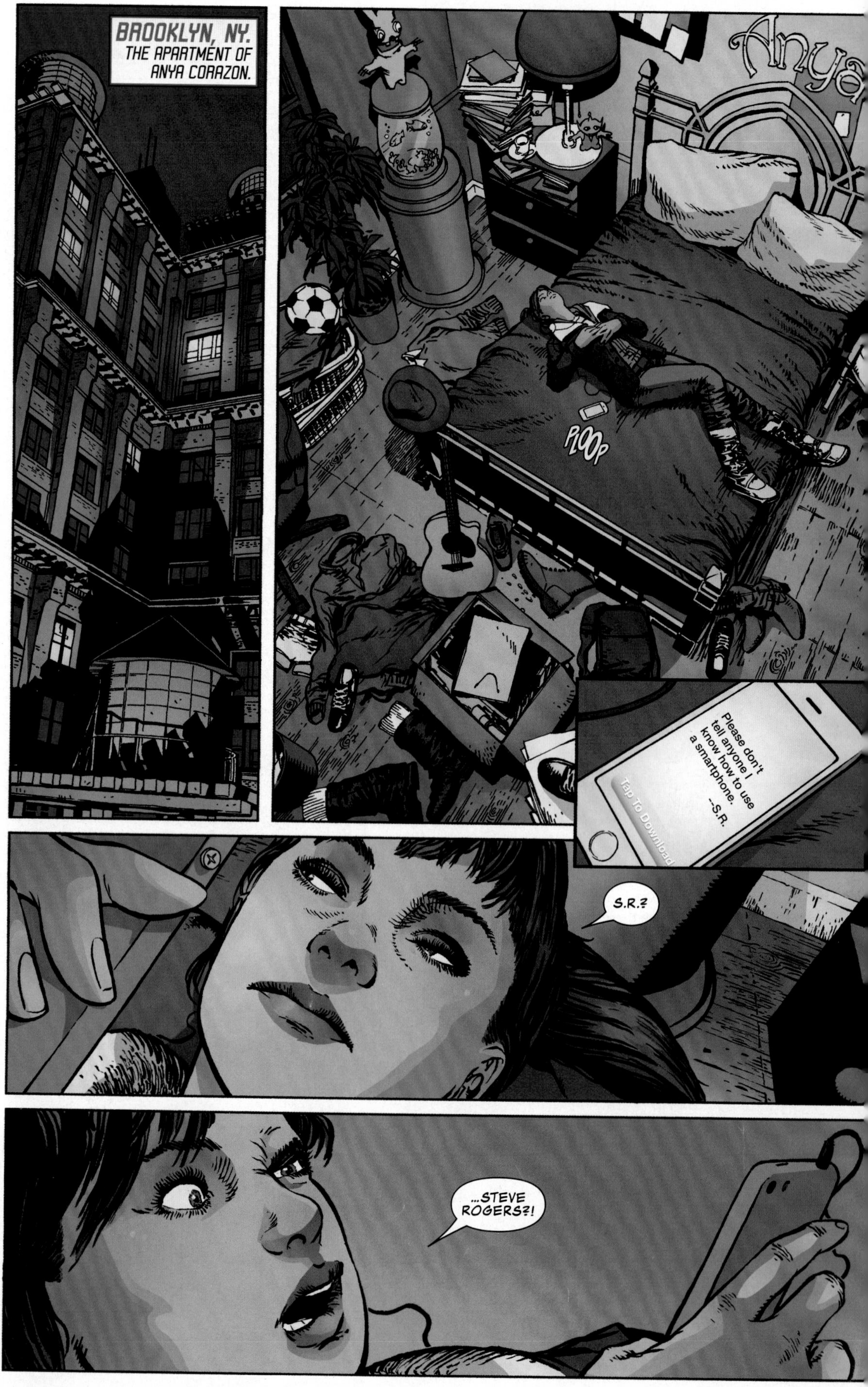
BROOKLYN, NY.
THE APARTMENT OF ANYA CORAZON.
Anya
PLOOP
Please don't tell anyone I know how to use a smartphone.
--S.R.
Tap To Download
S.R.?
...STEVE ROGERS?!

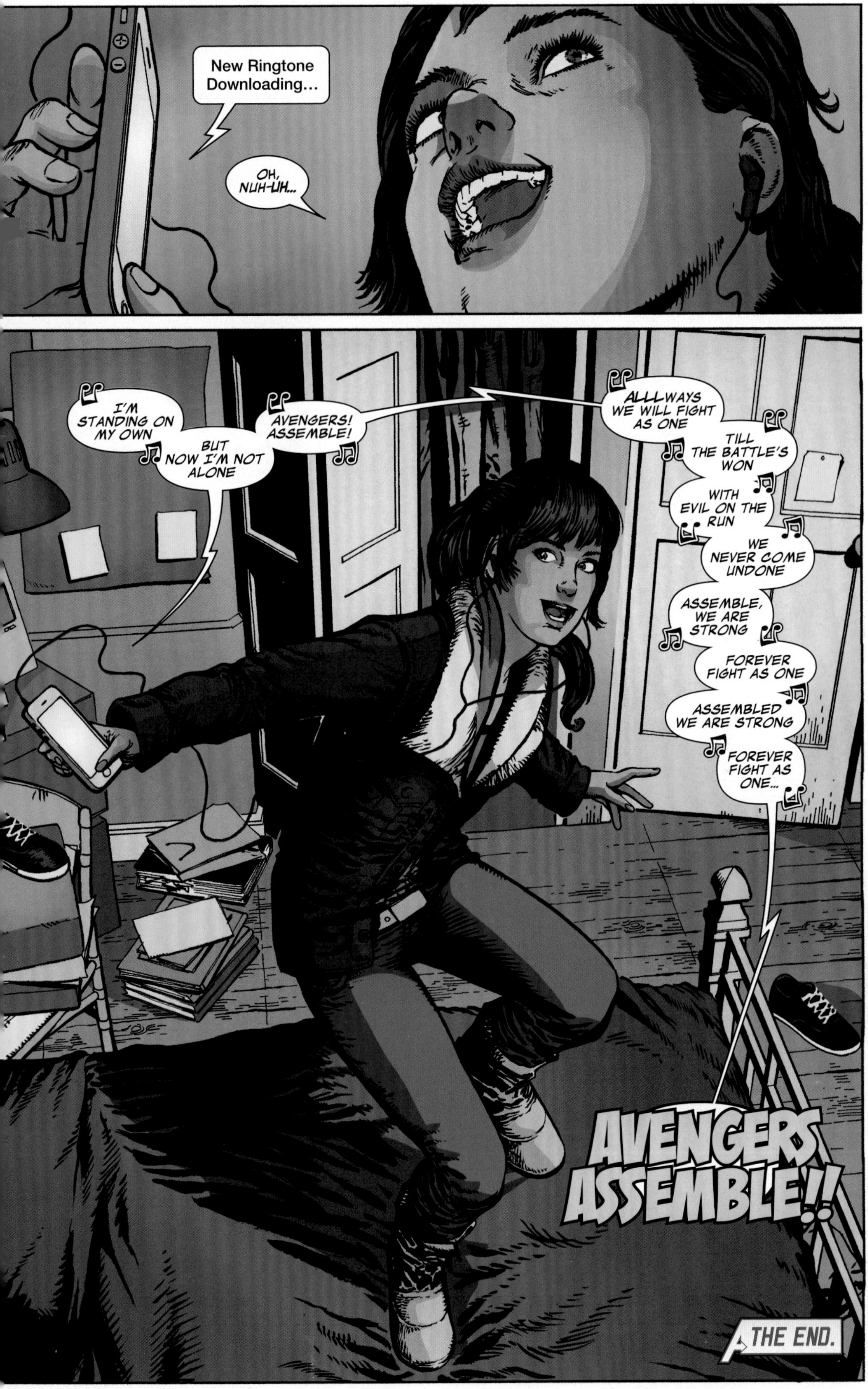
New Ringtone Downloading...
OH, NUH-UH...
I'M STANDING ON MY OWN
BUT NOW I'M NOT ALONE
AVENGERS! ASSEMBLE!
ALLLWAYS WE WILL FIGHT AS ONE
TILL THE BATTLE'S WON
WITH EVIL ON THE RUN
WE NEVER COME UNDONE
ASSEMBLE, WE ARE STRONG
FOREVER FIGHT AS ONE
ASSEMBLED WE ARE STRONG
FOREVER FIGHT AS ONE...
AVENGERS ASSEMBLE!!
THE END.

Goodnight Team Happy
Goodnight Team Sad
Goodnight Team Captains
Whose kale drinks taste bad

Goodnight to the Widow
And the red in her ledger
Goodnight to Clint Barton
Our favorite bet-hedger

Goodnight June
And teacher's cocoon

Goodnight Hyperion
Goodnight Shang-Chi
Goodnight to smartphones
Timing coffee (not tea!)

Goodnight Tom Brevoort
And thanks for the raps
Goodnight to the intern
Who writes the recaps

Goodnight Als
Goodnight Jens
Goodnight with thanks
For lending your pens

Goodnight Lauren
Goodnight Warren
Goodnight all colorists,
Domestic and foreign

Goodnight Stefano, Pete, Matteo and Barry
Goodnight AIM operative, dumb-like-mud Larry

Goodnight Kashmir Vennema
(Whose name sounds like enema
Don't think we'll see you
On screen at the cinema)

Goodnight to the Tower
And its weird kitchen sink
Goodnight to the artists
Who provided the ink

Goodnight Raff, Bags, Edwards and Jon
Goodnight Dan Buckley, who keeps the lights o

Goodnight powers
And flamboyant costumes
And goodnight to Clayton,
Who letters our BOOMs

Goodnight Brian Bendis
Who saw us out of the chute
Then moved on to great things
With Rocket and Groot

Goodnight Thor
Goodnight Corps
Goodnight to heroes
Who make our hearts soar

Move close for this one
Sit up and pull near
For I drop to a whisper
To wish good night "Mjölnir"

Goodnight to the bullpen
Goodnight to the flatters
And goodnight to YOU
Who made all this matter

Goodnight grumpy Logan
Goodnight Logan's hair
Goodnight my Avengers
...everywhere.

Until we next Assemble,
with love, gratitude and apologies to
Margaret Wise Brown, I remain,

Yours
Kelly Sue DeConnic
@kellysu

3 1901 05265 8749